Serving the Present Age

MCGILL-QUEEN'S STUDIES IN THE HISTORY OF RELIGION
G.A. Rawlyk, Editor

Volumes in this series have been supported by
the Jackman Foundation of Toronto.

Serving the Present Age

Revivalism,
Progressivism,
and the Methodist
Tradition in Canada

PHYLLIS D. AIRHART

McGill-Queen's University Press
Montreal & Kingston • London • Buffalo

© McGill-Queen's University Press 1992
ISBN 0-7735-0882-1

Legal deposit second quarter 1992
Bibliothèque nationale du Québec

Printed in Canada on acid-free paper

This book has been published with the help of a
grant from the Canadian Federation for the Humanities, using funds provided by the Social Sciences and
Humanities Research Council of Canada.

Canadian Cataloguing in Publication Data

Airhart, Phyllis D. (Phyllis Diane), 1953–
    Serving the present age

    (McGill-Queen's studies in the history of religion; 8)
    Includes bibliographical references and index.
    ISBN 0-7735-0882-1

    1. Methodist Church – Canada – History. 2. Method-
    ism – History. I. Title. II. Series.

BX8251.A57 1992   287'.0971   C91-090617-3

_25249_

This book was typeset by Typo Litho composition inc.
in 10/12 Palatino.

To my teachers
with special thanks to Jerald C. Brauer

Contents

Acknowledgments

Scholarly research is often considered a lonely and isolating endeavour. Acknowledging those who have contributed to the making of this book has reminded and reassured me that it need not be so. I am grateful for the company of friends who generously invested time and energy in my project. George Rawlyk, in whose series the book appears, responded above and beyond anything I expected when I asked him to "look over" my manuscript. I have greatly appreciated his incisive suggestions and his commitment to seeing it through to publication. Comments on the manuscript from Brian Fraser, Roger Hutchinson, Tom Sinclair-Faulkner, Timothy Smith, and Paul Wilson helped me to define the shape of the work, as did conversations with Marguerite Van Die and William Westfall. At the stage of more formal assessment for publication, one reader in particular (who later disclosed his identity as John Moir) provided constructive criticism of a number of key sections. In addition to being my indispensable teaching and research assistant for three years, Ian Manson was a sounding-board for ideas, and provided informed suggestions throughout the process of revision. David Illman-White carefully checked footnotes. Heather Gamester was both a good friend and ruthless copy editor, giving me sound suggestions for sharpening my prose style. Judy Williams, copy editor for the press, spotted many of my oversights and meticulously prepared the manuscript for the printer.

A number of institutions have assisted in the publication process. The staff of the University of Chicago's Regenstein library, Emmanuel College library (in particular Lynda Hayes), and the United Church Archives graciously handled my requests for information and materials. While I lived in Bourbonnais, Illinois, the Olivet library seemed almost a home away from home, providing me with a microfilm reader and a carrel. I have also appreciated the persons at McGill-Queen's University Press (whom I have yet to meet) who so pleasantly answered my many questions over the telephone. The Centre for the Study of Religion in Canada at Emmanuel College provided funds for research assistance. Funding support for publication came from the Jackman Foundation and the Canadian Federation for the Humanities.

By dedicating this volume to my teachers, I would also like to acknowledge those persons whose influence goes beyond their involvement in this particular project. That my life has moved in a completely different direction from anything I envisaged when I arrived at the University of Manitoba is in no small measure attributable to them. Alex Deasley's superb New Testament courses challenged me intellectually and were the catalyst I needed to think seriously about graduate work. Gordon Harland's encouragement and ongoing support have been vital during and since the time I studied with him. It was he who introduced me to the study of religion in North America and to the work of historians of Christianity at the University of Chicago. As a graduate student at Chicago I again found fine teachers. Martin Marty's breadth of knowledge, infectious enthusiasm, and seemingly inexhaustible energy were inspiring. He and Arthur Mann served as readers on a doctoral committee whose willingness to work through drafts in short order still amazes me. Most of all I am grateful to Jerald Brauer, my adviser at the University of Chicago. Reading his work on revivalism sparked my interest in studying this phenomenon. He showed unflagging interest in my ideas and has been a constant source of encouragement and practical counsel. I hope that my own work as a teacher reflects something of the quality of teaching which I have been privileged to enjoy.

And finally there is Matthew, who has given me love, joy, and harmony.

Serving the Present Age

Introduction

In every age of well-marked transition there is the pattern of habitual ...
practice and emotion which is passing, and there is oncoming of a new
complex of habit. Between the two lies a zone of anarchy, either a passing
danger or a prolonged welter involving misery of decay and zest of young
life. In our estimate of these agencies everything depends upon our standpoint of criticism.   Alfred North Whitehead[1]

From his parsonage home in Quebec the sixteen-year-old son of a
Methodist preacher anxiously followed the religious news. It was
1875. D.L. Moody and Ira Sankey had just returned to North America
triumphantly after an evangelistic tour of Britain. Would they visit
within travelling distance of his home town? He fervently hoped
so, for despite the good parental examples and careful religious
instruction of his upbringing, he did not consider himself to be a
Christian. Without conversion, which he had not yet experienced,
he feared he would be eternally lost. His apprehension was heightened by reports of a new outbreak of cholera in the region, and the
prospect of a visit from the evangelists was consoling. "Somehow,"
he wrote nearly fifty years later, "I could hardly think of being
converted except in a revival campaign."[2]

Such was the reminiscence of one of Canada's most prominent
social gospel leaders, Salem Bland, a person not usually noted for
his interest in revivalism. As he reflected on the incident years later,
Bland did not regard his earlier religious assumptions as exceptional
or abnormal. On the contrary, his response was, he suggested, "a
natural result of preaching and literature – before and for some time
after." But Bland's views had changed significantly over those fifty
years. Though still appreciative of much that Moody represented,

he captured the shift from his youthful anticipation of revival in the title of one of his later articles: "While Moody Preached the Workers Suffered."

Bland's spiritual pilgrimage from revivalism to the progressivism of the social gospel in these years was not uncommon. During the course of the nineteenth century, revivalism had fired the growth of Methodism in Canada, helping to make it the largest Protestant denomination in the country around the time of Confederation. Revivalism gave a distinctive piety to Methodism by shaping its understanding of religious experience, guidelines for personal and public behaviour, expression of religious ideas, and associations for cultivating the religious life. This revivalist piety, even more than doctrine or polity, became the identifying mark of Methodism in that century. Revivalism's emphasis on an experience of personal conversion was critically important in helping Methodists define who they were. But during the late Victorian era, the features that had characterized the pattern of Canadian Methodist piety began to undergo a transformation. By the time of church union in 1925, Methodism's most prominent leaders were espousing an approach to piety that was essentially and sometimes explicitly non-revivalist.

The late Victorian period is generally recognized as a challenging one for the Christian churches in North America. The doctrinal controversies accompanying new ideas and social changes shattered the evangelical consensus that had been forged earlier in the nineteenth century. Two major parties emerged out of the breakup of the old evangelical empire. One of these is often presented as fundamentalist in theology, conservative in social outlook, and heir to the name "evangelical" earlier shared by most Protestants in North America. The other is characterized as liberal in theology, progressive in its social outlook, and increasingly reluctant to lay claim to the evangelical tradition which had shaped its past as well.[3]

Still, a great deal about the collapse of the nineteenth-century evangelical consensus remains unclear despite the many recent historical and sociological studies of revivalism and revitalization movements. In his survey of that literature, Leonard Sweet suggests that the fragmentation of the evangelical tradition is poorly understood because little research has been done on evangelicalism in the late Victorian period. Studies dealing with that era, he concludes, are the weakest link in reconstructing the history of the evangelical tradition in America and determining why a consensus which was strong in the mid-nineteenth century was in shambles by 1915.[4]

Consideration of Methodism's role in this development has been particularly scant, perhaps because Methodism seems to have emerged relatively unscathed, at least by comparison with other denominations. While this may be true if doctrine or polity is taken as the barometer of upheaval, a study of patterns of piety reveals a very different picture. Methodist identity was closely tied to a revivalist model of piety throughout the nineteenth century. As Methodists recalled their past, revivalism linked the origins of their denomination, its subsequent statistical success, its distinctiveness as a movement, and memories of the religion of "the fathers." Late-nineteenth-century challenges, manifested in some denominations by controversies over doctrine and polity, tested Methodist assumptions about their tradition of piety. When looked at in this way, Methodism may have, in fact, been among the most profoundly affected by the realignment within Protestantism at the turn of the century.

An approach to the religious life that Methodists saw as their distinctive contribution to Christianity remained tied to the concept of "revival." An emphasis on revival persisted in the denomination with a tenacity that is difficult to account for apart from its importance as "tradition." Revivalism did not play an identical role in successive stages of Methodism as the movement diversified to meet the spiritual and educational needs of a growing and more affluent membership. But as part of "the tradition of the fathers," it was difficult to leave behind. This is important to keep in mind from the outset, for in looking at transitions in the approach to piety it is not my intention to try to gauge the level of religious enthusiasm demonstrated by Methodism's early converts in comparison with adherents a century later. The zeal and piety of the present never seemed to match that of the previous generation. Was there a continuous decline in religious fervour, or should one rather interpret the sources in the spirit of the editor of *Punch* who, when a reader complained that *Punch* was not as good as it used to be, replied, "It never was"?

The assumption of a deterioration of religious faith endemic in a call for its "revival" creates certain problems if revivalism is looked at in too strictly linear terms of "origins" and "decline." To analyse its impact on Canadian Protestantism, one must also be careful not simply to identify the impact of revivalism at a particular time with the level of the overt display of enthusiasm which often accompanied it. Caution is also called for in considering a concern for nurture of children, rather than conversion of adults, as evidence of decline in the importance of revivalism. By so doing, some have concluded that even by the 1860s revivals appealed only to minority groups and that results were unimpressive.[5] While concern for the salvation of children became more acute during the course of the nineteenth century, the spiritual outcome of nurturing was still defined primarily in terms of a piety which continued to reflect the ethos of revivalism.

The works of two scholars have been particularly helpful in shaping my approach to revivalism. Jerald C. Brauer's studies of American revivalism suggest the importance of moving beyond analysing revivalism only in terms of the technique by which a person *becomes* a Christian – the picture which comes first to mind with images of frontier camp meetings or special revival services conducted by a revivalist. He understands revivalism as more than a way of becoming a Christian; it is an approach to religion that colours the perception of being and remaining Christian as well.[6] Though revivalism shares much in common with both Puritanism and Pietism, it differs in significant ways from both of these earlier movements, emerging as a distinctive phenomenon in the eighteenth century.

Brauer compares the conversion experiences engendered by Puritanism and revivalism to illustrate the differences between them. While Puritanism's divergence from Anglicanism was evident in its approach to ritual, doctrine, and ecclesiology, what initially set the two apart was Puritanism's insistence on a conversion experience for every believer. Dissatisfaction with the English Reformation was rooted in a different underlying religious experience manifested in actions, ideas, and associational forms. Revivalism shared with Puritanism this insistence on the conversion experience. Conversion accounts from the Great Awakening, the first phase of revivalism in America, indicate a structural similarity with Puritian conversion narratives in both Old and New England.[7]

Despite this similarity in the basic structure of the conversion experience, the context, role, and consequences of conversion within the two movements differed.[8] The revival context was no longer a covenantal community guided by an elite ministry with aspirations of creating a holy commonwealth, as was the case with Puritanism; revivalism focused on the individual rather than the community. The role of conversion shifted, existing for its own sake in relation to the salvation of the person being born again; the conversion experience itself became central and all-pervasive, notwithstanding that one was converted in order to live a godly life. As for the consequences, revivalism fostered an approach to the Christian life that differed sharply from Puritanism as well as the sacramental piety of the Catholic, Anglican, Lutheran, and some Reformed traditions. The emphasis on conversion influenced the sermons, hymns, prayers, and other ritual forms adopted by revivalist groups. The propriety of liturgical and institutional forms took second place to their efficacy in converting sinners. Revivalism's pervasive influence touched even the ministry and the Scriptures. Focusing attention on revival results coloured judgments of both the success of the work of the pastor and the soundness of interpretation of biblical texts.[9] This approach to revivalism, which sees it as encompassing a distinctive approach to piety, forms the basis of this study.

Revivalism's contribution to Methodism's sense of identity also raises questions about the transmission of religious traditions, generally seen as a task of "conserving." In this regard Edward Shils's work on tradition has intrigued me. He emphasizes the dynamism and change of tradition rather than the sense of "sameness" which is usually associated with tradition as "the way things have always been." He defines tradition as the recurrence, in approximately identical form, of structures of conduct and patterns of belief over several generations.[10] This process involves incorporating new elements which are not exactly the same as past beliefs but which coexist with beliefs and behaviour of the past.[11]

Religious traditions are just as susceptible to change as other traditions. There is always pressure for innovation when a tradition encounters new issues, movements, attitudes towards ecclesiastical authority, doctrines, versions of sacred writings, variations of liturgy, and arrangements between spiritual and earthly powers.[12] Many of these innovations are initiated in the name of improvement. Change is most often sought by those who are deeply concerned with the tradition's continuation and satisfied with much of it, not by those who desire to do away with the old tradition.[13] Such change usually involves a modification of the symbols and images by which tradition is received. Without the capacity for change, continued vitality is doubtful. Shils notes that traditions must continue to fit the circumstances in which they operate in order to survive. However, this can open the door to deterioration if the "keepers" of the tradition convince members to conduct themselves in a different way or no longer present the tradition at all, or if a new generation adopts a different pattern of belief as more acceptable.[14]

Shils pictures the movement of tradition through time as like an old house which has been gradually renovated over the years: despite the changes it is still thought of as the same house.[15] This changing sameness is strikingly similar to the way that revivalism operated as "tradition" within Methodism. The ideals of the religious life were proclaimed as being in continuity with the piety fostered by the early Methodist revivals. To use Shils's analogy, by the late

Victorian period Methodism's revivalistic piety was like a familiar old house – not exactly as it was when new, perhaps not even as interesting despite all the renovations, but still recognizable as the same structure.

This attitude towards the old house began to change perceptibly around the turn of the twentieth century. Methodism had always prided itself, as a well-known hymn of Charles Wesley had put it, on "serving the present age." When it arrived in British North America it was an organization well suited to its environs. However, the cultural transformation that accompanied the dawn of a new century and the widely held perception that Canada was entering a new era raised questions about the adequacy of the old ways to serve this new age. Methodism's growing interest in progressivism revealed outdated features in the old homestead and made a move to a more modern dwelling attractive. Though there continued to be some in the Methodist family uncomfortable with the move and occasionally casting longing glances at the house which was no longer theirs, most were happy with their new location and their new neighbours. The move from revivalism to progressivism seemed to be a fairly easy one, perhaps because (though Methodists might have been reluctant to admit it) a discriminating eye could spot a number of the most cherished things from the old place interspersed with the new furnishings.

The picture of the transformation of the revivalist tradition and the reconstruction of religious identity that I have sketched here will be detailed in the following chapters. I will argue that, far from being untouched by the challenges of the late Victorian period, the Methodist tradition was radically affected by the collapse of the nineteenth-century evangelical consensus and the breakup of the Protestant empire built upon it. To analyse that collapse only in terms of denominations which divided organizationally as a result obscures its implications. The magnitude of the upheaval within Methodism may have been so pervasive that organizational resistance to it was ineffective. No longer viewed as the dominant force within the "evangelical" party, Methodism instead became frequently associated with a group accused of being unsympathetic to evangelical aims. Methodism, which once boasted that revivalism was its unique contribution to creating the evangelical consensus, was transposed from key participant to outsider.

Out of the old consensus emerged at least two distinctive approaches to the Christian life. Methodists perceived themselves as being presented with a choice of ideals and aims not viewed previously as incompatible: saving "souls" or "the social order." Many were no doubt dismayed to be classified as the spiritual progeny of "personal" rather than "social" gospellers and characterized as having had in the past an interest in building a Kingdom only in heaven, rather than one on earth as well. At its best the Methodist tradition had striven for both personal piety and social concern. But as twentieth-century Protestants divided their energies along lines of support for salvation of "souls" or "the social order," Methodists increasingly became identified with a social Christianity. Meanwhile the stories and rituals of their past were absorbed during the course of the twentieth century by other religious traditions which focused more narrowly on salvation of the individual.

Historians studying Canadian Protestantism have focused on the coalescence of religious concerns in this period. Some have pointed to the vital influence of Spencerian and Hegelian idealism on this process. One key study links philosophical idealism to the social gospel movement and credits it with shattering the old orthodoxy of ideas aimed at instilling theological students (and others through them) with traditional piety.[16] Because of idealism, the study submits, philosophical and sociological concerns replaced theological interests; idealism was thus instrumental in forging the consensus upon which the United Church of Canada was built.[17]

To describe the emerging consensus without giving due attention to the strains within evangelical Protestantism created in its wake is to tell only part of the story. How did speculative idealism, even granting its devastating influence on orthodoxy, invigorate those who became active in the social gospel and church union movements? How were these new religious ideas popularized? To what extent were they connected to traditional beliefs and practices to transform them into acceptable alternatives?[18] It is important to recognize the links between the early social gospel movement and evangelical ideals. Not only Salem Bland but others who will be introduced here – S.D. Chown, W.B. Creighton, T. Albert Moore, and Ernest Thomas – were progressives who began their ministries with confidence in "the old paths" of revivalism. The piety of the leading Methodist theologian in the quarter-century prior to the First World War, Nathanael Burwash, was also shaped by the world view of revivalism. For them, as for most Victorian Methodists, the first impulse was to recapture the revivalist tradition, not to reject or repudiate it. By 1925, however, revivalism's place was no longer assured. Methodism began to find its traditional place within evangelical Protestantism increasingly uncomfortable.

This study examines the changes in Methodist piety which resulted in the eclipse of many of its revivalist features by those who presented and received the tradition. It also depicts the main features of the new progressive ideals that were articulated as a more adequate way "to serve the present age." I have focused on two types of sources: the denominational press and sermonic literature. Part of John Wesley's genius was the connexional organization of his movement – the effective linking of its various departments and agencies. Successive generations of denominational leaders found that the press was invaluable in this regard. In particular the weekly paper, the *Christian Guardian*, was highly influential in shaping the mind of Canadian Methodism in the nineteenth and early twentieth centuries. The pulpit was, of course, another important transmitter of religious tradition. I have examined many sermons and addresses of several key Methodists who considerably influenced the general direction taken by the denomination. Though a distinction must be made between the "ideal" admonitions of press and pulpit and the "real" practice of piety, the models of piety proposed by those regarded as the spiritual guides and guardians of tradition must be taken seriously. While complete congruity between the two never occurred, a shift in one usually resulted in a change – either of conformity or reaction – in the other.

Focusing on the Methodist tradition in this way obviously has limitations. Concentrating on the religious press and the most visible denominational leaders highlights developments in Central Canada and (despite my own Maritime roots) reflects the "Upper Canada" bias of my sources and of the movement itself. Canadian Methodism was statistically centred in Ontario; over three-quarters of its members lived there. Another bias of these particular sources is reflected in the phrase "tradition of the fathers," seemingly a favourite expression for leaders of that time. Only limited attention is given to specific women in shaping piety, although their role is evident in the sections on the significance of voluntary societies. I have wondered whether the "tradition of the mothers" was anything like the "tradition of the fathers" – indeed, whether the progressivists' emphasis on "muscular Christianity," sacrificial service, and the importance family life in the effort to bring in the Kingdom of God suggests the reaction of the male clergy to what Ann Douglas has called the "feminization" of religion. But consideration of that thesis awaits further study.

I have limited this study primarily to examining the internal dynamics of Methodist religion, although many other areas of life impinged on it. The development of corporate capitalism, to name but one example, had a profound impact on the major cultural institutions in Canada. Religion was no exception. Given the interconnection between revivalism and middle-class culture that scholars have noted, a Marxist interpretation of developments would provide a different and stimulating analysis. So too does the use of a theory of secularization such as is illustrated by Ramsay Cook's provocative work, *The Regenerators*. Religion was not impervious to social and intellectual changes. [19]

Nevertheless, the response of religious groups to those changes was coloured by their past. And for Methodism in Canada, revivalism was a vital part of that past and a lingering influence in its attempt "to serve the present age." It shaped the interaction between tradition and innovation, transforming new beliefs and practices into acceptable alternatives as part of a search for a usable past.

CHAPTER ONE

Revivalism as "Tradition": The Making of a Methodist

You have nothing to do but to save souls. Therefore spend and be spent
in this work.   John Wesley

O praise the Lord, my soul, for He
Made sin and death before me flee;
And in his mercy gave me rest
When He made me a Methodist.   Methodist song[1]

On the day that John Wesley died, his followers in the British North
American province of Canada formed their third Methodist class
meeting. It was 1791 and in this large region, formally divided that
year into Upper and Lower Canada and later renamed Quebec and
Ontario, Wesley's movement could claim only one organized circuit,
one preacher, and, by one historian's estimate, about sixty members.
At the time of Wesley's death, the combined forces of Methodism
in all of the British North American provinces were hardly more
impressive. The Maritime provinces, Newfoundland, and Upper
and Lower Canada together mustered only four circuits, six preachers, and a membership of about eight hundred.[2] Yet a little over a
half-century later, the total membership of the various branches of
Canadian Methodism exceeded that of any other Protestant denomination in the country.[3]

It was the use of an approach to evangelism called revivalism
which played an integral part in this dramatic statistical accomplish-
ment. In Britain, Wesley's group had been been tagged with the
name "Methodist" because of the regularity with which it performed
religious exercises such as worship, fasting, partaking of Holy Communion, and acts of charity. But it was the "methods" of revivalism

which soon identified the movement, particularly in North America. Though Methodists did not introduce revivalism to North America, they quickly recognized its effectiveness in meeting the needs of communities which were predominantly frontier and rural. It was an effective strategy for converting men and women to Christianity and to Methodism. But revivalism was more than simply a recruiting technique. It became instrumental in shaping Methodism's perception of both its tradition and religious identity. In the century after Wesley's death, Methodist lore recast him from high-church Anglican to revivalist par excellence. When Methodism celebrated its Canadian centennial in 1891, Wesley was presented as "the foremost of all revivalists whom the Church has ever witnessed" in the special volume published by the General Conference for the occasion.[4] The Methodist itinerants in Canada were pictured as following in Wesley's footsteps. The stories of the heroic days of early Methodism in British North America chronicled revivalism's importance, weaving a colourful tradition out of the stories of Methodism's circuit-riding preachers and the zeal of their early converts.[5]

News of a visit from a Methodist itinerant brought onlookers from miles around to the meeting, often held in the home of one of the settlers. The new preacher introduced them to Methodism in a religious service wherein an appeal for conversion was couched in the language of revival. One of the first itinerants, Nathan Bangs, vividly described typical frontier meetings where even the introduction left no doubt of the preacher's evangelistic purpose: "My name is Nathan Bangs. I was born in Connecticut, May 2, 1778. I was born again in this Province [Upper Canada], May, 1800 ... I am bound for the heavenly city, and my errand among you is to persuade as many of you as I can to go with me." He explained that it was his practice to stand to sing and kneel to pray and invited those present to do the same if they wished. Then he preached on the text "Repent ye therefore, and be converted, that your sins may be blotted out, when the times of refreshing shall come from the presence of the Lord."[6]

Bangs was only one of the itinerant preachers who ventured to spread this gospel under conditions of extreme hardship. Methodists remembered their early itinerants as men (and occasionally women) who had given up the comforts of home and even their health to preach the Methodist message.[7] Conditions improved somewhat as the century progressed. A long-serving Canadian itinerant, William Case, recalled in a letter to Bangs the changes that had taken place in the decades since they commenced their work. Writing in 1855, Case marvelled at trains travelling as fast as forty miles an hour, comparing this to the times when they had travelled on horseback through dense forests at two-and-a-half to four miles an hour.[8] Long distances between the many preaching points and being continually on the move made the life of an itinerant preacher a difficult one. Assignments to a circuit being for at most a two-year term, the short interval of time between appointments corresponded to the assumption widely held among Methodists in the early nineteenth century that the primary role of an itinerant was to be an evangelist.

Whatever the personal costs to the preachers and their families, the revival message expounded by itinerants proved to be an effective way to spread Methodism. The Ottawa circuit was likely typical of how hundreds of British North American communities were introduced to the new movement. Recounting in his autobiography the story of his family's decision to became Methodist, Nathanael Burwash described how revival services attracted persons with no formal church affiliation as well as those from other denominations. Though Burwash's grandfather had been a devout churchman whose oldest children were baptized in the Church of England, the family was persuaded after a revival in 1826 to unite with the Methodists. Burwash attributed the rapid growth of the movement to its revivals. The little country circuit where he grew up increased from an initial forty members to ninety after the 1826 revival. By the time the figures were adjusted to include those converted after another revival ten years later, membership had risen to well over six hundred.[9]

As Methodism expanded, it drew its leadership from men and women converted in a revival ethos. It was at a revival service in a home near Amherst, Nova Scotia in 1779 that a young man named William Black was converted. It was Black who was largely responsible for spreading Methodism throughout the Maritime provinces.[10] An effective use of revivalism characterized the work of itinerants like Black and Freeborn Garrettson and was a key ingredient in the growth of Maritime Methodism.[11] Despite initial suspicions of protracted meetings,[12] Methodists in that region eventually reconsidered some of their earlier reservations about large gatherings. Influenced by British Methodism at the beginning of the nineteenth century, they saw themselves as more religiously "decorous and respectable" than their counterparts in Upper Canada. Ironically, as they became more socially respectable in the 1840s, they also became more evangelical.[13]

By mid-century the camp meeting found its way into Maritime Methodist life and circuits were swept by revivals.[14] Around the same time, Maritime Methodism's main educational institution, the Wesleyan Academy at Sackville that became Mount Allison University, was the scene of revivals. One meeting was apparently successful in persuading nearly all the student body, mostly teenage boys drawn from other denominations, to come forward to the altar for conversion. Several prominent Anglicans were dismayed when their children reported that they believed that in the process they had become Methodists. [15]

Methodism expanded to western Canada in ways similar to developments in eastern and central Canada. George Young, sent in 1868 as the first Methodist missionary to work with the white settlers of the North-West, began the story of his work in Manitoba with an autobiographical sketch that told of the "two births of which I have been the subject ... [t]he first on the last day of the year 1821, and the second in October 1840." [16] He transported this revivalist message with him from Ontario to the west. Women like his wife, Mary, were instrumental as well. Writing shortly after she died, George Young recalled that her "ruling passion was to work for the salvation of souls; and this feeling seemed to deepen and become intensified as her years increased." [17] When superintendent James Woodsworth reported a 109 per cent increase in the number of Methodists in the region between 1886 and 1890, he attributed the largest portion to "the direct product of our ministers and people by the use of the time-honored means and methods peculiar to our Church." [18] As a historian later put it, "their ritual was simple, their doctrines few and fundamental and their sermons were aflame with a consuming passion for the salvation of souls. They were physically vigorous, mentally alert, spiritually devoted, saying as they went, 'This one thing I do.'" [19]

Lesser-known Methodists, converted in similar settings, were the mainstay of Methodism. Visits from the circuit-riders were sometimes infrequent and it was the laity who prepared the way for revival successes. Methodist parents modelled the piety presented by the preacher; the work of an itinerant simply crowned their efforts. As children approached adulthood there were sometimes not too subtle pressures to choose a converted marriage partner. W.H. Withrow's romanticized account of the life and times of Barbara Heck captured this aspect of Methodist upbringing in his reconstruction of conversations that took place after the Hecks' beautiful daughter Katherine caught the eye of Reginald Pemberton, "a youth of noble spirit and manly, generous character" and son of the most powerful Anglican family in the community but, alas, unconverted.

The story had a happy ending, for when William Losee, the first itinerant to Upper Canada, preached at the home of the Heck family,

Reginald was converted. His father was angered that through the "rantings of a Methodist fanatic" Reginald had "degraded himself by weeping for his sins and crying for pardon" alongside another youth who had the reputation of being rather wild and reprobate. Colonel Pemberton lost a son and daughter and the sympathies of his wife to the Methodists, but eventually was won over himself. Reginald became a Methodist itinerant and married Katherine, with her mother's blessing. According to Withrow's account, despite the hardships of the itinerant life, Barbara Heck "would intrust her daughter's happiness to the keeping of the manly youth, who, even though disinherited, she would have preferred as a Methodist preacher to the heir of all the Pemberton estate without that richest grace of manhood, a converted heart."[20]

Methodists quickly outgrew house meetings and moved first into small chapels, then into larger and more impressive buildings. In these more commodious surroundings, revivalism continued to play an important part in Methodist religious life. Appeals for conversion were made in Sunday services as well as in "protracted meetings" where revival services were scheduled for a period of days or even weeks. The quarterly and annual business meetings of Methodism were also the scene of revivals. Summer camp meetings provided another setting for revival preaching.[21]

The impact of revivalism in shaping Methodism in Canada went far beyond expanding its membership rolls. It indelibly marked the religious identity of its adherents. In particular the conversion experience, associated with revivalism, characterized Methodist piety long after the pioneer days. Revivalism continued to colour the picture of Methodism in the minds of those both inside and outside the movement. Thomas Carlyle had once caricatured the British Methodists he observed as a people who were always looking at their own navel and saying, "Am I saved? Will I be damned? Am I happy? How can I get another blessing?" Though likewise ridiculed by many in North America, Methodism's introspective revivalist piety not only influenced its own members but also extended beyond denominational boundaries.

So linked was the new movement to a particular approach to the religious life that some used the word "Methodist" as shorthand for an expression of popular religion which in the nineteenth century crossed all denominational lines and permeated much of Protestant church life. It gave a distinctive character to Protestantism in North America, so much so that several historians have used the term "the Methodist age" to refer to the period between the Great Awakening of the 1740s and the First World War.[22] When the more sacramentally inclined looked to find a culprit for what they saw as the sad state of affairs wrought by revivalism's influence, they pointed the finger at Methodism.[23]

By the end of the nineteenth century, a common focus concerning the ideals of the religious life persisted within Methodism, transcending social, economic, and regional diversity.[24] Central to this was a piety which, while owing much to John Wesley, had been affected by the substantial changes which revivalism had brought to North American Protestantism, changes which had taken Methodism in directions that the sacramentally inclined Wesley had not envisaged.[25] Methodism presented an approach to spirituality which manifested itself distinctly in the religious experience to which its practitioners aspired, guidelines for personal and public morality, the articulation of religious ideas, and the associational forms by which piety was cultivated. Revivalism continued to influence Methodism in the late Victorian Canada through these expressions of piety.

The accounts of the spiritual pilgimages of leaders who came to prominence in the closing decades of the nineteenth century indicate the continuing importance of an understanding of religious experience that owed much to Methodism's revivalist tradition. One of the most interesting of these accounts was recorded by Nathanael Burwash in his unpublished autobiography. By the time of his death in 1918, he had become one of Canada's most important religious leaders through his work as professor of theology at Victoria College, Canada's leading Methodist theological school. Given his influence within Canadian Methodism, his conversion experience is worth examining in detail.[26]

Burwash was in a sense a product of the success of Methodist revivalism. His father, Adam Burwash, became a Methodist after the Ottawa circuit revival of 1826. A revival on the same circuit a decade later counted among its converts the John Taylor family, recently arrived immigrants and members of the Church of Scotland before becoming Methodists. It was one of the Taylor daughters, Anne, who married Adam Burwash in 1838. Their first child, Nathanael, was born a year later and raised in a home where Christian nurture instilled revivalist piety.

Burwash's parents were instrumental in his religious upbringing, each in a particular way. His father was one for whom the inner life of religion was "the ruling centre and controlling matter in his whole life" and whose care for his children was guided by his concern for their conversion. Nathanael remembered his father praying in the granary "times without number ... talking aloud to God praying for his boys, for the church and for a revival of power." He recalled his mother's piety as more comprehensive, combining an ambition for her children's intellectual development along with their conversion. However, she too had been "converted clearly in a great revival" and "appreciated fully the importance of the fundamental change of the new birth and directed her labours to that point."[27]

Daily family prayer in the morning and evening was the usual practice in the Burwash home, with additional spiritual discipline provided through studying scripture, answering catechism questions, singing hymns, and hearing exhortations.[28] As part of the emphasis on religion in the home, Burwash claimed his mother was always on the lookout for the "seeds of sin in the passions of childhood." Writing near the end of his life, Burwash suspected that modern theologians might no longer approve of his mother's methods, yet he remained convinced of her theological astuteness: "sin," he wrote, "was there by the fallen nature, and conscious conviction of its presence must prepare the way for its cure by redeeming love."[29]

Burwash's reflections on his childhood counter the assumption often made that concern for the salvation of children marked a decline in revivalism's importance. This was hardly the case in the Burwash home. The influence of revivalism may have become even more pervasive when the model of the religious life was presented by a revivalist preacher as well as by parents dedicated to Christian nurture defined by revivalist piety.[30] The home provided a context for impressing on children from a very early age the necessity of a definite conversion experience. Parents extended to their children an invitation to be converted which might later be acted upon in a formal and more ritualized setting.[31]

There was no significant period of religious indifference or resistance to conversion in Burwash's spiritual pilgrimage. By the time a visiting preacher arrived in 1846 to hold protracted meetings in the small Canada West community of Baltimore where his family had moved, Burwash already felt under conviction of sin – at the age of seven! "I was under deep conviction," he recalled. "I cannot remember the time when under mother's earnest teaching it was not so. I cannot remember the time either there nor afterward when I did not earnestly and daily pray to God for the forgiveness of sin. But I could not call myself a child of God. I could not say that my sins were forgiven. And this in the Methodist teaching of the day was the essential point."[32] Burwash went forward to the altar at a revival service, but felt no assurance that his sins had been forgiven. From that time on he prayed every night that God would spare his life until he had that assurance[33] – what Methodists called "the witness of the Spirit."

Burwash's struggle continued after he decided to prepare for the ministry at Victoria College, then located in Cobourg, not far from Burwash's home. A step towards resolution of his spiritual difficulties came in 1852 during the Christmas vacation of his first year at college. During revival services conducted by one of his classmates, "all the convictions of past years came back with renewed power." As a result of his friend's preaching, "in a moment like a flash of light" Burwash saw that "God was declared to be gracious and merciful through Christ, forgiving iniquity, transgression and sin."[34] He was still reluctant to regard this as conversion, hesitating even to give his name for church membership. It was almost a year later in the fall of 1853, during a college revival, that the assuring "witness of the Spirit" finally came to Burwash.

What he described as "the perfecting of his conversion" was not an isolated incident at Victoria that year. The successful camp meetings and city revivals of 1852–3, sparked in large measure by the visit of the American evangelist James Caughey, had brought an influx of candidates for the ministry.[35] These zealous new converts discovered rather quickly that there were plenty of lost souls to be saved at Victoria College. Of the nearly three hundred students enrolled, Burwash calculated that fewer than 25 per cent were "professing Christians." By the end of the academic year that situation was drastically reversed; fewer than 5 per cent were left unmoved by the revival which swept through the college.[36] Burwash himself was at last "fully and publicly committed to Christ and his church for life-service."[37]

Burwash was only one of the students converted in that college revival who rose to prominence in the denomination. He became a church member in May 1854 in the company of such other newly converted students as Albert Carman, who went on to become General Superintendent. With what Burwash described as "the ablest, oldest and most advanced students all converted," the revival was instrumental in setting the high moral and religious tone which became "an established tradition of the college."[38] Along with scores of ministerial candidates were several laypersons who over the next decades provided the church with strong leadership.[39]

Burwash's ministry was characterized by a passionate drive to encourage conversion. As he prepared for the first service in his first circuit, he prayed that God would give him a convert as a sign of approval that he was "in the right way." Assurance of his calling came quickly, for when he gave the "old Methodist invitation to penitent sinners to come forward seeking salvation" on the first Sunday evening, a poor day labourer responded and "found peace in believing."[40] He was grateful that the early years of his ministry had been spent in the Bay of Quinte area among local preachers whose ideal for the church was continuous revival. This religious environment shaped his short career as pastor and influenced his work as a professor. Although he made no claim to be a successful evangelist, he maintained that "evangelism became my ideal of the ministry and largely influenced my teaching in all the after years."[41]

The long struggle which preceded Burwash's conversion may have been unusual, but the importance he attached to the experience was normative for the Methodism of that time. Social gospel leader Samuel Dwight Chown described in his autobiography how a concerned friend had pleaded with him for six months to join a class meeting, thinking that if he went, Chown would seek forgiveness for his sins. Since he suspected that his friend might be right about the consequences of attending the class meeting, he refused to go. However, he made a promise to his dying father that he would attend a class. Shortly after his father's death he was converted, at the age of fourteen, at revival services held in 1868 at Kingston's Sydenham Street Church.[42]

Revivals were a familiar feature of religious life in the Ontario circuits to which Chown was appointed. One of his assignments in North Gower was to assist Richard Hammond, described by Chown as a specialist in successful evangelistic work. The young preacher spent 1875 helping Hammond in revival meetings and later conducted services on his own. Describing the work of guiding scores of people to the decision to lead a Christian life as the "supreme joy,"[43] Chown adopted what was for his time an innovative approach to evangelism. With the Salvation Army bands making inroads in Ontario, the Methodists responded by forming "bands" of their own to participate in evangelistic work. Chown was assisted in one of his most successful revival campaigns by a band organized by a Methodist minister, David Savage. As a result of these services the inquiry room of the Methodist church in the small community of Sydenham where Chown was pastor was visited by over 200 seekers, of whom he believed 150 were "soundly converted."[44]

A conversion experience was attested to by persons who held very different opinions regarding other issues which faced the church. The biblical scholar George Workman, a graduate of and later professor at Victoria College who after the early 1890s was almost constantly in trouble for his liberal theological views, was one such person. Writing to C.T. Scott, one of Workman's detractors, Burwash was quick to remind him of that occasion: "Geo. C. Workman like C.T. Scott is one of my boys and almost if not the very first who was converted at [Victoria] College after I commenced my work there."[45] For both Workman and Burwash, the methods of higher criticism and evangelism apparently were not mutually exclusive. As late as 1906, Workman was among the revival workers when the American evangelist Reuben A. Torrey visited Montreal.[46]

Conversion was central to the piety of both men and women in Canadian Methodist circles. For women it became tied to a conception of "evangelical womanhood" which shaped the way that women aspiring to it formed friendships and chose activities. Conversion became for them the defining experience of their lives; it marked the beginning of a commitment to nurturing the Christian life that involved intensive self-examination of daily activities and "useful" social involvement.[47] The diary of Annie Leake reveals a young girl's desire for conversion that is similar to the young boy Burwash's in many respects. At the age of eleven she experienced the first of three unsuccessful attempts at being converted. In 1857 at the age of seventeen she sought conversion at a protracted meeting in Parrsboro, Nova Scotia and received the assurance of the Holy Spirit a few days later. This life-altering experience marked the beginning of her commitment to Christian work. After teaching in Nova Scotia and Newfoundland, she served between 1887 and 1893 as the first matron of the Woman's Missionary Society rescue home for Chinese prostitutes in Victoria.[48]

Because so many Methodists dated their conversion to revivals, it was difficult to replace special meetings even by calls for conversion in regular Sunday services. The line of argument of revival supporters is illustrated by an editorial in the *Guardian* in 1885 which described a meeting where "an excellent official brother" spoke against special services because of the abuses associated with them. However, when someone requested that all those present who had been converted in such meetings stand, all, including the critic of the special services, rose to their feet.[49] Ten years later, the same argument was used to support the involvement of the Epworth Leagues of Methodist youth in revival work. The writer noted that some pastors and evangelists estimated that as many as two-thirds or three-quarters of church members had been converted at revival meetings, a statistic cited as clear demonstration of their necessity.[50]

The last decades of the nineteenth century saw no shortage of role models for conversion. The obituary notices in the *Guardian*'s "Our Righteous Dead" column confirm that the experiences of Burwash, Carman, Chown, Workman, and Leake were in tune with the piety of men and women of lesser-known accomplishments. Conversion's central role in Canadian Methodism is indicated by the repeated references to it, often with specific details, in the vast majority of the *Guardian*'s obituary accounts. In some cases details of the "second birth" were given where there was no date mentioned for the first.[51]

The presence of so many men and women who had experienced conversion reinforced the emphasis placed on it in the pulpit and press. The anxiety which Salem Bland felt as a teenager because he had not yet been converted is significant not because of its novelty but because of its normalcy. The young man who later became so prominent as a social gospel preacher could in 1875 conceive of only one sure way to become a Christian – to be converted at a revival. He described this as a natural result of the preaching and literature of the late Victorian period. One can certainly understand why he arrived at that conclusion.

Methodists thought of conversion as a life-altering experience evidenced by the "fruits of regeneration" which grew out of it. They closely intertwined guidelines for personal and social behaviour with what they variously called Christian perfection, sanctification, or holiness. Wesley himself had promoted the doctrine of Christian perfection as "the grand depositum" of Methodism, but among his followers it was a constant source of confusion and contention. As to whether it was a definite, instantaneous, and distinct "second blessing" (conversion being the first), or a process with various crisis points along the way, Methodism could find no lasting consensus.[52]

Theological tensions over holiness developed afresh in the 1850s. The revival which swept through many Canadian communities brought to Methodist altars those already professing conversion but now seeking a subsequent experience of sanctification. At highly successful holiness camp meetings and revivals held in the Maritimes, Canada West, and Quebec, James Caughey and Phoebe and Walter Palmer invited thousands to experience sanctification. The assurance of Christian perfection which Wesley himself had hesitated to claim was less of a stumbling block for those who accepted the logic of Phoebe Palmer's "altar theology." To those reluctant to profess perfection, she pointed out that Romans 12:1 instructed them to present their bodies as a living, continual sacrifice. By placing "all upon the altar," she had been able to claim the scriptural promise of Matthew 23:19 – that the altar sanctified the gift, cleansing the believer of sin that remained after conversion. This was "a shorter way" to holiness, she argued, than that proposed by those who viewed the pursuit of perfection as a lifelong process.[53]

For those seeking perfection in the Christian life, revivals thus came to hold much promise even for converted Methodists like Nathanael Burwash. The emphasis on religion in Burwash's home notwithstanding, he claimed to have been unaware at the time of his conversion of a second definite experience for which he should strive. The doctrine of holiness apparently had not been a prominent feature of Canadian Methodism as he knew it before the revivals of the 1850s. It was shortly after his public profession of faith in 1854 that he heard a sermon on holiness. It marked the beginning of a new spiritual struggle that lasted for many years.[54]

Methodists who listened to the preaching of James Caughey, the Palmers, and other holiness teachers became caught up in the quest for a "higher Christian life." Readily available devotional literature complemented holiness preaching and many Victoria College students dedicated themselves during the summer to circulating the *Guide to Holiness*, a publication with which the Palmers were closely associated. Burwash believed that because of the periodical, holiness teaching became an important part of Methodist religious life in Ontario. Both father and son subscribed, Nathanael describing himself as "a constant reader."[55]

When Burwash started work on his first pastoral charge in Belleville in 1861, he took with him a conviction that "a more perfect Christian life than I had hitherto attained was a possibility and still more a duty."[56] Books on the inner life by John Wesley, John Fletcher, Madame Guyon, and William Arthur, combined with a daily half-hour of prayer, brought him to the realization that a gracious God would not deny him both saving and sanctifying grace and that God was willing to provide that grace. As he read Wesley's sermons, he began to see everything in a new light. Peace did not come exactly as he expected it – he admitted that he did not attain or receive "the blessing of perfect love or entire consecration or any other name"; yet he could say, "I saw my God as I had never seen before and that humbled before Him I only willed to be what he would have me be."[57]

Burwash was probably unusually introspective, yet his story indicates that the quest for holiness was by no means the concern of a few obscure individuals or "holiness cranks." The *Guardian* and the denominational publications extended the influence of popular holiness teachers with suggestions to clergy and laity for development of "the higher life," for instance the use of the Methodist hymnbook as a "manual of devotion."[58] Sermons and addresses on the subject of holiness dealt with the externals of religion as well as cultivation of the inner life, earning for Methodism an often well deserved reputation for preoccupation with rules and prohibitions.

A strict code of personal behaviour grew out of Methodism's pursuit of perfection. But it became increasingly problematic to impose it on the entire membership once it grew and diversified in composition. The difficulties were evident in discussions about the "amusements" or "footnote" controversy. Delegates to the 1886 General Conference added to the *Discipline* a footnote that prohibited such activities as the drinking of alcoholic beverages, card-playing, dancing, circus-going, and theatre attendance. The matter was not resolved until the footnote was dropped at the 1910 General Conference. In the meantime it created a considerable stir. Writing in 1902, the editor of the *Guardian* was dismayed that the footnote was generating a controversy out of proportion to its merits and was diverting attention from more important issues.[59]

For many it was the cause of temperance that was of greater consequence than the footnote. Wesley had condemned excessive drinking and all but the medicinal use of "spiritous liquors" (distilled alcohol). Methodists in Canada had long been disturbed by problems which they attributed to alcohol abuse. The temperance societies which they helped to organize in the early nineteenth century exuded revivalism's spirit of reform.[60] During the course of the century, they moved from a position of moderation in the use of wine and ale to total abstinence, deeming even moderate drinking unbefitting the holy life. After a long debate, the sacramental use of wine was questioned, initiating a search by the *Guardian* for good recipes for unfermented wine and creating a market for American Methodist T.B. Welch's grape juice, developed in 1869.[61]

The temperance issue forged a strong link between revivalism and reform. Many Methodists moved easily between a staunch defence of special revival services and working for temperance reform. Their social ethic was consistent with the individualism implicit in the revivalist presentation of conversion and Christian perfection, though temperance workers became increasingly aware of the sociopolitical complexities of the temperance question and broadened their sphere of activity accordingly. The temperance cause reaped the benefits of revivalism, according to S.D. Chown, who had signed the pledge to abstain from the use of intoxicating liquors even before he could write his own name. He consented to his signature and received the picture pledge in the basement of the Sydenham Street Church in Kingston "upon almost the same spot where years afterward I accepted Jesus Christ as my friend and Saviour." During revival meetings, it was the custom "to consolidate our gains" by summoning the people together for the signing of the pledge against strong drink. Chown reported that he had "found great advantage in this."[62]

Prominent temperance worker Nellie McClung also saw a link between revivalism and reform. Inspired to join the movement by the example of her future mother-in-law, Annie McClung (a convert of Phoebe Palmer's camp meeting on the Millbrook circuit), she found that revivalism sometimes succeeded where temperance education failed. Her temperance charts "had shown certain facts, as true as the multiplication tables, and given warnings. It showed the right way, but had no power to make people choose the right way. It appealed to the head alone, and because of this it failed." She recalled that drunkards did not reform and bar-rooms did not empty in the small Manitoba community where she was teaching until after a visit from the Judd sisters, evangelists from Ontario.[63]

E.H. Dewart, editor of the influential *Christian Guardian* from 1869 to 1894, whole-heartedly agreed. Though no less insistent than the later social gospellers that religious principles should be applied to the solution of social problems, concern for personal salvation governed his approach to reform. "True reformation must concern itself with the individual," he insisted. "It must exert a power capable of saving him. All the efforts and agencies which have become corporate, or which are recommended as light-giving and life-ennobling, have their source in human nature regenerated by spiritual power. The churches, as the organ of that power, have much more to do with the reformation of society than has science or legislation."[64] Apart from the salvation of the individual, it was impossible to attempt to save society; without having experienced salvation, a person could not do God's work in the world.[65]

Dewart and many other Methodists regarded sinful human nature as the cause of evils that neither social nor political readjustment could remedy. It was the church's obligation to regenerate individuals as well as to rebuke both public and private sin: the Christian church was "to fulfill its mission in the world, not by assuming the functions of the State, but by being the instrument of bringing men from sin to holiness, and from the power of Satan unto God."[66] But there was, Dewart feared, a new and quite different attitude creeping into the work of reform. He could not endorse proposals for social change which assumed that if people were only well fed and clothed, crime would disappear. This, in his view, challenged the message of repentance and made preaching about conversion superfluous.[67]

Since Methodists expected that a genuine conversion would be accompanied by a changed life, the experience marked not an end but the beginning of an active piety. New converts were admonished to become "useful Christians." With this mandate for religious activism, revivalism sparked the growth of voluntary associations which opened new doors for women in particular. Their work in Sunday schools, missionary societies, reform movements, and charitable organizations gave them opportunities to influence life outside the domestic sphere. Daily life was invested with religious significance as men and women aspired to conform their personal behaviour, homes, and communities to evangelical ideals.[68]

Revivalism shaped Methodism's understanding of religious experience by underlining the importance of conversion as the first step of the Christian journey and the prelude to both personal and social righteousness. Revivalism also affected the expression of religious ideas, for it profoundly influenced Methodist theology. Wesley saw doctrine as derived from the Bible, and for Methodists, as for Protestants generally, the Bible held a distinctive place of authority. Yet Methodists recognized that Wesley had taken a step in a new direction when he presented his doctrinal standards not in the form of a creed or a confession of faith but in a series of sermons that elucidated not only right belief and right action but right experience as well.[69] The experience of the Christian would test and confirm the promise of salvation offered in the Scriptures.[70]

A century later, Canadian Methodists continued to see this as Wesley's contribution to the history of doctrine. In Burwash's introduction to the fifty-two sermons that made up *Wesley's Doctrinal Standards*, he insisted that to understand them properly the reader had to keep their "experiential character" constantly in view. This would enable the reader to see that Divine truth drawn from the Word of God was not merely a subject for intellectual contemplation or speculation, a philosophy or a theory of religion, or even a plan of salvation. It was a presentation of the gospel as experienced by Methodist preachers and exemplified in the Methodist class meetings.[71]

The "peculiarity" of the Methodist tradition as Burwash presented it did not lie in its doctrines of justification, regeneration, and faith, for all these had been clearly defined and preached since Martin Luther and John Calvin. Methodism had moved beyond the sixteenth-century Protestant reformers by "the concentration of all these into *one experimental crisis* of religious life, from which a consciously new life dated its beginning." Conversion was the name given to this experience. In retrospect, Burwash added, it was possible to trace this crisis experience in religious persons of all ages, but in the past it had been obscured – even during the Reformation era. God had reserved it for the age of Methodism "not first to experience this form of religious life, but, for the first time since the days of the Apostles, to make it the central idea of a world-wide Gospel preaching." Though the Wesleys were not the only ones to preach the message of "conscious salvation" in the eighteenth century, "in Methodism alone did this fact of experimental crisis in the religious life enter into the very heart of its standard theology, and exert a *formative influence* on its entire body of doctrine."[72]

It was in this context of their own tradition's history that some Methodists viewed the controversial issue of doctrinal development. In an address to the Theological Union of Victoria College in 1879, E.H. Dewart explained that an old doctrinal definition was like an old coin: it bore certain impressions which connected it with the people and conditions of life which had produced it. The development of doctrine was for Dewart a positive step, involving a fuller and more explicit statement of faith. Wesley himself had greatly contributed to it. His exposition of the witness of the Spirit and Christian perfection merited special mention, in Dewart's view, as Methodism's distinctive doctrines. But like Burwash, Dewart emphasized the importance of both biblical teaching and experience: Wesley "read the Word of God in the light of living experience of men and women who had felt its converting and sanctifying power."[73] While insisting on the importance of right doctrine, Dewart questioned whether subscribing to creeds and confessions was the most effective guarantee of orthodoxy. For him the history of Methodism was practical evidence that "a true personal experience of the saving grace of Christ will do more to preserve from 'divers and strange doctrines,' than subscription to the most elaborate Articles of Religion or Confessions of Faith."[74]

Evangelicals had long been divided by the issue of the extent of human responsibility in salvation. Those who sided with Methodists in positing greater scope for the operation of free will were called "Arminians" in recognition of their affinities with Arminius, one who had earlier taken exception to the implications of the Calvinist doctrine of predestination. Salvation, insisted Arminianism, was available to all, not a limited number of "the elect."[75] An experiential approach to the Christian life was at the heart of what Methodism saw as the distinguishing mark of its Arminian doctrinal positions. As one article explained, Methodism was a religious revival, not a new theology, but Arminian theology was "the only possible conception of the doctrines of grace in a great revival."[76] A contributor to the *Methodist Quarterly* suggested that Methodism's uniqueness lay in the assumption that Christianity was "the life of the soul" rather than an organization or system of doctrine. The movement had acquired its "peculiar color and texture" by its having been "moulded and fused in the heat of revival fires" and "elaborated under that tender and gracious influence which has dominated in Methodist history from the beginning, and must constitute the factor to which all else is subordinate so long as Methodism is true to her glorious antecedents."[77]

That revivalism had given to Methodist theology a distinctive flavour was a view still shared by major denominational leaders in the late nineteenth century. As delegates met in 1884 for the first conference of the newly united Methodist Church, Albert Carman reminded them that "what is peculiarly known as Methodism begins with and culminates in the lively doctrines of practical, personal, experimental and spiritual religion and grace." What Carman called its "working doctrines" included conviction of sin, repentance, acceptance of Christ, regeneration, assurance, sanctification, and the baptism of spiritual power.[78]

Carman presented these practical and experiential doctrines so as to set them apart from theoretical and philosophical approaches to theology. There was more than a hint of disdain for a more sacramental approach to piety. Methodism differed from "ecclesiasticism" with its "proud assumption of priestly office and sacrificial merit, the figment of apostolic succession; and thereby figment on figment, the only availing ministerial ordination, and the consequent baptismal regeneration." He likely felt assured that the relative inferiority of this "ecclesiasticism" could be easily demonstrated to any thinking person when he asked, "How long would it take such doctrines and such a system to save a man, to convert a world?"[79]

While Albert Carman's presentation of Methodist theology set it in the context of a revivalist past, the work of Nathanael Burwash translated the tradition's experiential approach to Christianity into a theological method.[80] Burwash stated the crux of his approach to theology succinctly in his opening lecture at Victoria College (by that time relocated in Toronto) in October of 1893. "We must get at, not volumes of theology constructed to hand," he advised his students, "not creeds and dogmatic canons, but the original facts with which theology deals: – the living sin, the living Christ, the living salvation, and the living God himself. Do not be carried off on minor issues. Theories of Inspiration, Atonement, Inerrency, are not the essence of the subject. But God, Christ, Sin and Salvation are. Where shall we find our facts as to these? In the Bible and in the hearts of humanity."[81]

This methodology guided Burwash's two-volume *Manual of Christian Theology on the Inductive Method*. Completed in 1900, it brought together the ideas he had developed over the course of his thirty years of teaching at Victoria College. In the preface, Burwash explained that the underlying principle of the work had come to him when, as a young pastor, he tried to help those struggling with scepticism. Finding little or no help in the apologetic works of the eighteenth century (which only tested his own faith), he explained, "[my] sole anchorage in this conflict was the inner assurance of faith. In the quiet of closet communion all doubt as to the essential truth of Christianity as a faith of the heart in God and in His word disappeared before the assurance of faith. It was soon clear to [me] that this rather than rational, scientific, or historical investigation, must in the very nature of the case be the basis of the faith of the great majority of mankind."[82] Although Burwash considered his work to be a reconstruction of doctrine, it shared the experiential basis of theology of Methodism's revivalist past.

Revivalism, then, contributed to a distinctive way of understanding religious experience. It shaped both guidelines for behaviour and expression of religious ideas. Its pervasive influence in the late Victorian period is also seen in the denomination's associational forms. Camp meetings and protracted revival services in local churches come quickly to mind as the main institutions of revivalism. These particular associational forms did not always remain prominent, a development which some historians have interpreted as signalling that revivalism in general was in decline.[83] Yet not even the most ardent supporters of special revival services considered them a substitute for the regular evangelistic work of the pastor and laity.[84] Many aspects of regular church life presupposed a vital connection to the religious world view associated with camp meetings and protracted meetings. The class meeting and nurture of children are two significant examples which illustrate revivalism's continuing influence on the life of the church in the late nineteenth century.

Wesley's approach to spiritual formation was developed out of his modification of the Anglican special-purpose religious societies. The class meeting grew out of societies which Wesley organized for mutual support and encouragement of men and women within the Church of England who banded together because of their "desire to flee from the wrath to come." Once Methodists became dissenters from the established church, the function of the class meeting changed in important ways from Wesley's original vision. No longer able to presuppose the support of the Anglican parish system, Methodists at first relied on these meetings to provide pastoral care between infrequent visits of the circuit-riders. Methodism's itinerant system also ensured that a minister would be appointed to a local congregation for only a short period of time. This created opportunities for class leaders to gain considerable power and prestige by providing continuity in the religious life of the congregation. For a person who wanted to become a Methodist preacher, leadership of a class meeting was one of the first tests of a call to the ministry and an important part of theological education.

The class meeting had helped to give Methodism an identity distinct from the Church of England. However, the requirement that to be a Methodist one must also be a member of a class created confusion. In 1854 Egerton Ryerson challenged this condition for church membership. Although his argument was based on the difficulties that young people experienced when placed in a class of "greybeards," his concern that Methodism be recognized as a denomination, rather than a voluntary society, likely influenced his thinking on the subject. The requirement of class attendance was a reminder of the days when Methodists were part of the Church of England. It was a condition that no other denomination placed on its members.[85] Yet loyalty to the class meeting persisted. Some years later when Henry Flesher Bland tried to persuade the 1878 General Conference to do away with the class attendance requirement, again "the attempt at greater inclusiveness was overwhelmingly defeated."[86]

The class meeting was affected by the preoccupation with personal experience that sometimes accompanied revivalism. Class attendance and revivalism have often been perceived as riding the same roller-coaster, a decline in class attendance being attributed to the decline of revival. But, ironically, the success of revivalism may have contributed to one of the most debilitating problems of the class meeting. David Lowes Watson has linked the decline of the class to an increasing preoccupation with inward piety that distracted attention from practical good works and the means of grace. He suggests that while personal spiritual development and evangelism were functions of the early Methodist class meeting, neither served as its primary purpose. The excessive attention to religious experience (arguably related to the impact of revivalism) resulted in meetings that were repetitious and thus onerous to many, distorting Wesley's purpose for the class and undermining its long-term vitality.[87]

In Canada the class meeting quickly became the setting for the personal introspection and evangelism to which Watson refers. The existence and vitality of class meetings as "nurseries of piety"[88] cultivated the type of religious experience associated with Methodism's revivalist tradition. One of the peculiarities of the class meeting, according to the *Guardian*, was that it assumed "the existence of spiritual life and personal religious experience." Without "experimental knowledge of salvation in the hearts of the people," the paper predicted, the class meeting would become formal and lifeless, if sustained at all.[89]

That the class leader and members often proved to be effective evangelists is illustrated by S.D. Chown's account of his conversion, noted previously. Conversion was not a prerequisite for membership in a Methodist class; rather the class was one of the contexts in which a person might expect to experience conversion. Chown had intentionally avoided the class to resist conversion.[90] The peer pressure of the class was intense, for the meeting largely consisted of members relating their religious experiences under the watchful guidance of the class leader. This approach to spiritual formation was carried on by several generations of Methodists. Each week, leaders of class meetings similiar to those conducted by Nathanael Burwash at Victoria College gave participants an opportunity to describe their religious life. The leader might then comment, correcting errors and pointing the way to higher attainment.[91]

Imagine how the unconverted must have felt, with church membership tied to being placed in this situation week after week! It is not difficult to see why the writer for the *Canadian Methodist Quarterly* concluded that when its "peculiar functions" were faithfully worked out, the class meeting was one of the most efficient evangelizing agencies the world had ever known. "Our whole denominational history is largely a recital of the diffusion of saving grace," he wrote, "originating in the unpretentious but powerful influences of the class-meeting ... Many who, under the message of the preacher, have been convinced of sin, have been enabled through the personal and individual dealing of the faithful and competent class-leader to enter into the liberty and peace of the children of God. In this respect the class-room may well be regarded as the inquiry room of Methodism."[92] With the class, Methodism had devised a way of cultivating a revivalist piety on a weekly and regular basis, in doing so passing on its distinctive tradition of piety to the next generation. Since both young and old were often members of the same class, it was not only "beneficial to those who have advanced beyond the threshold of piety," but also "exceedingly advantageous to the lambs of the fold."[93]

How vital was the class meeting by the late nineteenth century?

This is difficult to assess by looking at denominational publications. There were those who felt that the class meeting had lost and would never regain the position which it had when its work was substitute for regular preaching and pastoral care.[94] Others maintained that it was still a power in Methodism and had never been in better shape.[95] Whatever its vitality, participating in a class meeting remained an official test of membership and attempts at even small changes (such as the issuing of tickets annually rather than quarterly proposed in 1890) were defeated.

Competing with the class meeting were associational forms which, as part of the regular work of the church, vied for the time and attention of Canadian Methodists. In North America, voluntary associations were an effective means of extending denominational influence in a context of disestablishment. The Sunday school became one of the most significant of these, involving thousands of adults and children as teachers and students. The Sunday school replaced the opportunities for children and adult members to explore the religious life together (which the class had provided) with systematic and specialized approaches to religious education of children alone.

Some have viewed the popularity of the Sunday school as evidence that by the latter half of the nineteenth century Canadian Methodism had substituted gradual growth in grace for the definite conversion experience associated with revivalism. Yet one must move cautiously in identifying support for Sunday schools as a repudiation of revivalism and the type of piety it aspired to foster. The first Sunday schools were organized to teach poor children basic literacy, morals, and manners. But by the 1820s and 1830s the focus shifted to preparing children for conversion. One historian queries whether "character education," "theological literacy," or "values training" ever replaced the identification of Sunday school with conversion. The Sunday school emerged as the most enduring of the associational forms that accompanied nineteenth-century revivalism. Concern for conversion of children was its "mainstream of energy."[96] In the Sunday school students not only learned the Ten Commandments and the Lord's Prayer; they "absorbed the values and precepts of evangelical Protestantism" and "imbibed their teachers' expectation and learned the behavioral manifestations of religious conversion."[97]

The question of Christian initiation – how children were to be brought into the church – remained contentious well into the twentieth century.[98] The Canadian Methodist church continued to baptize infants while denying the doctrine of baptismal regeneration; for Methodism the new birth of regeneration was linked to a distinct conversion experience. For those who could accept neither conversion nor baptismal regeneration as a way of bringing children into church membership, Horace Bushnell's theory of Christian nurture was a tempting alternative. The *Guardian* described him as one of the most original and thoughtful theologians America had produced, but still warned readers (long after the publication of *Christian Nurture* in 1847) to use his ideas with caution and discrimination.[99]

Methodist leaders generally took that advice, qualifying Bushnell in ways that weakened the force of his organic analogy of the development of the Christian life. One Bushnellian advocate, in a paper presented to a Sunday school convention and printed in the *Guardian*, maintained that the religion of childhood was largely imparted: it "comes from God; and the Christian parent and the Christian Church, by its ministries of ordinance and teaching in various ways, become the agencies through which it is conveyed ... Like the poor blind man on the street, who may either be led into danger by the deceitful guide, or into the safety and plenty of home by the benevolent and kind-hearted, the little child may either be raised to the grandeur of angelic purity and blessedness, or led on to infamy and ruin."[100] To accept this approach to the Christian life, one had to reinterpret the conversion experience, for a child could not know sin or "feel the pangs of guilt like the hardened sinner who, under deep conviction and heartfelt penitence, is turning to God." The terms "conversion" and "born again" could not "in the very nature of things involve the same class of experiences at all."[101]

Yet personal testimony to such new approaches to conversion – and even in some cases interest in child conversions – seems to have been uncommon in the 1880s. The *Guardian* was dismayed at the church's indifference to children younger than twelve to fourteen years who wanted to be converted during a revival, arguing that this was tantamount to offering them to the howling wolves before welcoming them into the fold.[102] One writer described the ideal Christian experience: a person always walking in the ways of righteousness and requiring no conversion. However, he admitted, such cases were uncommon and apt to be looked on with suspicion. Seldom were they presented in the pulpit, since they conflicted with traditional theories of regeneration.[103] At least partly persuaded by Bushnell and romantic views of the innocence of childhood, some questioned whether the conversion experience needed to be preceded by the life of sin that revivalism's presentation of conversion seemed to presuppose.[104] Though theoretically such success with children would preclude adult conversion, many felt no compulsion to choose between the two: a strong supporter of revivals such as Dewart could still praise the efforts being made to convert children.[105]

Unlike Bushnell's nurtured children who were never to know a time when they were not Christians, Methodism, for the most part, still wanted its children to have a recognizable conversion experience. Writing in 1882, Burwash pointed out that it was Methodism that had brought the modern church back to the "Scriptural definition of regeneration as *the conscious crisis of religious life.*" It would be a sad day for the denomination, he continued, if it were to forsake "this clear foundation of conscious experience" for trust in "any occult work, supposed to be wrought secretly, by unconditional grace, and in unconscious states of existence" – a not too veiled reference to baptismal regeneration. He maintained that the whole of contemporary evangelical Christianity had embraced the central idea of Wesley's theology: that "the new birth is this conscious crisis of religious experience preceded by repentence, conditioned upon faith, wrought by the Word and Spirit of God, and completed in the full assurance of Sonship." For Methodism to depart from this view would be "to reduce the work of the church to a process of *education,* as distinguished from the work of *evangelization.*"[106] Canadian Methodism's foremost educator obviously regarded the latter as the more important of the two.

These "regular" means of cultivating piety did not preclude concomitant support for the "extraordinary" means of seasonal revivals. However, the methods by which revivals were encouraged did undergo significant changes during the course of the nineteenth century. The camp meeting, still highly regarded in some regions of the country, waned in popularity, though holiness teachers like the Palmers demonstrated its attractiveness as a place of grace for the already converted.[107] Those who organized the holiness camp meetings were deeply committed to the conversionist aims of revivalism, for the pursuit of Christian perfection was for those already professing an experience of conversion. The emerging Methodist middle class was disdainful of the emotional excesses commonly associated with camp meetings and protracted meetings. But often ordered revivals rather than no revivals was the solution critics proposed.[108] The most respectable could respond to an invitation to "the higher Christian life" issued by many late-nineteenth-century evangelistic campaigns.

And so, in these various forms, revivalism continued to play an important role in shaping Canadian Methodism in the late nineteenth century. Social gospeller Salem Bland, looking back at the last three decades of that century, found it difficult to discover anything that compared with the vitality of "the mighty tide of life-changing influence that was rushing through English-speaking lands" during an era he described as "the golden age of evangelism." He remembered attending as a young minister annual conferences in central Canada that were "peculiarly distinguished by evangelistic meetings, not only indoors but in the streets."[109] Most Methodists in those days, he recalled, still entered the church as a result of conversion; the embers of this warm experience, though they might cool down, could always be fanned by revival into a blaze.[110]

Descriptions of church life sketched by reports of special events sent in to the *Guardian* corroborate Bland's recollections. In addition to revival reports from small rural circuits, readers were kept up to date on large campaigns planned for Montreal and Toronto, scheduled stops for major Canadian and American evangelists in the 1880s and 1890s. Hugh T. Crossley and John E. Hunter were two of the most successful. After their graduation from Victoria College, they were assigned pastoral charges. Each, knowing the other only by reputation, decided to write the other a letter suggesting that they form an evangelistic team. When the letters crossed in the mail, they took it as a sign of God's blessing on the venture. With the consent of their Conferences, they formed a partnership in 1884.[111] Over the next twenty-five years, their names were conspicuous in the reports of the special services held in large towns and cities. Even "the Methodist Cathedral," Toronto's Metropolitan Methodist Church, reported regularly revival services lasting sometimes as long as four weeks.[112] During the course of one such month-long campaign, it was estimated that Crossley and Hunter held fifty-five meetings and spoke to between 75,000 and 100,000 people.[113]

Revivalism's popularity added to the difficulties of those who proposed that Methodism rely on regular services and religious education to recruit new members. Despite complaints about the excesses of enthusiasm which sometimes accompanied revivals, Methodism's statistical success, for which it was assumed revivalism deserved credit, remained a powerful argument against those who disparaged them. In the late Victorian period, revivals (especially those promoted and controlled by denominational leaders) were generally approved.

Moreover, the piety associated with revivalism was integral to Canadian Methodism's self-understanding, for revivalism remained tied to Methodism as "tradition." This was a point made often by the *Guardian* and echoed in other Methodist sermons, addresses, and publications. E.H. Dewart maintained that no church had employed special services or protracted meetings to the same extent as Methodism. Though initially ridiculed, the wisdom of "the fathers" in choosing revivalism as a means of carrying out evangelistic work was no longer questioned. Those who had at first criticized revivalism had since adopted its methods. Whereas other churches might credit their success to an educated ministry, earlier organization, or greater material resources, Methodism owed to the spirit of revival "more than to all other causes, its greatest achievements in all periods of history, and its important position among the churches at the present time." According to Dewart, Methodism would not have been successful without revivals, for they had afforded ample scope for preaching and the laity's zeal.[114]

Of course not all Methodists agreed with this presentation of their past. There were those who contended that revivalism was fine for days when scarce clergy resources or poorly organized societies made them a necessity; now larger centres of population had created a different situation. But Dewart believed that it was still necessary to set apart a special season where particular effort was made to convert sinners. To those who preferred steady growth through the regular services his answer was "ordinary means abound, but ordinary allurements of the world do more abound."[115] He saw the future of Methodism as linked to the fortunes of revivalism: "Methodism was born in a revival of religion, the great majority of its ministers and members were converted in revival services, and the cessation of revivals among us would be a certain sign of declension and loss of power."[116]

Methodists watched with pride as one denomination after another adopted methods which they viewed as their own. Sermons, addresses, and publications claimed revivalism as Methodism's special contribution to evangelical Protestantism. The assumption of a shared revivalist piety was at the heart of their conviction that the evangelical denominations were growing more alike. Dewart noted that accounts of conversions and sins forgiven were no longer considered presumptuous. Many sang and talked at conferences and Bible studies just as Methodists did at class meetings. Others used evangelists and lay-readers in their services and permitted women to preach and testify. The spirit of Methodism, he concluded, had largely permeated all the other denominations, and he informed the readers of the *Guardian* in 1888 that this was "no time to surrender or hold with a feeble grasp, doctrines, usages, and methods of operation stamped with the seal of Divine approbation for more than a hundred years ... As the toilers go to their respective fields of labor for another Conference year, let our motto be 'the world for Christ,' and a glorious revival all along the line."[117]

It is the connection of revivalism with the origins of British North American Methodism, its subsequent statistical success, memories of the piety of "the fathers," and its distinctiveness as a denomination which are important in understanding the tenacity of the concept of "revival" within Canadian Methodism. Revivalism shaped the tradition that Methodism passed on from one generation to the next. A piety profoundly influenced by revivalism gave Methodists a sense of their identity. That piety continued to be much in evidence in the late Victorian period. The numerical strength of Methodism in Canada at that time resulted in a great deal of diversity among its membership. Not every Methodist can be assumed to have had exactly the same religious experience as Nathanael Burwash and Annie Leake Tuttle, nor did all adhere to the Discipline's behaviourial proscriptions. Yet one is left with the impression that Methodism succeeded in presenting a model of the religious life which its practitioners could regard as "normative" and distinctly Methodist. If not all could attest to achieving it, they were at least able to detect deviation from it.

No religious world view can avoid encounter with alternative ways of seeing and doing. Methodism was no exception. Even as it applauded its success, late-nineteenth-century Methodism found itself challenged on two quite different fronts. There were those who in the name of fidelity to the past began to use the traditional language of piety, perhaps inadvertantly, in innovative ways. There were others who in the name of progress questioned the continued use of revivalist language. Methodism in Canada was to be profoundly influenced by both.

CHAPTER TWO

Old Paths and
New Gospels

"When *I* use a word," Humpty Dumpty said in a rather scornful tone, "it means just what I choose it to mean – neither more nor less."

"The question is," said Alice, "whether you *can* make words mean so many different things." Lewis Carroll[1]

All conservatism, G.K. Chesterton once remarked, is based on the idea that if things are left alone, they will stay unchanged. To challenge this notion he observed that when left alone a white post soon becomes a black post; to maintain a white post one must always be painting it again – and, hence, always be having a revolution. Many Methodists in Victorian Canada came to learn by experience the lesson of the white post: it was not easy to preserve tradition in precisely the same terms it had been received, despite the use of many of the same words to present it.

That the likelihood of such adjustment was not evident to all is illustrated by the *Christian Guardian*'s response to the publication in 1886 of Henry Drummond's *Natural Law in the Spiritual World*. The considerable interest in the book prompted questions about its impact on Methodist theology. The editor assured readers that "there is no sign of a probability that the Methodist Church will have any occasion to change its ground respecting free will, human responsibility, and universal redemption" on account of Drummond's book, "or any other book that is ever likely to be written."[2] Such confidence in the face of the massive social change and intellectual innovation of the time is remarkable; yet it seems, in one sense, to have been well founded. Compared with divisions which followed some other denominations' encounter with new scientific and historical ideas, Methodism appears to have come through relatively unscathed.

This rather easy adjustment to modernity has sometimes been attributed to an anti-intellectualism rooted in revivalism which stifled theological development or to a catholicity of spirit deriving from Wesley's "if your heart is right, give me your hand" – Methodists either had little theology to be challenged or were not inclined to fight over what they did have. There is some merit in these observations. Canadian Methodist leaders believed that theology grew out of religious experience. Consequently, they directed their energies more towards cultivating that experience than towards expounding it in systematic theological terms. Carrying on Wesley's ecumenical spirit, they co-operated with others in evangelistic efforts. They were reluctant to quibble over doctrine and willing to transcend denominational barriers. But to look only at doctrine and polity for evidence of disruption does not tell the whole story. Because of the tradition of revivalist piety and the centrality of religious experience for it, the challenges confronting Methodists were of a different nature.

Methodism's encounters with two new religious movements illustrate its unique problems. Conversion and sanctification as presented by the Plymouth Brethren and the holiness movement were seen by some Methodists as threatening to the church at the grassroots or popular level, and potentially as dangerous as either evolution or higher criticism. The Methodist idea of conversion was completely at odds with that of the Plymouth Brethren. And holiness teachers promulgated versions of sanctification seen as suspect and even dangerous to some and simply embarrassing to others. The approach to religious life heralded by these two movements differed significantly from the revivalist piety which had been central to Methodist identity and the ethos of nineteenth-century evangelicalism. Their impact on Canadian religious life was much greater than their small number of adherents suggests. Even denominations with no direct organizational links to these new movements were influenced by them in a variety of ways. Their popular appeal was enhanced and extended when some of the major urban revivalists disseminated their distinctive doctrines. Resistance to these innovations helped to transform Methodist piety (in a less dramatic but no less fundamental way than did the gradual acceptance of evolution and biblical criticism) and to break up the nineteenth-century evangelical consensus which Methodism had helped to define.

Despite differences of opinion on the general nature and function of revivalism in American culture, historians have agreed that it changed Protantism in North America. In the United States, the "transformation of Evangelical Calvinism into Evangelical Arminianism" reoriented religious world views during the Second Great

Awakening. The widespead displacement of Calvinism by Arminian views was brought to a climax by the mid-century revivals.[3] Canadian developments paralleled this transition, and Methodists proudly attributed this adoption of their ideas by others to the impact of revivalism.

Appeals for conversion highlighted the Arminian doctrines of free will and human ability, eroding traditional Calvinist theology. By the 1860s, all the Calvinist denominations except the Scotch Presbyterian, Antimission Baptist, and German Reformed groups seemed to have moved towards an implicit espousal of Arminianism.[4] But was the victory for Arminianism as complete as we tend to assume, or did the ambivalent or dissatisfied find a new way to combine Calvinist assumptions with an appeal for conversion? The possibility that revivalism in a new guise may have offered Calvinism a very effective resistance to this "Arminianizing" is a possibility that has been given little attention. Revivalism's effectiveness may have persuaded some Calvinists to accept features of Arminianism as it already existed. It may also have sparked the creation of an alternative approach to piety which eventually challenged, in the form of fundamentalism, the dominant position which Methodism held within evangelicalism.

The Plymouth Brethren movement drew its inspiration from the millenarian ideas of John Nelson Darby, an Englishman who first organized bands of followers in Ireland and then, more successfully, in Plymouth, England. Darby travelled widely in Europe and North America. He spent long periods of time in Canada and the United States, visiting seven times between 1862 and 1877. He concentrated his activities in Chicago, Detroit, and St Louis, travelling from these cities to New York and Boston by way of Canada. Most of his work in Canada was restricted to the Ontario area between London and Toronto. In both countries, he found his most receptive audiences among Baptists and Presbyterians, particularly the "Old School" Presbyterians – those who had most strongly resisted revivalism's Arminianism.[5] Darby himself remained, as one historian describes him, "an unrelenting Calvinist" whose interpretation of the Bible and history "rested firmly on the massive pillar of divine sovereignty, placing as little value as possible on human ability."[6]

Interest in Darby and the Plymouth Brethren has centred on their interpretation of history: a division of time into "dispensations" and the expectation of the "premillennial" return of Christ to establish an earthly kingdom. Many interpretations of the last times were forwarded in the early nineteenth century, but by the end of the century the dispensational premillennialism of John Nelson Darby dominated American millenarianism. It became one the most important theological components of twentieth-century fundamentalism. This distinctive eschatology gained acceptance with ministers and laypersons. They felt no obligation to sever their old denominational ties, for the Plymouth Brethren claimed that their movement was "non-denominational." Methodism was a major exception to this pattern of permeation. Methodists seemed to be relatively uninterested in dispensationalism, though the few who did accept it tended, unlike Presbyterians and Baptists, to leave their denomination. This reaction has puzzled some historians.[7] Was there something about the Plymouth Brethren belief system, besides its dispensational view of history, that was fundamentally at odds with the Methodist tradition?

Speculation about the end times was not the only reason for the early antipathy of Canadian Methodist leaders to the alternative model of piety presented by the Plymouth Brethren. This is a critical factor in understanding Methodism's later ambivalence towards (and in some cases outright rejection of) twentieth-century fundamentalism. At the heart of Methodism's criticism of the new movement was a disagreement about conversion. Conversion is generally assumed to have been a common concern of both Methodists and the Plymouth Brethren, rather than a point of contention. Ernest Sandeen, for example, says that "all Evangelicals insisted that conversion was prerequisite to Christian faith, that only those who had passed through the experience of the 'new birth' could consider themselves Christians."[8] Darby's discounting of human ability, for instance, did not mean that he found no place for conversion. The "new birth" was central to his description of the dispensation between the First and Second comings of Jesus. It was by conversion that a person entered the spiritual community of the church and became a recipient of the biblical prophecies and promises addressed to God's people living in the dispensation of grace.[9] However, to group "all Evangelicals" too quickly together in their interest in conversion may cause us to miss a clue to Methodism's problems with the Plymouth system.

E.H. Dewart's response to the arrival of the Plymouth Brethren is a striking illustration of how Methodists saw the new movement. In 1869, just a few months before he became editor of the *Christian Guardian*, Dewart published a scathing attack on the Brethren in a pamphlet entitled *Broken Reeds; or, The Heresies of the Plymouth Brethren Shown to Be Contrary to Scripture and Reason*. Then a young minister in Ingersoll, Ontario, he defended his decision not to participate in the local evangelistic services that were creating such considerable excitement. At first glance, his introductory paragraphs seem to contradict the whole-hearted and unwavering support of revivalism (including "union meetings" held with other denominations) that he soon after demonstrated during his long tenure at the *Guardian*. To explain, he discussed the heresies of this group of "Evangelists," "Revivalists," or "Lay preachers." (These were titles which the Brethren used instead of pastor, minister, or preacher, recognizing no distinction between clergy and laity.)

Dewart's objections to the work of the evangelists in Ingersoll make no reference to their unusual eschatology and so are interesting in this respect. Though their criticism of the institutional church and its ministers disturbed him,[10] his major objection at this time lay at the pulse of Methodist revivalism: the conversion experience. It was in their exposition of the "new birth" that Dewart found tell-tale signs disclosing their affiliation with the Plymouth Brethren (which they denied). "Here was the same flippant, easy, and withal earnest exposition of Plymouth doctrine – the same air of oracular self-satisfied infallibility – the same 'finished salvation' by a literal substitution of Christ's sufferings for ours – the same hits at repentance and 'doing' anything in order to salvation; and the same absence of any direction to sinners to confess their sins or pray for forgiveness, and of the need of the Holy Spirit."[11] Most Methodists would have, like Dewart, recognized the approach to conversion these new evangelists were belittling as their own.

Dewart insisted he had no prejudice against lay preaching, revivals, or sudden conversions.[12] His objection lay in these evangelists' teaching "on the manner in which Christ's death avails to procure our salvation, and on the still more practical question of how a sinner is to obtain forgiveness."[13] They taught that Christ had suffered the *actual* penalty for the sins of those for whom he died, thus freeing them from that penalty. Dewart argued that such a view of the atonement made faith unnecessary, led either to a doctrine of universal salvation or to the unconditional salvation of an elect number, and made the work of atonement a commercial transaction.[14]

Those seeking conversion were advised by the Brethren that repentance and prayer were unnecessary until after they were born again. These actions were "splendid sins," for nothing a person did before regeneration was acceptable to God or conducive to salvation. They believed, claimed Dewart, that "a man is wholly wicked, or wholly sanctified. With them, a man who has believed and repented in any degree is saved. A man who is not saved can have nothing good in him."[15] Plymouth evangelists taught sinners to *believe* so as to receive the "finished salvation" that Christ had purchased for those that believed the declarations of the Bible. Dewart concluded: "Stripped of all confusion ... this view of faith amounts to this, – You are saved because you believe you are saved."[16]

This "new gospel," Dewart admonished, taught the unconverted "that salvation is a perfect and finished thing; that, as soon as we believe, we are complete in Christ, fully sanctified as well as justified." It was a total misconception of the nature of salvation as he understood it. Salvation, he countered, changed both a person's relationship to God and that person's character; it implied growth and development. For Methodism, the witness of the Spirit and fruits of regeneration provided assurance and evidence of salvation. In contrast, Plymouthism's "new gospel" answered the question "How do I know that I am an accepted child of God?" by placing the ground of assurance solely on the declarations of Scripture that referred to forgiveness through the blood of Christ's atonement.[17] "The seeker is told that if he believe – not on the person of Christ, but – in the fact that Christ 'paid his debt' and 'blotted out' his sins upon the cross eighteen hundred years ago, he is already saved."[18] There was little room here for repentance or the witness of the Spirit, both important in the Methodist understanding of conversion.

This "new gospel" was, suggested Dewart, just what sinners had long been looking for – how to be saved without repenting and giving up their sins. And no wonder converts were multiplied by such a system! Visiting a Brethren service, he could discover no signs of "the seriousness and influence, that are associated in most minds with the idea of a pentecostal revival." Their piety was "a very narrow, morbidly-sentimental type, with a good deal of a certain kind of cant, and very little of manly, scriptural, catholic godliness." Despite their racy preaching and their new, livelier songs which created such a sensation, Dewart remained unconvinced that much good was accomplished.[19] Little wonder that he protested that the preaching of these evangelists was not true *in the sense in which they used the words*.[20] Although their revival language sounded much like "Methodism," the Brethren's approach to conversion signalled a way of becoming, being, and remaining Christian that was inherently at odds with Methodist theology.

Time did little to persuade Dewart to change his mind. As editor of the *Christian Guardian*, he took the Brethren's views to task[21] and his paper provided a sympathetic forum for Methodists who disliked the rival evangelism. Letters to the editor warned readers to be on the lookout for these "pretended non-sectarian teachers":

In some cases they worm themselves into churches, and particularly Sabbath schools and Bible classes, where they can exercise their influence and stealthily introduce their pernicious teachings. In times of revival effort they show themselves, and, where they are not altogether lacking in discretion, merely pray or speak as they have opportunity; but a close observer will detect their Plymouthism in the marked absence of confession of sin, in the use of the pet phrase "the finished work of Christ," and in great emphasis on the "believe theory."[22]

The *Guardian* familiarized readers with the evangelistic methods of those propagating the "believe theory" approach to conversion. One correspondent described a steamboat encounter with them. A friend had warned him beforehand to take care lest he fall into the hands of the Plymouth Brethren. He managed to avoid them on the first leg of his journey, but a conversation with two strangers on the way back turned into an argument over Plymouthism. One man mentioned that he resided in Michigan, but immediately added that heaven was his home; the other claimed that they "knew they had eternal life." That they had a distinctive approach to conversion was evident to him by the way they spoke. "They were anxious to know if I were equally privileged with them – if I were 'saved,'" he reported. "I meekly told them that I humbly trusted I was, having found Christ about fifty-six years ago, and that through mercy I had been kept from wickedly departing from the Lord. But my terminology did not seem to satisfy them. Said one of them, 'You *trust* that you are;' but urged that I must *know* it."

After this exchange, the two young men recited passages from the Bible which contained the word "know" used in relation to the experience of Christians, "all having been duly marked with ink in their pocket Bibles." Upset by these beliefs, the writer said, "When they thrust their open Bibles before me with the finger on the marked passages, I waved even the sacred Book away ... Such a use of the Bible is almost a profanation." He concluded that while invited evangelists were often a great blessing, many of the Plymouth type were an unmitigated curse.[23]

Concern over the influence of Plymouthism extended well beyond the pages of the *Guardian*. In chronicling the history of Victoria College, Nathanael Burwash credited Plymouthism with having worked a subtle and dangerous change in religious life in the 1860s by reducing the work of the Spirit in the religious life to an intellectual process. Burwash described Plymouthism as a form of rationalism. Its danger lay "in the substitution of the confidence secured by an intellectual process ... for the deep and regenerative convictions and revealing light of the Holy Spirit." Plymouthism had lost sight of the work of the Spirit "by which alone we are truly 'born again.'" What Burwash called "believe the Gospel" evangelism did not lead to assurance of faith through the witness of the Spirit, as taught by John Wesley.[24]

Daniel Steele, an American Methodist theologian and professor at Boston University, saw Plymouthism as a form of antinomianism. Burwash agreed. The Brethren's insistence that repentance and prayer should not precede believing was, he suggested, comparable to the Moravians' error in Wesley's day. They had taught believers to be still, to wait for Christ rather than going to church, communicating, fasting, praying, or reading the Scriptures. But even Moravian teaching had more room for the operation of the Spirit than these modern antinomians, for whom salvation was the result of the operation of the intellect. [25] In his preface to the Canadian edition of Steele's *Antinomianism Revived; or, the Theology of the So-Called Plymouth Brethren Examined and Refuted*, Burwash described Plymouthism's views on atonement, faith, and the agencies by which the Kingdom of Christ would be advanced as an antinomian curse. Plymouthism, he contended, was one of Christianity's greatest enemies because it was creating "weakness from within, which is far more dangerous than can be any attack from without." [26]

Plymouth evangelists soon divided the communities where they worked. In one such case in the southwestern Ontario area around Sarnia, two Plymouth Brethren were initially welcomed in November 1872. But their preaching soon sparked intense interdenominational acrimony, setting the Methodists and Free Church Presbyterians against the Congregationalists and Baptists. Again the most controversial aspects of Plymouthism were the instructions its evangelists gave to those who sought conversion and its teaching about assurance of salvation. [27] Letters to the *Sarnia Observer* reported that these evangelists sneered at asking sinners to pray and repent – the prayer of a sinner was of no more effect than the barking of a dog. Instead sinners "were told again and again that they had nothing to do but believe." And, despite strong opposition, their impact on church-goers was widespread. They impressed even those described as "intelligent men, who had made a profession of Christianity for years." [28]

One of the harshest critics of the Brethren evangelists was the Rev. James Duncan, a Free Church Presbyterian minister whose congregation held joint Sunday school and prayer meetings with the Methodists. In a series of articles for the *Sarnia Observer* he criticized the visitors for preaching about the necessity of "perfect assurance" of salvation. He was dismayed that there was no reference made to the Holy Spirit's work in enabling persons to see their sinful condition. The Holy Ghost might just as well not exist, he added, for sinners had only to "believe in the Lord Jesus Christ." [29]

Not all the criticisms were one-sided. Plymouth Brethren evangelists disparaged Methodist revivals for requiring a long sorrowing period that led to self-righteousness and made a virtue of feeling.

They objected to the Methodist practice of asking seekers to come forward for prayer. They criticized the prominence which Methodists gave to testimonies of the conversion experience, attacking in particular the testimonies of women "as if this was a questionable and unscriptural thing." Aware that Brethren evangelists cited "Let your women keep silent in church," the *Guardian* countered with biblical references to women's involvement. The editor concluded that it was utterly unwarranted to say that Christian women had no right to witness for Christ and to exercise "whatever gifts of usefulness God has given them."[30]

Methodist warnings were not enough to stop the spread of Plymouth evangelism. In his 1869 pamphlet, Dewart had predicted what historians have confirmed: the gospel according to the Plymouth Brethren was very appealing to Calvinists.[31] In a review of Daniel Steele's *Antinomianism Revived*, Dewart noted the incompatibility of Wesleyan Arminianism with the Plymouth system. He wondered, however, whether Calvinists would be able to reject its conclusions. Steele had observed that prominent ministers in the United States were preaching the tenets of Plymouthism. There were reports that Henry Varley, D.W. Whittle, George F. Pentecost, and other leading evangelists were in strong sympathy with "this peculiar theology" and that D.L. Moody had learned his system of Bible study from the English Brethren.[32]

In Canada the gospel according to the Plymouth Brethren was preached by ministers and evangelists with no formal connection to them. One *Guardian* correspondent attending a revival meeting organized by Presbyterians, Baptists, Episcopalians, and Methodists found that all but the Methodists preached Plymouthism: to be saved one had only to believe that sin had been blotted out at Calvary. If you believed, you were saved, and the Bible itself was evidence that you were saved. Concerned that the "leaven of Plymouthism" had already influenced the younger clergy in those denominations, especially the ones interested in evangelistic work, the writer assessed the impact of their teaching as widespread: "Plymouthism, of late years, has run mad, and you will now find busybodies on the [railway] cars, in public places, and holding meetings."[33] The lay-workers' effective use of tracts also transmitted the ideas of Plymouthism. By 1884 Dewart complained that Plymouthism was met with "in such a form as may justify one in saying that it is 'in the air.'"[34] It even attracted promising young Methodist ministers like Salem Bland. For a time he corresponded with Lord Cecil, a peer from a prominent British family who devoted his life to Brethren evangelism.[35]

In an attempt to counter the influence of Plymouthism, Canadian Methodism's leaders made comments which on the surface appear to disparage revivalism. These remarks are more accurately interpreted as a rejection of a specific type of revivalism, one regarded by Methodism as a new and dangerous rival. According to Rev. Alexander Sutherland, the Canadian Methodist delegate to the British Wesleyan Conference in 1886, it was a "pernicious influence," a "jelly-fish religion which, under the guise of a so-called evangelism – (loud cheer) – has caused not a few to turn aside from the old paths." Sutherland asserted that Plymouth evangelism ignored repentance and made faith a mere assent to a proposition rather than trust in a living Christ. It substituted assurance by logic for the witness of the Spirit and put an imputed righteousness in the place of renewal by the Holy Ghost.[36]

Leading Methodists became critics not of revivalism in general but of what from their perspective seemed to be the perverted form of it associated with the "believe theory." Those Methodists who still strongly supported revivalism, and who proudly claimed that their own tradition had emerged from it, were concerned that heretical elements had been added. The critical response of Methodism to the Brethren's "believe theory" of conversion suggests that the religious situation was more complex than either a transition from crisis conversions to nurtured faith or salvation of the social order. It involved more than a rejection of revivalism because of embarrassment over emotional excesses.[37] It entailed rather the difficult task of coming to terms with the coexistence of two distinctive notions of what conversion entailed. The propositional piety of Plymouthism threatened to undercut the Methodist tradition, for it challenged its more experiential piety. For those converted by the approach of the Plymouth Brethren, salvation was grounded in intellectual assent to biblically derived propositions that enabled a convert to answer the question "Are you saved?" with a degree of confidence that Methodism's "witness of the Spirit" seemed unable to give.

Canadian Methodists who took John Wesley's teaching about Christian perfection seriously had more difficulties in store. They paid close attention to personal and public behaviour after conversion as an expression of holiness. However, this presentation of holiness in terms of Christian perfection was antithetical to the Brethren's concept of a "finished salvation":[38] with the creation of "the new man" at the time of the new birth came perfect holiness accomplished by Christ's death. At Calvary, the Brethren believed, all sin – past, present, and future – had been blotted out.[39]

Twentieth-century fundamentalism was to gain a reputation for being ambivalent and even antagonistic to social reform – what Timothy Smith has called evangelicalism's "great reversal." This would not have surprised late Victorian Canadian Methodists. They feared that those who held the idea of a "finished salvation" would tend to treat faith like a charm to secure salvation. This would give a secondary place to practical works of righteousness.[40] A different understanding of the conversion experience and the relation of ethical behaviour to it signalled a changing approach to social reform. It may have contributed to the "great reversal" no less than the pessimism of the complex dispensational philosophy of history to which it is generally linked. The Methodist approach to the Christian life involved possibilities for both personal and social progress that were incompatible with the "believe theory" and inconceivable in the premillennialist schema of history. The rival evangelism with its "believe theory" and suspicion of practical works was fostering a piety strangely unfamiliar to leaders of Canadian Methodism but, with its attention to conversion and holiness, all too easily mistaken for theirs.

Difficult questions about holiness came from other quarters as well, as the interest which the 1850s had witnessed surged again in the 1880s and 1890s. In 1893 one correspondent to the *Guardian* claimed that there had never been a time in the history of the Christian church when the subject of holiness was so widely discussed. No longer simply a Methodist concern, the pursuit of holiness had become interdenominational. The writer was astonished at the increase in holiness literature and meetings, and the growth of associations for the special promotion of holiness that were "moulding the religious sentiment of the age."[41] But there was still no agreement on how holiness was attained or what it entailed. In Canada, Methodists found that Wesley's view of Christian perfection (which some had found problematic to begin with) was now criticized by proponents of alternative holiness theories. As a result a number of distinct movements emerged. These new groups elicited mixed responses of puzzlement, ridicule, and anger, even from those who regarded themselves as holiness advocates.

The story of Ralph Cecil Horner, whose teaching gave rise to a new denomination, the Holiness Movement Church, illustrates well the difficulties which holiness created for Methodism.[42] Born in 1854 in Clarendon Township, Quebec, Horner was converted in 1872 at a Methodist camp meeting near his home. Shortly thereafter he experienced what he called "entire sanctification." His graduation from Victoria College in 1887 probably came as a relief to the professors there, for it was, he says, "a great trial to [them] to have me look them in the eyes and ask them if they had the experience of entire sanctification."[43]

Horner also tried the patience of the committee which conducted his ordination interview. He was convinced that he had been called to be an evangelist; he insisted that he had been "born in a revival and could not be satisfied without seeing sinners coming to Jesus for salvation."[44] This raised some troubling issues. A report of the proceedings submitted to the *Guardian* noted that Horner had been accepted for ordination only after a "considerable discussion occasioned by his unwillingness to take the usual ordination vows." According to the report, he finally agreed.[45] However, his interpretation of the events of his interview a few years later was quite different, fuelling the bitterness of a dispute which ended with Horner's 1894 suspension and later expulsion from the ordained ministry of the Methodist church.

The "prostrations" (falling to the ground) of those under the influence of the Holy Spirit, emotional displays, simultaneous praying aloud, and the noise which accompanied Horner's ministry all contributed to his difficulties with Conference leaders. But failure to submit to ecclesiastical authority was deemed at least as much of a factor. Conference proceedings and Horner's own account indicate that though there was much in the ordination vows to which Horner could agree, he balked at two questions. He was asked about his call to the office of a minister; Horner felt called as an evangelist. And the final ordination question tested his willingness to submit to the authority of the Methodist church; he wanted to be subject only to the will of God.[46] Horner claimed to have agreed to ordination only reluctantly, swayed by the chairman who asked that he trust the committee.[47] Though Horner understood his appointment that year (as one of two Methodist Conference evangelists) to be a recognition of his special call, the Conference insisted then and after that there was only one ordination – to the regular ministry.

In 1890, instead of reappointment as Conference evangelist, Horner was given a pastoral charge. He no doubt felt betrayed. He refused to accept the position and resisted all attempts to control his evangelism. Matters escalated in 1894 when some of his supporters in the Ottawa area purchased a Baptist church for his holiness meetings.[48] The Conference accused him of holding services and collecting money without consulting his superintendent. Though he defended himself by claiming that he had received a special ordination in 1887, the examining committee read from the Journal of that Conference to show that he, despite reservations, had received the same ordination as the others. T.G. Williams retorted that Horner had received a regular ordination, "a fact well known to every intelligent Methodist, as there is only one form of ordination in our book of Discipline."[49]

However, it was not easy for Methodists to rid themselves entirely of Ralph Horner. His teaching about sanctification had been praised by leading Canadian Methodists. Even T.G. Williams had recommended Horner's defence of the possibility of a second distinct "blessing" to *Guardian* readers.[50] He was not alone in his endorsement of Horner's ideas. In 1891 General Superintendent Albert Carman wrote the introduction to Horner's *From the Altar to the Upper Room*. Perhaps Nathanael Burwash was most embarrassed of all. Just a few months before Horner was deposed, the *Guardian* had published Burwash's laudatory review of Horner's *Notes on Boland; or, Mr. Wesley and the Second Work of Grace*. He had informed readers that anything "more completely exhaustive and more perfectly conclusive" than Horner's exposure of Boland's misrepresentation of the doctrine of perfection could scarcely be conceived; a few slips only slightly marred the perfection of the work. Burwash concluded, "We feel proud of Mr. Horner as a Canadian Methodist preacher."[51]

Though it deplored his methods, the Methodist church did not censure Horner's theology. And so the problem persisted. Many continued to regard Horner as an authority on holiness and were upset if their pastor criticized him. As one perplexed correspondent pointed out, Horner's books had once been recommended in the denomination's publications by the best-educated and most reliable leaders in the church.[52] To remedy that confusion, in 1895 the Conference condemned prostrations and simultaneous audible prayers, both practices associated with Horner's revivals.[53] But Horner's influence remained strong.

Horner's insubordination and his controversial evangelistic methods were not the only problem where the issue of holiness was concerned. A second movement developed independently in another region. This time attention centred around Nelson Burns, the Canada Holiness Association (organized in 1879) of which he became president, and the *Expositor of Holiness* (founded in 1882) which he edited. Born in Niagara, Ontario in 1834 and raised in a Methodist home, Burns became a teacher in 1857 after completing his university education at Genesee College near Rochester, New York. Not convinced that teaching was his life's work, he believed God was calling him to the ministry. He was appointed to a Methodist circuit in the London Conference in 1862 and was ordained in 1866. Finding little success in his first five years as an ordained minister, Burns decided to return to teaching. He later attributed his pastoral problems to

his failure to emphasize the holiness which he himself had experienced after reading a book by Phoebe Palmer. His second attempt
at pastoral ministry in 1876 ended two years later after opposition
to his holiness preaching forced him to resign. He was never again
on the active list of the Methodist ministry and was formally deposed
in 1894.

Looking at the charges and counter-charges exchanged by Burns
and his Methodist detractors over the issue of holiness, it is easy to
sympathize with the latter. It must surely have been difficult for
them to try to evaluate the issues raised by the proliferation of
holiness literature and associations.[54] Even in Burns's own version
of the controversy in his autobiography written some years later,
one can see why Methodist leaders found his brand of holiness
doctrinally objectionable. He tended to identify any challenge to his
own leadership as an attack on Divine guidance. His attitude only
exacerbated the problems.[55] He also had a habit of vindicating his
position by drawing attention to the misfortunes which befell those
who opposed him. When E.S. Stafford, a prominent Methodist pastor in Toronto, died of a brain tumour a few years after preaching
against Burns's theory of Divine guidance, Burns remarked, "there
is some probability, in my mind, that the disease in the brain had
something to do with the abnormal strain induced by his attempt
to grapple with and successfully settle the mighty question [of Divine
guidance]."[56]

The radical perfectionism implicit in Burns's idea of Divine guidance was rejected in numerous sectors of both the American and
Canadian holiness movements.[57] Consequently the publication of
the February 1885 issue of the *Expositor of Holiness* caused quite a
commotion. There Burns stated his position on the "mistake question": when God was accepted as absolute guide, no regrettable
mistakes could occur in that person's life.[58] Editorials and correspondence in the *Guardian* criticized the article,[59] as did prominent
Methodists across North America. General Superintendent Albert
Carman responded by writing the *The Guiding Eye*.[60] James Harris,
one of the founders of the Canada Holiness Association, was concerned by the "rise of a new element in the teaching and spirit of
the President" after the 1883 camp meeting, and announced in the
Guardian that he was withdrawing his membership.[61] Daniel Steele,
a highly respected leader of the holiness movement in the United
States, warned Canadian Methodists of the dangerous teaching of
the Canada Holiness Association.[62]

The conferences most directly affected by Burns and the Canada
Holiness Association tried to put a stop to their teaching in 1893.
The Niagara Conference brought charges of heresy against Albert

Truax, one of Burns's major defenders. They suspended and deposed him from the Methodist ministry the following year.[63] After attending the trial, E.H. Dewart reviewed the charges against Truax for readers of the *Guardian*. Truax's view of Divine guidance, his critics had alleged, led to a disparagement of Scripture and Christ by lowering him to the level of ordinary mortals. The Conference also accused him of saying that the Spirit had directed him against holding family prayers, preaching that Christ was merely an example and questioning whether Jesus was conceived by the Holy Ghost. Convinced that Truax's writings contained a "false system of belief, which goes a long way towards Unitarianism," Dewart supported the action of the committee to suspend him.[64]

As for Nelson Burns himself, the Guelph Conference investigated his case for a year before trying him in 1894. The charges were similar to those made against Truax: ignoring the leading doctrines of Methodism by teaching that Scripture was not the only rule of faith and practice, the divinity of Jesus was non-essential, and the will of God might and should be known exclusively by the direct guidance of the Spirit. All charges were upheld and Burns was deposed from his position as an ordained Methodist minister.[65]

A third new type of holiness teaching was less contentious than the methods and beliefs of Horner and Burns, but it too raised questions because of its links with "believe theory" evangelism.[66] Those associated with the Keswick movement, named after the British site where the conferences began in 1875, became active exponents of holiness interpreted as a suppression rather than an eradication of sinful nature. Keswick holiness presented a tempting alternative to Wesley's approach to sanctification, particularly for the Calvinist wing of evangelicalism which found the Methodist tendency towards "perfectionism" troublesome.

Initially, Methodists saw the Keswick movement as a welcome alternative to the other more vexing types of holiness teaching.[67] But even as Dewart lent editorial support to the movement, he raised some telling questions. Keswick teachers sometimes spoke, he noted, as though believers were passive instruments. They dismissed "sinlessness," a notion which they associated with Methodist holiness. In view of his long-standing reservations about the Plymouth Brethren, Dewart was also understandably dismayed that Keswick supporters seemed to suggest that premillinerianism was a necessary component of holiness teaching.[68]

Official Methodist support for the Keswick movement wavered when H.W. Webb-Peploe, one of its leading figures, declared himself in opposition to Wesley's teaching on holiness. At a Keswick convention in 1896, he stated that sin must remain in all believers until death; Wesley had deceived himself and other by teaching otherwise. This, insisted Webb-Peploe, was the Keswick platform.[69] A growing divergence between the Keswick movement and Canadian Methodism was apparent in the *Guardian*'s description of their devotional literature as more mystical than moral. It was unlike Wesley's emphasis on "perfect love" which, when applied, was simply Christian ethics.[70] The *Guardian* regretted that since the Keswick movement had banned discussion of art, literature, social science, and political economy, it was unlikely to make the impact originally anticipated.[71]

It is difficult to assess the impact of these holiness movements. Was the divisiveness which they created more damaging than the source of vitality lost by Methodism's inability to incorporate their diversity? Throughout the holiness controversy, denominational leaders refused to admit that Methodism no longer stood by its "grand depositum" – Wesley's doctrine of Christian perfection. They denied any formal repudiation of it by any branch of the Methodist family. They insisted that the doctrine remained "in our hymn-books, in our Discipline, in our Gospel songs, and, best of all, in the experience of thousands of our people quite as clearly as in the days when Wesley rescued it from the errors and neglect into which it had fallen."[72]

However, these same leaders made no secret of their opposition to holiness "fads and fancies" and saw no need for special publications and organizations. "We need the holiness fervor and the practice of perfect love," they maintained, "but it is not wise to organize the holiness people apart from the Church ... True holiness and perfect love are the central fire of the Church's energy, and true holiness people are in the heart of the Church, and not out of it. We do not want the holiness as a disorganizing element, as the seed of a new sect, but as a vitalizing element in the Church."[73] Ironically, their pleas for patience in dealing with diversity coincided with conference actions to expel Horner, Burns, and others who contributed to it.

There is no doubt that the Plymouth Brethren and the holiness movement presented Methodism with unique challenges and created much confusion in the late Victorian period. In view of the varying models of religious life they presented, the confusion is understandable. Many evaluated these innovations from the perspective of traditional Methodist piety and, in some cases, resisted them from that perspective. However, in certain significant cases, that piety also provided a basis from which Methodists appropriated new ideas. The response to evolution, philosophical idealism, and biblical criticism suggests that a world shaped by the persistence of revivalism enabled some Methodists to move relatively easily towards theological liberalism. Methodist tradition, with its emphasis on experience as component of theological method, played a significant role in this process.

The impact of Darwinian evolutionary theory on Canadian intellectual life has sometimes been posited as having had devastating effects on traditional Christian orthodoxy as a result of the questions which "preyed upon the minds of many young men and women at Anglo-Canadian universities during the 1870s and 1880s."[74] Some historians have claimed that a reconciliation of evolution and religion was effected by John Fiske and others. Others have questioned this easy transition, maintaining that such accommodations were "perhaps most satisfactory to their own psychological needs." Historians who argue the latter position point to the university periodicals of the time, where little solace is derived from apologists; suggestions that a reconciliation would be worked out they see as superficial and defensive at best.[75]

There is no doubt of the pervasiveness of the idea of evolution. It changed people's outlook from a static to a more dynamic world view. But was the picture for orthodoxy in the last quarter of the nineteenth century altogether gloomy? Beyond the universities, there is little evidence of an inclination to grapple with the implications of evolutionary theory.[76] While optimism may have been premature and even unfounded, there is every indication that it was genuine and widespread. It is unlikely that many church-goers lost their faith as a result of Darwin. It is even more unlikely that many of those who did turned to philosophical alternatives such as Hegel's idealism to see them through their crisis of faith.

The popularizers of theistic evolution played a key role in transforming specialized scientific ideas into widely held social attitudes. While their presentation failed to convince many in the scientific community, they won out with the public.[77] Those who calmly insisted that evolution and theology were compatible exceeded in numbers and influence those who argued the reverse. By 1885 Henry Ward Beecher could announce that the controversy between evolution and Christianity had ended. The popular view of evolution which resulted is described by one historian as "a benign, optimistic, theistic variety of the theory." By the 1890s, evolution had become almost a fashionable creed, equated with progress, advance, and improvement.[78]

The way that the *Canadian Methodist Magazine* and the *Guardian* dealt with evolution supports the latter interpretation. The names of Asa Gray, John Fiske, Henry Ward Beecher, Henry Drummond (despite reservations about his "determinism"), and other popularizers of theistic evolution appeared frequently in Methodist publications. The *Guardian* admitted that the initial reaction to evolutionary theory had been uneasiness and fear. It had seemed that evolution superseded all necessity for a creative agency, but then science itself had come to the realization that evolution was simply the way God worked in nature. The editor concluded: "If the principle of the survival of the fittest counts for anything, Christianity has vindicated its adaptation to human want as nothing else in this world has done."[79] At any rate, the truth and value of Christianity did not rest on the verification of a scientific theory. So far all the evidence had gone against the spontaneous origin of life. But even if in some future time scientific investigation indicated something different, Dewart insisted, "that would not justify us in denying a living God and Christ the Savior of sinners."[80]

A few years later Dewart seemed less confident that the battle with science had been won, but his quarrel was with evolution as a concept of development, not as a theory of origins. It was not enough to admit that God existed at the beginning of evolution, for "if it is assumed that evolution is the invariable method, in the realm of mind and morals as well as in that of matter, by which all results are achieved, such a theory throws obscuring shadows over the belief in a personal God."[81] He had begun to sense the misrepresentation of Darwin in the popular understanding of his theory. By encompassing a theory of progressive moral development, evolution restricted the freedom of God to act in history. It made God's action unnecessary by substituting the rise of humanity for the Fall of Genesis. This gave to the direction of history an optimism which Darwin himself had not guaranteed.

Dewart's successor as editor of the *Guardian* shared some of his concerns. If, as the evolutionists implied, sin was merely accidental, natural, inevitable in upward progress, and animal in origin, A.C. Courtice found it difficult to see how guilt could be a reality. From this viewpoint the theory was scientifically, philosophically, and scripturally defective.[82] But even with these reservations, his attitude towards science was generally positive, for it was grounded in religious experience. He urged Christians to familiarize themselves with the ideas and the methods of both science and theology, observing "the means by which they make their way out to a firm and assured faith." He reminded readers, "That a man should seek to solve some of these problems for himself does not imply that he is in danger of slipping off that one sure foundation, the consciousness of salvation through a personal union with Christ by faith. That salvation and that union have been established in the experience of men as surely as any teaching of science. And no advancement in thought can ever overthrow the glorious foundation truth of Christ's gospel."[83]

It is likely, then, that a good number of Methodists appropriated Darwin's evolutionary theory not by the route of Hegel's idealism, but by a way which they considered in keeping with Wesley's theology – confidence in the reality of their religious experience. Indeed, Hegelian philosophy remained suspect. It was associated by many with pantheism. Pantheism, not atheism, was the danger of the day, reported philosopher Borden P. Bowne of Boston University in 1900 as he addressed Victoria University's Theological Conference. As for theism, he believed the outlook was brighter than it had been twenty-five years before.[84] Another American Methodist, John J. Tigert, contrasted Methodist theology with the theology derived from Tübingen's historical criticism. This Tübingen school was "essentially an attempt to rewrite history on the basis of Hegelian a-priori philosophy." He informed *Guardian* readers that it had nothing in common with Methodism. In fact Wesley had anticipated Schleiermacher and those theologians "who would verify the entire dogmatic system by analysis of the implicit presuppositions and contents of Christian experience." Their approach, unlike Hegelian philosophy, was in harmony with "the genius of Methodism in its special emphasis upon Christian experience."[85]

Even Methodists who are sometimes identified as philosophical idealists had reservations about Hegelianism. Salem Bland, for example, described his first visit to a Theological Alumni Conference at Queen's University as the watershed of his intellectual life. There he encountered the work of Hegel and the two Cairds, Edward and John, a bewildering experience which he said made him uncertain whether he was standing on his feet or on his head. Bland claimed that though Hegel helped him to come to an understanding of evolution and history, he never completely accepted his views. Speculative idealism seemed too deterministic, with "no room for the will – just a slow but irresistable development." His discovery of the philosophy of Rudolph Eucken of the University of Jena came as a relief. This form of idealism supplemented Hegel by recognizing a place for the will and emphasizing the need for spiritual control of life.[86]

S.D. Chown , like Bland, credited Eucken with taking him beyond the idealism of Queen's University. Linking his ideas more closely to traditional Methodist themes, he reported that even those who had little interest in evangelistic work were concluding that escape from a sinful or apathetic life was found only by a complete break with the past. "It is still more gratifying to notice," he continued, "that the most pronounced trend in philosophy to-day is away from necessity into freedom and away from the material into the spiritual. Eucken, who as you know at present stands out as the greatest and most conspicuous philosophic thinker in Germany, emphasizes the importance of conversion and proceeds to say that 'from of old the raising up of a new life was the main achievement of religion and the most convincing proof of its truth.'" Chown viewed "the philosophic situation" as "full of comfort and strength for orthodox Christianity," for "the new life that Christ offers is certified to and demanded by experience and observation, by philosophy and literature."[87] While, for some, speculative idealism may have shattered the "old orthodoxy of ideas ... aimed at instilling students with a traditional Christian piety,"[88] for others, idealism reinforced orthodoxy and became useful only when interpreted in the light of traditional piety.

And so Canadian Methodists appeared to have successfully resolved most of their theological difficulties with science and philosophy. However, waiting in the wings was yet another issue of far-reaching consequence. The extension of scientific methods into new areas of inquiry had a considerable influence on biblical studies. The principles of "higher criticism" had been advanced for years in Europe and by the late 1800s were making headway in North American circles. In 1881 the publication of the Revised Version of the New Testament publicized new ideas about the Bible. In the fanfare accompanying its distribution, reports of discrepancies in the documents used for the translation created a storm of controversy. It was clear that no "original" edition existed.[89] Biblical scholarship was also popularized through circulation of a wide array of study materials for summer Bible Institutes attended by teenagers and college students, the International System of Sunday School Lessons, and the home study program of the American Institute of Sacred Literature, to name only a few.[90]

The spread of biblical criticism appears to have moved rather slowly in Methodist circles. Nathanael Burwash did not accept the theory of the dual authorship of the Book of Isaiah until the mid-1880s and was still careful to distinguish his "reverent criticism" from the destructive type associated with the rationalistic German critics.[91] Even this cautious approach to biblical criticism took several more years to work its way into Canadian Methodist pulpits. According to Salem Bland, the controversy over the Bible had scarcely rippled the surface of Methodist church life by 1890s. George Workman's trouble with Victoria College over his views on Messianic prophecy was a portent of things to come, but, as Bland recalled, the incident was not widely publicized at the time. Describing himself as an above-average student, he recalled that as late as 1892 he knew "absolutely nothing about [biblical criticism] except that it was rationalistic, if not atheistic, and I thought it unnecessary and dangerous."[92] He doubted whether anyone in his congregation at that time "knew what the higher criticism was – had ever heard of it."[93]

The Queen's Theological Alumni Conference of 1893 introduced Bland not only to Hegel but to biblical criticism as well. Although Bland eventually became associated with the most liberal theological wing of Methodism, his initial response to this approach to the Bible was hardly an instantaneous conversion:

Reckless iconoclast, as I fancy, some regard me now, I delivered my soul with little hesitation then in a sweeping and cocksure condemnation of such investigations. I denounced them as unnecessary, useless, and disturbing to plain Christian folk. If there are scholars, I protested, who must pursue such unprofitable inquiries, much as rats and mice must keep on gnawing otherwise their teeth would grow so long as to force their jaws apart and doom them to starvation, why should they not keep their researches to themselves or, at least, rigidly within such highly professional publications as no ordinary practical and common-sense Christian would be tempted to read.[94]

Biblical criticism was perhaps Bland's most significant discovery at Queen's and it soon began to challenge his traditional religious views. Bland recalled that he experienced five or six years of resistance, fear, and misgivings before he found "firm footing again on the other side of the slough through which I had wallowed." It took even more time for him to apply the principles of interpretation which had transformed his conception of the Old Testament to the New Testament as well.

The issue of higher criticism was unsettling in some Canadian Methodist circles,[95] but tradition again coloured the response. It was, for example, a consideration in the twenty-year controversy with George Workman. Workman was roundly criticized in the *Guardian* for the views on Messianic prophecy that resulted in his resignation from Victoria in 1892. Since the church was reluctant to declare him "unorthodox," the matter dragged on for years, unfairly keeping him under a cloud of suspicion.[96] At the same time, Workman was one of the harshest critics of the "gospel of doubt" he found in Goldwin Smith's *Guesses at the Riddle of Existence*. He described the results of this "rationalistic" higher criticism as negative, unproductive, and misleading.[97] Like Burwash with his "reverent criticism," Workman believed he had found a place for critical inquiry that did not destroy orthodoxy. Workman was confident that the church had nothing to fear from this type of biblical criticism.

Workman combined confidence in a non-"destructive" higher criticism with a belief that evangelicals would put its methods to good use. In his statement to the Regents of Victoria College in 1892, Workman insisted that he had taught nothing that was not strictly evangelical, that he had no covert doctrinal novelties, and that while his attitude to inquiry was "truly liberal, my spirit, as well as my practice, is as truly conservative."[98] Similar assurances of loyalty to evangelical principles sounded from the theological colleges. They shaped the attitude of Methodists to biblical criticism, which, despite a degree of polarization, was remarkably optimistic.[99] Just as the methods of science were no threat when rightly used, so the evangelical faith had nothing to lose and much to gain from a critical study of the Bible – rightly conducted. Thus S.D. Chown, newly elected as General Superintendent, could speak confidently in praise of liberty and staunchly defend the action of the 1910 General Conference that had ensured that biblical criticism would be taught in the colleges of Canadian Methodism. But Chown may also have calmed the fears of the hesitant by the way he phrased his praise for freedom of thought. "Let every man feel free to reconstruct any epoch of Old Testament history, but," he cautioned, "he had better say nothing about it until he has attained to its spiritual significance and can pluck the fruit from the Tree of Life for the healing of the people. I am prepared to let the pendulum of thought swing me far out into the realm of modern knowledge, but I would rather die this moment than allow it to swing my feet off the Rock of Ages."[100]

Plymouth Brethren evangelists, holiness teachers, scientists, philosophers, and biblical scholars presented a sometimes bewildering array of innovation. Methodism's way of experiencing conversion, its "grand depositum" of holiness teaching, the perception of the nature of change in the world, and even the Bible came under fire from different quarters. Generally Methodists seemed satisfied with the outcome of these encounters, but there was a growing realization that the range of innovation was creating a situation where the old words were no longer being used in the old way. Some, like the Plymouth Brethren, challenged Methodist conversion by presenting an alternative route to it; the evolutionary theory of moral development threatened to make it unnecessary. E.H. Dewart was as wary of Nelson Burns, who claimed that the Spirit was speaking to him in direct revelations, as he was of liberals who denounced creeds and doctrines. The authority of the Bible to which he wished to appeal to check the extravagances of the former was being eroded by the latter. Both undercut biblical authority; neither was using an honest and straightforward approach. "Words that are true," he regretted, were "used to insinuate something that is really not true."[101]

Dewart was not alone in his puzzlement over the use of religious language. Evangelicalism in general, and Canadian Methodism in particular, were about to undergo a process of change that parallels what often happens to systems of belief. Sociologist John Porter has suggested that a certain amount of imprecision is characteristic of a widely held belief system, since its vocabulary is used so frequently. The loss of precise meaning makes it easier for persons to feel that their private interpretations conform to a general social consensus, despite the subtle transformation that takes place in their assimilation of social beliefs.[102] Dewart had spotted some significant differences in the use of the evangelical vocabulary. As active participants in the highly influential evangelical consensus, many Methodists did not notice (or were willing to overlook) these differences. But their reluctance to evangelize with the Plymouth Brethren and the expulsion of troublesome holiness advocates were tell-tale signs that the old consensus might not be able to withstand the pressure of a serious challenge to its world view.

Most Methodists did not seem bothered by what we might now term the cognitive dissonance in their attempts to find a place for new scientific, philosophical, and historical methods. Was this really a crisis of faith? As James Turner has noted, such a crisis was not inevitable. Using the idea of "love" as an analogy, he observes that we still agree to commit ourselves to another for life despite the many "apostasies" that suggest the difficulties; we speak in terms that would seem to be non-rational.[103]

It may be more accurate to say with A.D. Gilbert that the "crisis" was one of plausibility rather than of faith. For, he notes, the crisis of faith seems to have produced very little actual *loss* of faith. There was no serious defection of members. But attracting those who did not already presume the prevailing world view was another matter.[104] For a denomination whose tradition was linked to revivalism, the situation at the turn of the century was critical. Methodists prided themselves on serving "the present age." Revivalism had served the nineteenth century well with its ethic of self-control, self-denial, and "usefulness." This ethic was a critical factor in the survival of many small communities.[105] But were the mores and methods of revivalism still suited to "the present age"? Indications were that the language of revivalism might not be adequate to explain the new age ushered in with the twentieth century.

CHAPTER THREE

New Horizons and a New Evangelism

It is sweet to fathom the design of the Godhead in the midst of general cataclysm.   Joseph de Maistre

City life is like a spider's web – pull one thread and you pull every thread.   J.S. Woodsworth[1]

Canadian history at the turn of the twentieth century defies easy categorization. Seen from one angle, it manifests the mind-set and mores of the "Victorian" age. But from another angle it demands a new "Progressive" or "Modern" label, for much of the Victorian world had been left behind. Canadian Methodist literature of that time reflects this sometimes frustrating mix of old and new. To find familiar evangelical phrases in the sermons and writings of Methodists who thought of themselves as guardians of the past comes as no surprise. But what are we to make of the persistent use of the same language by those regarded as the most forward-looking denominational leaders?

The use of religious language in a period of sweeping changes raises a question: can large-scale and seemingly abrupt ideological shifts take place with only a slight formal modification of familiar patterns of thought? One historian has suggested that this may indeed be the case if the modified variant of a familiar idea has an affinity with very different beliefs and propositions. Familiar patterns of thought thus become embedded in the new. The intimate connection between old and new is almost unrecognizable in this new gestalt.[2]

Could this be what happened to Canadian Methodism at the turn of the century? With what seemed to be only a slight modification of a familiar pattern of religion, Methodists juxtaposed revivalist piety with progressivist presuppositions; yet in doing so they created a way of looking at the religious life that to us appears to be a radical divergence from the past. In retrospect it seems clear that an important juncture for Canadian Methodism – and for North American Protestantism in general – had been reached. Looking back at the cultural shift that took place, we can hypothesize: what happened to Methodism was part of a broader cultural "organizing process" (similar to what took place during the Second Great Awakening),[3] a process which affected virtually every social institution. Evangelical Protestantism saw the end of the old consensus which Methodist revivalism had helped to shape. Meanwhile the new "organizing process" set in motion the formation of new alliances forged from fissures that had been developing for decades. Initially, however, even the progressivists saw themselves as merely faithful transmitters of the revivalist tradition of "the fathers."[4]

While all of North America underwent this cultural reconstruction in the early decades of the twentieth century, the process in Canada was distinctive in a number of important ways. Events had taken Canada along a somewhat different course from its neighbour to the south. The economic realities of Canadian life immediately after Confederation at first fell short of the promises of politicians and railway promoters. At this time there was, suggests one historian, little more to hold together Canada's ad hoc, confused, and partly contradictory developmental policies than a vague desire to imitate the economic progress of the United States. By that standard Canada's economic growth after 1867 did not measure up, despite the railroad, free homesteads on the prairies, an open door to immigrants, and the tariff protection of the National Policy.[5] Hopes for Canada's future were clouded as several hundred thousand moved to the United States between 1880 and the end of the century. As one observer noted, if the Canadian-born population were counted it was Boston, not Winnipeg, that was the third largest Canadian city.[6]

The beginning of a new century coincided with a remarkable turnabout in Canada's fortunes. Business had come of age in the United States by the late nineteenth century, but the scale, structure, and organization of economic activity in Canada remained small, owner-operated, and competitive.[7] After 1900 market forces, capital, new technologies, and mergers combined to produce a Canadian version of the "big business" that we think of as part of the nineteenth century in other industrialized nations. The "Laurier boom," fuelled by Canada's natural resource industry, brought almost uninterrupted economic growth between 1900 and 1913. The long-awaited immigrants finally arrived to fill the prairies. The availability of jobs in Canada stemmed the tide of emigration to the south and the flow of capital northward indicated that even Americans were convinced of Canada's future. News of large profits was common-place and there seemed to be no end to prosperity. Laurier's boast that this would be "Canada's century" suddenly seemed to have more substance than most election promises.

With economic prosperity a pattern emerged in Canada that was well underway in the United States. Aided by a range of techno-logical innovations, business underwent an organizational revolu-tion that signalled the passage of capitalism from a competitive to corporate stage.[8] Mergers, acquisitions, and trusts became more commonplace. Multifunctional and multilocational corporations gradually took over small businesses run by a single proprietor or a few partners. Between 1909 and 1911, 275 individual Canadian firms were merged into 58 corporations. The wealthy and even the middle class poured their money into new investment strategies, disregarding warnings from the church about "speculation."

Repercussions of this business revolution were felt in the political, intellectual, and cultural spheres. By propagating new ways of look-ing at the world and modelling new life-styles, corporate capitalism began to reshape everyday life. The principles of "scientific man-agement" and assembly-line production transformed the workplace. The growth of the service sector created myriad career opportunities for women. The middle class mushroomed with the addition of "white collar" workers to its previous complement of skilled workers, shop owners, small manufacturers, farmers, and members of profes-sions.[9] Technology revolutionized the home as well. Increased pro-ductivity brought the price of such new consumer items as washing machines, and eventually even automobiles, within reach. By the turn of the century, advertising had developed into a sophisticated art of persuasion designed to create a desire to consume rather than simply to inform the public about goods and services.[10] Railroads transported many from the country to the city; newspapers, mass marketing, and motion pictures standardized urban culture and car-ried it to the country.

Over economic reconstruction hung the spectre of wasteful du-plication and needless competition. Farmers, bankers, workers, manufacturers, politicians, and reformers shared (for different rea-sons) a disenchantment with competition. Under the banner of "pro-gressivism," they made plans to meet the challenges of this new world.[11] Given its diversity, it is not surprising that the progressive movement presents a confusing picture of leaders mixing old vision with new methods to achieve different goals. What progressives shared was a growing sense of the corporative nature and connectedness of life that challenged the unrestricted market economy and unbridled individualism of the nineteenth century. They were willing to intervene in the economy – and in people's lives if necessary. With what one historian describes as a mix of the ethos of nineteenth-century Protestant evangelicalism and the new methods of science and large-scale organization, they attempted to restore community and common purpose. [12]

While the promise of prosperity accompanying change was welcome, virtually every social institution, including the churches, experienced dislocation as well. They shared a sense of uneasiness as unsettling reports of economic disparity filtered in from Europe and the United States. Newspaper accounts familiarized Canadians with the evils of British and American cities, and there was growing evidence from Canadian cities to give them credence. Some dismissed them as having little to do with Canada; most had no alternative but to listen, learn what they could of strategies and attempted remedies, and then protect themselves as best they could.

In a sense Canadians first experienced progressivism vicariously, since the full impact of economic change came later than in England or the United States. Other countries' proposals for reform were modified to suit the Canadian situation even before the full brunt of social change was felt. This trend was evident in religious circles. Canadian Methodists displayed a lingering confidence in evangelism that, under these circumstances, was warranted: the old methods were not put to the test as quickly as elsewhere. But they also welcomed and encouraged such "new measures" of evangelism as mass evangelism, city missions, and social reform. But older assumptions about the goals of evangelism were entwined with them. [13] Many Methodists had no quarrel with progressivism's proposition that the situation called for "applied Christianity"; but initially the Christianity that they "applied" was still one shaped by revivalism.

Methodists instinctively drew on what had worked for them in the past to meet the challenges of the city and the west: they modified what had worked so well in rural villages and small towns. [14] Among the proposals to save the city and win the west (and, indeed, the world), none was more prominent initially than the evangelistic campaign. Considering the failure of this style of evangelism to accomplish its aims, it is tempting to read the enthusiasm for it as a desperate effort to shore up a dying way of religious life. However, to do so overlooks the initial success of these campaigns, which bolstered confidence that the "old paths" were best in these new and sometimes troubling times. An intermingling of old and new is apparent in the work of the professional evangelists. In one sense they merely conducted protracted meetings on a grander scale. Yet they also introduced ideas and practices which challenged Methodist revivalism in significant ways.

Revivalism was no stranger to the city, for the mid-century revivals in the United States had been predominantly urban-centred. Support from the rural areas actually lagged by comparison.[15] Though Canadian cities were smaller in size and in number, several were the scene of successful meetings held by James Caughey and the Palmers. Operating in the city soon changed both Methodism and revivalism. The responsibilities of larger congregations made it difficult for a minister to find time to hold revival services. In the early days of the itineracy, a circuit-rider might deliver a sermon to a preaching point as few as four times a year before going off to Conference to be appointed to a new circuit. As one historian put it, "Four powerful sermons, ringing the changes from conviction of sin all the way to perfect love would take care of an entire year's preaching."[16] The settled pastor, who replaced the roving saddle-bag preacher as one of the by-products of Methodist success, preached new sermons to the congregation every week. Some ministers found preaching at revival meetings a bit distasteful; for others the logistics involved in organizing a successful city revival simply made it too taxing.

The solution seemed to be the professional evangelist, who was much in evidence in the revivals that swept across rural and urban areas of North America in the late 1870s and early 1880s. One historian estimates that the appearance of evangelists and revival teams became more common in Canada after 1884.[17] A number of Canadian evangelists, including the most celebrated team of Crossley and Hunter, visited the major population centres. D.L. Moody, one of a number of prominent American revivalists invited to Canada, created a considerable stir during his 1885 visit to Toronto.[18] A year later Sam Jones and Sam Small, a Methodist team from Georgia, attracted even greater numbers (according to the *Guardian* more than had ever attended religious services in Toronto). They awakened an intensity of interest in personal religion that has "seldom, if ever, been experienced in Toronto before."[19]

Not all Methodists were excited about the innovation which professional evangelism represented. The Maritime correspondent to the *Guardian* reported in 1887 that "our brethren in these eastern parts are considerably exercised on the subject of special evangelistic agencies, somewhat on the matter itself, but more as to the best methods." The controversy centred on the use of tactics such as the team approach of Crossley and Hunter and revival prayer bands.[20] These evangelistic teams received a quite different welcome in the west. Crossley and Hunter in 1888 as well as D.L. Moody and J.A. Burke (a substitute in that campaign for Sankey) in 1897 were among the evangelistic teams which drew massive crowds and front-page attention in Winnipeg.

Manitoba Methodism accepted what some saw as new methods of evangelism as in keeping with tradition. The reports of revival services in the *Winnipeg Daily Tribune* and the *Manitoba Free Press* routinely noted the presence of local ministers and Wesley College professors on the platform before a crowd which would have included large numbers of Methodists. The correspondent who described the proceedings of the 1897 Annual Conference in the *Guardian* was pleased to note in his report that "it is quite evident that the present generation of preachers in the Manitoba Conference believes in the old-fashioned Gospel, and the old-fashioned methods in revival services, and doing so, success in soul-saving will surely be ours as it was in our fathers."[21]

The use of revival "specialists" opened a new round of a debate which had drawn sporadic attention since at least the 1850s: should the denomination use professional evangelists? Some argued that to do so marked a departure from one of Methodism's fundamental principles: every pastor was an evangelist who was expected to keep John Wesley's charge to Methodist preachers, "You have nothing to do but to save souls." Consequently, Methodism had produced surprisingly few major full-time evangelists. Every bishop, college president, presiding elder, and circuit-rider was to be a winner of converts.[22]

At their annual conferences in the 1880s and 1890s, Methodists disagreed among themselves about the relationship between the roles of "evangelist" and "pastor." Yet they still agreed on the importance of a converted ministry. Conversion remained a prerequisite for ordination. The highlight of an annual conference was the well-attended public service for ordination candidates at which the ordinands were generally expected to give an account of their conversion and call.[23] The remarks of pastors and professors invited to address the gathering often reaffirmed conversion's importance. At the 1880 Toronto conference ordinands were warned that "no man can be a true minister who is not a converted man ... 'Ichabod' may be written on the door-posts of the Church if conversion is not a requisite for the work." The fledgling preachers were also advised to aim always at conversion and be more anxious about it than anything else, for it was "the Samson lock of strength."[24] Decades later these sentiments were re-echoed: in 1906 ordinands were reminded that the first requirement of the minister was conversion and divine call, not education or social position. The Methodist church, which had really begun in the conversion of John Wesley, would come to an end, the speaker predicted, when it no longer had a converted ministry.[25]

Even in its new city environs, Methodism was reluctant to give up its traditional concept of the minister as both pastor and evangelist. Its leaders approvingly conserved the image of converted ministers seeking to secure a converted membership. Continuing to hold firm to the conviction that every pastor was an evangelist, Methodism attempted to find a place for some specialized evangelistic work carried on in co-operation with and under the supervision of the regular ministry.[26] Special agencies, such as the non-denominational Canadian Evangelization Society, were cautiously recommended,[27] though the hopes for that particular society were short-lived. Many of its workers, often rightly or wrongly identified as "Plymouth," reportedly disparaged the evangelistic endeavours of the regular ministry – a blow to Methodist preachers who prided themselves on that score.[28]

Such complaints about Plymouthism, heard in passing amidst the euphoria of successful ventures into mass evangelism, are striking in view of the divergent approaches to evangelism which developed in the twentieth century. The dissension which surfaced after Sam Jones and Sam Small visited Toronto was one indicator of the differing assumptions underlying co-operative ventures in evangelism.

The dissimilarities between the Jones-Small team and those identified with "Calvinist" evangelism were recognized by the evangelists and many among their audience. Sam Jones contrasted his theology with Moody's by explaining, "Mr. Moody lingers about Calvary more than I do. I linger more about Sinai."[29] Jones rejected what from his perspective was a Calvinist error: that sinners could do nothing except believe before undergoing conversion. "The mere believing that Christ died to save sinners doesn't amount to much," he remarked. "When you come into heaven your entering depends upon what you've been doing down here; there's nothing said about the blood of Jesus."[30] There was also a striking emphasis on moral reform, especially the cause of temperance, in the preaching of Jones and Small. As one historian of revivalism notes, Jones in particular was thought of by his contemporaries as a preacher of a social gospel.[31]

Such distinctions became more than matters of theological subtlety when Jones and Small arrived in Toronto. E.H. Dewart noted that among the clergy, only Methodist ministers regularly participated in their campaign. Absent were those who had gathered around Moody and Calvinist evangelists suspected of being Plymouth sympathizers. He remarked, "most of those to whom we refer were strongly for Christian union at former evangelistic services, where the theological teaching they preferred was taught by the evangelists."[32] His own preference for Methodist revivalism was obvious in his praise for Jones's preaching with its "full recognition of man's part in salvation, and of the necessity of forsaking sin, which we have not seen equalled in the teaching of any other modern evangelist." There was a marked contrast, he suggested, "between Mr. Jones and the evangelists of the Plymouth and Calvinistic schools. He evidently has no faith in the notion that 'nothing either great or small remains for us to do.'"[33]

Dewart remembered a time around mid-century when revival services had been little known in Canada outside Methodist circles. E.P. Hammond and D.L. Moody were among the evangelists who had since "revolutionized public sentiment." As he viewed religious life in the 1880s, Dewart interpreted changes in preaching, pulpit style, and singing as signs that the spirit of Methodism had pervaded the religious movements of the age. Delighted as he was at this "vindication" of Methodist revivalism, he was disturbed by some evangelistic practices which had become commonplace. Were the evangelistic methods of the urban campaigns conducive to fostering the type of conversion experience that was so central to Methodist piety? Instead of Methodism's "time-honored method of inviting seekers to kneel at the communion-rail, or at the mourners' bench," some proposed that prospective converts attend an inquiry meeting or simply stand up. This procedure, he noted, failed to benefit the entire congregation. He wondered whether it was as helpful in the long run as the more "radical" Methodist way. In the campaigns of the new professionals, the seeker was now often asked simply, "Do you accept Jesus as your Saviour?" If the answer was in the affirmative (as invariably was the case!) the person was counted as a convert. This practice was unsatisfactory by Dewart's Wesleyan standards, for, he explained, "conversion is a work of grace wrought in the heart by the Holy Spirit. It is preceded and accompanied by godly sorrow for sin, and is attested by the direct witness of the Spirit of God ... We must see to it that the work of conversion is real, thorough, radical. And this can be best attained by our own method. When men and women have the moral courage to leave their seats and bow as penitents at the altar of prayer, it is evidence of the reality of conviction of sin, and a desire to flee from the wrath to come."[34]

The *Guardian* urged its readers to "ask for the old paths" by staying with the methods "stamped with the seal of the Divine approval for more than a hundred years." Yet Methodists admitted that the city could not replicate the ethos in which some of those old methods had been effective. There was a certain nostalgia for the camp meetings, but few expected them to gain a comparable place in the city. New times demanded new methods – this was admitted. Yet many could give only grudging endorsement to the new urban evangelism with its tinges of "Plymouthism," for it seemed to pervert and undermine the basic Methodist understanding of what the conversion experience entailed.

Always wary of Plymouthism, Methodists noted its adoption by more and more urban evangelists, though terms such as "easy religion" replaced references to the "believe theory." One Methodist described it as "a sort of hold-up-your-hand conversion" which had made Methodism in some places "as weak as water." He feared that "the incipient Plymouthism, and superficial doctrines taught by many so-called evangelists" were responsible for the opposition of church people to "positive conversion."[35] Another complained of "professional convert manufacturers" who never talked about the "old way" of conversion with its insistence on repentance and sorrow for sin. The new way, as he described it, was "to get the Christian to stand up, just to make it easy, and then sing a verse of a hymn to throw a glamor over the devil's eyes, so he won't mind allowing those still sitting just to stand up, or hold up their hands for prayer, and then take their names and hand them to the pastor – a fine lot of sheep to hand over to comfort the dear shepherd's heart."[36] But these warnings went unheeeded. By the end of the nineteenth century, interdenominational revival campaigns, often conducted by an evangelist employing the newest methods (deplored by Methodists as resulting in "easy conversions") had largely replaced the protracted meeting of the local church.[37]

Methodists soon realized that their disagreements did not end with the matter of conversion. Under the influence of Plymouthism, many evangelists presented the whole course of human history in a particular way. A distinctive view of history, dispensational premillennialism, had been a feature of the Plymouth Brethren movement from the beginning.[38] Propagated by popular evangelists and featured at interdenominational Bible Conferences, premillennialism quickly spread well beyond the relatively small number who formally joined the Plymouth Brethren. Sides formed as two distinct parties with fundamental differences of opinion on the goals and expectations of evangelism either accepted or rejected it.

Exchanges between Henry Parsons and leaders of Toronto Methodism after the Jones-Small revival are illustrative of this developing divergence. Parsons was pastor of Toronto's Knox Presbyterian church and was emerging as a prominent leader of those later associated with fundamentalism. He embarrassed Methodists at an Evangelistic Conference by announcing that it would take ten years to recover from the "setback" of what Methodists thought had been a "successful revival." E.H. Dewart, who had been very impressed with Jones and Small, was dismayed by Parsons's "unscripturally low estimate of the value of Christian work." He attributed this to "his peculiar belief that the evangelistic agencies of the Church shall never secure the conversion of the world."[39] He dismissed dispensational premillennialism, a theory which he and other critics interpreted as expecting the world to get worse and worse, despite Christian agencies, until Christ's second coming inaugurated the Kingdom of righteousness.

This view of history prevailed at the international meetings held at Niagara-on-the-Lake, Ontario.[40] The *Guardian* printed notices of these biblical and prophetic conferences which popularized premillennialism despite Dewart's theological reservations. At the time of the 1893 "Believers' Meeting," Dewart was in the midst of a controversy over George Workman's higher criticism. In the Niagara conference papers he found no sympathy for "modern rationalistic views of the Bible." In fact some, he admitted, might even think their opposition to biblical criticism was too indiscriminate. But it was premillennialism, not their approach to the Bible, which seemed to him to be the doctrine which created a bond of unity among participants at the Niagara meetings who formed what he called "a well-defined theological school." Unable to accept their premillennialism, he was disturbed at their tendency to assume that only those who held their particular view of the time, manner, and results of Christ's Second Coming believed at all in the doctrine of the return of Christ.[41]

A.C. Courtice, Dewart's successor as *Guardian* editor, was no more receptive to premillennialism. Sensing the threat that its approach to evangelism presented to Methodist revivalism, he questioned the emphasis that Moody and others were giving to education, for it detracted from their previous interest in evangelism. When Moody's energies turned from evangelism to educational work in the 1890s, some took it as a sign that conversions were less numerous. Courtice found it understandable that those who emphasized an imminent Second Coming, rather than the present work of the Holy Spirit to convict and convert, would become more interested in properly instructing the believer about the millennium than in converting the unbeliever.[42] He feared that Moody's new educational ventures undermined the work of existing agencies to evangelize the world and establish the Kingdom of God.[43] Picturing a steadily deteriorating world seemed to cast doubt on the effectiveness of the Holy Spirit's work, so central to Wesleyan teaching. Yet it was becoming increasingly difficult to engage an evangelist who did not preach dispensationalism.

The demand for professional revivalists threatened to undermine the traditional Methodist view of both the ministry and the Christian life. It forced the denomination to consider some difficult options. They could attempt to make more effective use of pastors and lay workers to evangelize; they could look outside the denomination (with the risk of hiring an evangelist with Calvinist or even Plymouth tendencies); or they could send out their own ministers as full-time evangelists.

To deal with the confusion created by freelance evangelists, Methodists decided to appoint Conference evangelists. Reluctant to issue a wholesale condemnation of non-Methodist evangelists, they also established guidelines for conducting revivals within Conference boundaries and tried to regulate them as much as possible. For most Methodists in the late nineteenth century, the end of conversion remained more important than the means – whether it be by way of an old-fashioned protracted meeting, the agency of a professional evangelist, a pastor, or a dedicated layperson.[44]

Professional revivalism, though important and conspicuous, was only one attempt made to deal with the new challenges facing the church. Concern for people in neglected locales and improverished areas of the city sparked the formation of new associations which soon competed with established denominations for members and financial support. Several of these grew out of the late-nineteenth-century holiness movement. One of the more visible was the Salvation Army, organized by two Methodists, William and Catherine Booth, who had been greatly influenced by Phoebe Palmer's holiness message.[45]

When British Salvationists arrived as immigrants in 1882, they found a promising situation in Canada. They arrived just in time to capitalize on the dissension created by the Methodist union of 1884. The Army grew impressively in its early years[46] and Canadian Methodists paid it close attention. Initial response to the work of the

Salvation Army in Britain, judging from the *Guardian*, had been favourable. When the *Guardian* introduced readers to the new movement in 1880, it praised its work, despite its being "out of harmony with good taste," as effective among "the lowest and vilest of the people" beyond reach of regular church agencies.[47] Dewart was particularly impressed with the similarity between its work and Wesley's and concluded that no Christian could do other than thank God for such an agency.[48] When the Army moved to Canada, many Methodists evidently came to the same conclusion and enlisted.

As the Salvation Army advanced in Canada, the *Guardian* grew wary. The paper continued to commend the Army's zeal and its work among the poor but now criticized its extravagances and questioned the quality of its pastoral care. Methodists detected a subtle shift in the Army's work: no longer satisfied to remain an evangelistic agency to revitalize existing denominations, the Army had become a rival.[49] Methodism now had more to lose than to gain from its success. Dewart predicted that a visitor to a Salvation Army fellowship meeting would find that most were Methodists or had had some Methodist training.[50]

Readers of the *Guardian* confirmed his suspicions. One wrote, "Take from the Army, in many of our villages, those who have been connected with the Methodist Church, who have either disgraced it, or whose goodness was like the morning dew and those with little piety, less self-control and least judgment – who generally go for the newest thing out and you will find that the residue is small indeed."[51] Other readers were even less charitable. They accused the Army of harming the Sunday school and encouraging immorality by keeping young people out late at night. One went so far as to say that he did not believe there was any religion at all in the Salvation Army, the whole thing being a farce and an institution of the devil.[52]

Champions and critics agreed that the Salvation Army presented a unique challenge to Methodism. Its aims, if not always its methods, appealed to many Methodists. Many young people, and at least one promising young minister, Salem Bland, considered joining.[53] Some proposed a union between the two that would combine their strengths.[54] Others proposed the organization of comparable evangelistic agencies and soon there were Methodist "bands" of various types of layworkers – circuit bands, prayer bands, gospel bands, Hallelujah bands. David Savage, a respected Methodist minister, was given permission to leave his pastoral work to organize one of the best-known and active of these, credited after only a few years with twenty thousand conversions.[55] In the 1880s two youth groups, the Epworth League and Christian Endeavour societies, were formed for young people to "promote personal piety and Christian service" among "earnest souls banded together by means of this solemn pledge for the glory of God and the salvation of their fellow immortals who are swiftly travelling towards eternity."[56]

Even as Canadian Methodism organized new associations so as not to be outdone by the evangelistic work of the Salvation Army, the Army moved in a new direction. General Booth's *In Darkest England and the Way Out* presented a new approach to the city in a book that attracted widespread attention after its publication in 1890. Reviewing the book in the *Guardian*, Dewart noted Booth's change of policy: "His former position was to seek to secure the salvation of souls first, and leave the bodily wants to be supplied afterward. Now he boldly declares that unless the pressing bodily wants be supplied the people must perish." Dewart conceded that attending in this way to the plight of the poor in London was commendable. Whether Booth's scheme would ever be carried out was another matter. Dewart had his doubts, especially after the resignation of Commissioner Smith, the most prominent Salvationist in social reform activities and the reputed instigator of Booth's plan.[57]

Others were more impressed. The *Canadian Methodist Quarterly* described *In Darkest England* as "the most surprising thing about the Army that has hitherto transpired." The reviewer pronounced it the most remarkable book of the season; some, he added, believed it to be the most remarkable book of the century, eclipsing completely the excitement created by *Lux Mundi*. The plan represented, in his view, an entirely unique scheme of evangelism.[58] *In Darkest England* was not without its critics, but on the whole it improved public relations and generated growth. The *Guardian* again reversed its position. Dewart described the Salvation Army's ten years in Toronto as remarkable; it had passed the stage where its sensationalism threatened to mar its usefulness.[59] Later editorials referred to it as the most important contemporary religious movement.[60]

This new phase of the Salvation Army's work once again prompted a parallel Methodist response. Denominational leaders asked themselves: could they do religious social work and do it better? They answered by throwing their support behind city missions. Methodism's interest in city missions predated *In Darkest England*[61] but was given new energy by it. In 1887 the mission that became the Methodist model was founded by Hugh Price Hughes, a London minister and editor of the *Methodist Times*. His mission offered an alternative to those who questioned the Army's effectiveness, particularly after a census found that the original barracks were two-thirds empty on Sunday evenings.[62] Interpreting this as a sign that the Army's approach had failed, British Methodism undertook its own work among the poor.

Canadian Methodists responded whole-heartedly to the "Forward Movement" of Hughes's city mission. The *Guardian* considered it instructive and suggestive for churches in Canada and made frequent references to its work.[63] The *Canadian Methodist Magazine* described his mission as part of a movement which was striving, as Hughes had put it, "to show the people that Jesus Christ is the best Friend they ever had, and that His principles will do more for them than Socialism; that Christianity should influence all aspects of social life, and is not "played out," but that it has a message for men and women, to-day, in this life as well as for the life that is to come."[64]

Visitors to the London city mission on a Sunday morning could expect to hear Hughes's assistant, Mark Guy Pearse, preach on "the relation of the individual to Christianity." The typical afternoon service would find Hughes linking the ethical teaching of Jesus to social issues. The evening service was, as Hughes described it, "strictly evangelistic." Despite his concern that some were so busy saving souls that they had no time to save men and women, the first annual report of his mission work stated that about five hundred had professed to find salvation. Not a single Sunday had passed without public decisions for Christ, including some striking conversions. All the work of the mission converged, he insisted, "to the supreme end of personal conversion."[65]

Hughes was sometimes criticized for his sensational methods, but the *Guardian* defended him. The paper praised his attempts to combine evangelism with the application of Christian principles to social problems. The mission was credited with increasing Methodism's interest in social and moral reform. Commendation for Hughes's new methods was coupled with a warning that if Methodism lived on memories and traditions alone, losing "the old fire and power" of its services, God would raise up some other agency to do the work it had done in the past.[66]

Convinced that the city mission offered a promising way to evangelize neglected urban areas, some of the wealthier Canadian Methodist churches funded similar ventures. In Winnipeg, a Sunday school teacher named Dolly Maguire organized a class especially for immigrant children. The class quickly outgrew the space provided. After a large lean-to erected outside the church and a rented tent both proved to be too small, the mission moved to a building near the CPR station. Outside the building a large sign in eight languages welcomed people with the words, "A House of Prayer for all People";

it soon earned the name "All Peoples' Mission." The mission provided religious teaching and, with additional staff after 1893, a broad range of social services. Besides Sunday school classes, there were prayer meetings three nights a week, house-to-house visitations, relief aid to the sick and the poor, an employment bureau, mothers' meetings, and night school. In 1907 social services expanded again under J.S. Woodsworth's superintendency.[67]

In Toronto a hall was built in 1894 by H.A. Massey in memory of his son Fred Victor, once active in city mission work. Five Methodist churches in the area supported the venture with workers and funds. The Fred Victor Mission provided gospel meetings on Sunday and Monday, social activities during the week, cheap lodging for homeless men, and a medical dispensary.[68] Links to urban revivalism were evident in the mission's evangelistic services and in the prominence of Mary T. Sheffield, a graduate of the special program for city mission workers at D.L. Moody's Chicago Bible Institute.[69]

The links between evangelism and city missions remained strong over the next two decades. The group of students from Victoria University who pondered how best to continue the spirit of revival after a visit from evangelist Gipsy Smith were inspired to city mission work as they met for prayer in the Mission Board Room of the Wesley Buildings. Describing a very emotional scene, J.M. Shaver reported that each student stood and "surrendered his all to the God Who called to him from the bleared face of the genius in the gutter, through the hopeless wail of the drunken outcast, weeping over lust and appetite beyond human control, through the thousands of poorly-paid young men and women for whom it was made easier to fall than to live a noble life, and from the little children who have ten chances of becoming criminals to one of becoming Christians." The next day the group met with the Fred Victor and City of Toronto Mission Boards to organize a co-operative program of social work.[70]

For Methodist women, excluded from ordained ministry, the missions provided unique opportunities for Christian service that even involved a salary, albeit a small one. This was the case for those who joined the deaconess order after its establishment in 1894. The Fred Victor Mission was the largest single employer of Methodist deaconesses, members of the most influential of the Canadian orders. In the years between its founding and the merger with its Presbyterian counterpart after church union, the Methodist deaconess order trained more than nine hundred women for teaching, nursing, and social work in Canada's major cities.[71]

For thousands of other Methodists, involvement in movements of social reform was a way of meeting the turn-of-the-century challenges.[72] The temperance crusade gained widespread support from reformers who connected alcohol use with poor working and living conditions. Other reformers tried to improve conditions by supporting the labour movement. The cause of temperance and labour attracted many who, like the city mission workers, were convinced that evangelism and social reform were inseparable. This connection was important, for it enabled religious activists to claim continuity with the past. Later social gospel leaders were able to retain support within sectors of Methodism that might otherwise have banded to oppose the innovative and sometimes radical pronouncements they forwarded. No denomination in Canada was more actively involved in the twentieth-century social gospel movement than was Methodism, but the nineteenth-century roots of this involvement owe at least as much to the social Christianity preached by city mission evangelists as to the liberal theologians who are usually credited.[73]

Despite a growing recognition of the church's social mission, Methodists began the new century convinced that "souls" necessarily superseded "the social order" as the primary (though not exclusive) concern. In the days of Dewart's editorship, the *Guardian* had repeatedly reminded readers that Christian work entailed more than devotional exercises, orthodox beliefs, and ritual observances; it involved carrying a Christly spirit into all relations of life making even secular life sacred.[74] Yet the spiritual mission was primary, and was not to be "subordinated or thrust aside by [the church's] philanthrophic efforts to improve the social and temporal condition of society." He believed that there could be "no lasting philanthropy, or benevolent sympathy" that did not spring "from the faith and love of renewed hearts."[75] Dewart was not alone in emphasizing personal salvation as the key to reforming society.[76] Public criticism from prominent ministers awaited those who forgot, as one labour supporter discovered. E.S. Rowe's plea in support of strikers was met with a sharp rebuke from W.S. Blackstock who retorted that if Rowe would only turn his attention to the salvation of souls with the same enthusiasm, he would be a great power for God in the church.[77]

The stances that leaders took on the matter of "regenerated individuals" as the nineteenth century drew to a close hold a few surprises. It was Albert Carman, now widely regarded as having been very conservative in his social views, who argued that Jesus was a social reformer as well as an evangelist, seeking to regenerate the surroundings as well as the souls of his followers. An article by "M.T.S." (probably Mary T. Sheffield) reported on a conference where Christian workers associated with Moody had been challenged by the idea of "the fatherhood of God and the brotherhood of man."[78] On the other hand, Salem Bland had not, apparently, undergone his conversion to the social gospel in 1899. He was still preaching sermons like "The Kingdom of God Realized Only in Individual Regeneration" where, while sympathizing with the cause of labour, he maintained that the Kingdom of God was spiritual and entered by being born anew. Responding to the criticism that the church should do more charitable work, he replied: "Well I for one don't think the chief business of the church is to open soup kitchens and clothe tramps or even deal out alms." Justice was more important than charity, he believed, but even that was not the business of the church. It should be concerned with the new spirit within rather than with outward arrangements.[79]

But change was in the wind. When Salem Bland accepted an invitation to teach at Wesley College in Winnipeg in 1903, he came face to face with the problems of immigration to the west. The experience changed a man already struggling with the new ideas of biblical criticism; it created a social gospeller. Those involved in the temperance and labour movements gathered additional denominational support when S.D. Chown was appointed as secretary of the newly formed Department of Temperance and Moral Reform in 1902. In that position he encountered new ideas that would change both him and the Methodist Church. The influential denominational paper was also in flux. The long editorship of Dewart was followed by several short ones. This changed in 1906; that year W.B. Creighton, who had been in charge of the paper during the illness of George Bond, was formally recognized as the new editor of the Guardian. He held this position until 1925 when he became the editor of the Guardian's successor, the United Church's New Outlook. The young assistant's sympathy for a progressivist gospel became increasingly apparent over the years.

As for General Superintendent Carman, he began to have doubts about some of the new directions the church was taking. In 1902, at the same General Conference which appointed Chown to the Department of Temperance and Moral Reform and approved the start of church union negotiations, he expressed concern over the small increase in membership in the previous four years. This ought not to have been the case, he believed, given the evangelical movements, the work of special evangelists, and the Forward Movements of mission societies and Epworth Leagues. He predicted that the church would soon have to ask "whether there is after all any better method for the salvation of souls than the old protracted meeting and the penitent bench used by the revival pastor among his own people. Surely we need well to look to it that we be not drawn aside from our main business and aim, the personal salvation of men, women and children, to other church efforts, however close akin, and however excellent in their character. Whatever other systems may accomplish, Methodism cannot fulfill its mission without continuous and abundant revival."[80]

The approach of a new century presented Methodists with a unique opportunity to experience this "abundant revival." Many thought a nation-wide revival the most appropriate way to usher it in. Plans for "the coming revival" all promised revitalization of religious life. But as the methods and message of these alternatives to evangelism were scrutinized, there were signs of developing fissures. Lines of demarcation were set as those who looked for revival weighed the merits of the "old paths" against a "new evangelism." Ultimately the debate took place in a context of disillusionment. The heralded revival failed to materialize.

Accompanying the idea of a religious awakening to celebrate the twentieth century was concern over a slackening in Methodist membership growth. Carman alluded to this in his 1902 General Conference address. To this was added the financial troubles created by the recession of the mid-1890s. In years past, revival had meant different things to different people. It was not only a means of converting persons but was also, at the practical level, a means of converting institutions to Christian principles, a boost to membership and subscription statistics, a way of enlisting people in religious causes, and a solution to financial problems.[81] In the case of Canadian Methodism's "Twentieth Century Forward Movement," that much remained unchanged. In fact, the *Guardian*'s report of the decision of the 1898 General Conference to inaugurate the Forward Movement gives the impression that the financial drive was the main concern and the suggestion of an evangelistic effort almost an afterthought.

At the General Conference in 1898, William Blair and Salem Bland's evangelism resolution was prefaced by a confident statement that the twentieth century would prove to be "the most glorious in the history of the Christian church since the century that witnessed the Incarnation of the Redeemer of the world."[82] If those grand hopes were dampened after the Twentieth Century Forward Movement failed to produce the anticipated number of conversions, it was not for lack of publicity in denominational circles. The special committee organized to "plan" the revival recommended that each region arrange sessions to promote it. They designated the second Sunday in October 1900 as "Revival Sabbath." It was to be followed wherever possible by special services.

The importance of revivalism in Methodism's past was not overlooked. The committee urged that there be "a general use, under wise adaptation, of the means and methods by which Methodism has achieved her former triumphs." The doctrines of repentance, justification, regeneration, and entire sanctification were to "be set forth with clearness and energy." The committee requested that during the campaign the denomination's periodicals be made "especially evangelical."[83] The *Guardian* co-operated by keeping its readers informed of what each region was doing. It reported on evangelistic activities of various local churches, gave advice to ministers on conducting revival services,[84] and drew attention to the drive by headlines such as "A WAVE OF SPIRITUAL REVIVAL NEEDED" and "A DEBT-PAYING REVIVAL NEEDED."[85]

To the dismay of those who had promoted it, the results of the much-heralded "Revival Sabbath" were disappointing. The *Guardian* noted that the beginning of the campaign had been duly observed in most parts of the Dominion, but included a telling detail when it noted that Toronto's effort consisted of special services in the Metropolitan Church conducted by the youth of the Epworth League.[86] Emphasis on revival continued into the new year and the *Guardian's* first editorials of the twentieth century affirmed its importance.[87] But for all the fanfare, the revival services organized for the fall and winter of 1900–1 came nowhere close to meeting expectations. The effort was by no means a complete failure, for the financial goal of a million dollars was reached and surpassed.[88] However, the monetary achievement was overshadowed by the membership statistics for 1901. To be sure, all areas of the country showed an increase in membership, but the rate of the increase was disappointing.

The general revival "ordered" by Methodist officialdom to celebrate the coming of the twentieth century had not materialized.[89] Warnings like those from the *Guardian* that Methodism would have "sold her birthright and gone back upon her magnificent history when she ceases to lead the world in evangelism"[90] were not enough to turn the tide. The numbers for 1902 were even more discouraging. So despite special evangelistic campaigns, the General Conference statistics for 1898–1902 showed the smallest increase of any quadrennium since the 1884 union.[91] As the campaign drew to a close, criticism of revivalism surfaced once again. Disappointment over the results of their own "Twentieth Century Forward Movement" added to the bitterness of dealing with the "Plymouth" alternative to evangelism that Methodists viewed as perversion of their tradition.

Many had looked to professional revivalism as a solution to the problems of evangelizing the city. Even those who thought that its commercialism was distasteful, its theology suspect, and its effectiveness questionable found it difficult at first to argue with the crowds it attracted and the converts it claimed. But Methodism's "decreasing increase" in membership seemed to suggest that the denomination was not benefiting from professional evangelism, at least not numerically.[92] There was talk of withdrawing support for the work of professional evangelists – support which had never been whole-hearted to begin with. Most recognized that the professional evangelists were not entirely to blame. The *Guardian* noted the church's preoccupation with organization and machinery, false liberalism in thought and practice, Sunday secularism, materialism, and reckless criticism from outsiders. But there was no doubt that the dependence on "special and professional evangelists" for revivals was partly to blame: the *Guardian* had "again and again warned the Methodist Church against the weakness which must result from her pastors failing to be everlasting evangelists."[93]

Ironically, the Twentieth Century Forward Movement – another revival, though a denominationally sponsored one – was the most publicized solution for the problem that revivalism had helped to create. The mixed results of such an enterprise did not go unnoticed. C.S. Eby wrote a series of articles criticizing the denomination's priorities, using Toronto's Metropolitan Church to illustrate. He reported that when the financial part of the movement was launched, a crowd was there to see the magnates and pillars of the church pledge a quarter of the denomination's goal of a million dollars. But the response to the evangelism proposal was quite different: "When the spiritual revival, that was to sweep the country, was to be inaugurated in the same Metropolitan, every great official and lay magnate was splendidly conspicuous by unanimous absence, and the whole left in the hands of the – Epworth League." The leaders themselves had found to their dismay that "a revival is not to be had when it is ordered."[94]

Despite the failure of the Twentieth Century Forward Movement, another evangelistic campaign was organized in 1903 to celebrate the bicentenary of Wesley's birth. It again linked revivalism to fundraising.[95] Carman published several open letters in support of what he called the first need of the church: "a revival in the sense of the olden time; a revival that saves men from sin, and stirs them up to hate it in all its forms and at its very beginnings; a revival where souls are truly and gloriously converted." He urged that the revival deepen spiritual life and "widen in statistical demonstration" as well.[96] In his view, nothing was more appropriate than to celebrate the bicentenary of Wesley's birth with an offering for missions, since the Methodist revival had kindled the missionary spirit of the last century.[97]

Again the financial returns were the most impressive result. Even before the appointed time for the simultaneous revivals, the *Guardian* seemed to be preparing readers for different results than they had anticipated. The paper issued a statement which was to became increasingly common over the course of the decade: the "coming revival" would be different from any that had preceded it. "We speak much at times of the old-fashioned revival," observed one editorial, "as if that is the thing that we must have at all hazards. It indeed was a great and glorious experience, and is a precious memory to many of us, but we would not limit the Spirit by saying that we must have another after its type. It may come after a different fashion, and with many differing features."[98]

Within Methodism tensions soon developed between those supporting revival and those doubting its appeal. Some seemed divided in their own minds on the issue. S.D. Chown published an article in 1897 on the positive uses of fear in calling for conversion. He concluded that "the pulpit needs to speak emphatically to-day upon the horrors from which men are saved, as well as the beauties of the life to which they are saved."[99] Just three years later, however, the *Guardian* reported that Chown's paper on "The Revival Power of Methodism: How Lost and How to be Regained" had aroused a lively discussion at a Toronto Methodist Preachers' meeting because "the message which it contained was so startling." In a turnabout of emphasis, Chown had announced that it was time to stress the positive rather than the negative side of religion – what a person was converted to rather than converted from. Maintaining that Christ said more about service than sin, he concluded that "the revivalist to-day must recognize the conditions, and apply the truth in new ways. The preaching will be less dramatic, and the conversions will be less demonstrative."[100]

This "startling" message was substantially the same as the one Chown presented to a Spiritual Conference at Victoria University the following month. Chown speculated that if Methodists imitated the methods which "the fathers" used, they would indeed have similar results – in areas where the problems of life were the same. However, the same effectiveness could not be expected in places where life was more complex.[101] Although the "revival that is coming" might be less dramatic than those of the past, Chown assured them that it would be "full of burning righteousness and intense spirituality."[102]

"The coming revival" was the subject of articles by another up and coming young minister who became a prominent member of Methodism's Department of Evangelism and Social Service. Ernest Thomas (who sometimes wrote under the pseudonym "Edward Trelawney") urged the church to look beyond the message of the past generation. The revival, he said, was already in their midst, present in the divine life that was struggling to find non-ecclesiastical expression in the work, for example, of the Conference of Associated Charities and Correction.[103] Thomas warned against identifying "a revival" with the work of evangelists like D.L. Moody or Reuben A. Torrey. Revivals had occurred before these evangelists arrived on the scene; furthermore there was an ongoing revival which had nothing to do with them or their methods. In what would become a frequent criticism of professional evangelists in the twentieth century, Thomas worried that Torrey had a tendency to define Christianity as his own type of it "rather more emphatically than some of us would."[104]

Despite these reservations, it was Ernest Thomas who wrote an appreciate report of Torrey's 1907 Montreal campaign for the *Guardian*. The biblical scholar George Workman, whose use of higher criticism had placed him at the centre of controversy, was named as one who had assisted those seeking conversion. Thomas noted this point to illustrate the way that persons representing diverse theological perspectives had worked together in evangelism. Interestly, as Thomas observed (and in contrast to the positive press coverage of earlier evangelistic campaigns), the secular press was critical of Torrey. Thomas defended Torrey's work against reports which left the impression that he was an "ardent, narrow theological controversialist, who appended to his polemic addresses a few mechanical words of gospel invitation." Such press reports, he insisted, "could hardly explain the attractiveness of the meetings."[105] Apparently Methodists still tended to close ranks when outsiders attacked something so close to the heart of their own tradition.

Uncertainty about the specific features of "the coming revival" was also evident in the *Guardian* during W.B. Creighton's first years as editor. When his son Donald, the well-known historian, wrote about him many years later, he emphasized his social gospel sympathies. He claimed that his father "had never been impressed by the revivalist traditions of the old Methodist Church."[106] But W.B.

Creighton's views on the subject of revivalism were perhaps not as clear-cut as his son recollected. Editorials before (and some even after) 1910 generally supported this form of evangelism. It is not disparagement of Methodism's tradition of revivalism that we find in these editorials; they seem, rather, to represent the struggle of a person who cared deeply for that tradition despite uncertainties about its continuing vitality.

Creighton agreed with those who regarded revival as the greatest present need of the church. He meant by "revival," he explained, just what "the fathers" meant, with insignificant modifications: not special meetings but a revitalization of religion. It had become fashionable, he realized, to speak condescendingly of the old revival meeting, but he warned that only a fool ever discarded an old method without having a better one to substitute. "It is all very well to talk of the old-fashioned 'explosive' type conversion (and a sneer lies in the very word), but where," he asked, "is the new type of conversion? It is easy to talk of developing in men 'a passion for righteousness,' but where is this 'passion for righteousness'? The old-fashioned revival would do more to develop a 'passion for righteousness' than anything else the world ever saw."

To those who believed in child conversion he replied, so did the fathers. Childhood training was not new. Universities, culture, official influence, and wealthy members had all contributed to Methodism's growth, but its strength had been its evangelistic power. He challenged readers by placing the matter of revival squarely before them: "If we have lost the power to save sinful men, let us face the issue fairly. If this power was only an illusion, let us not hesitate to speak forth our conviction. If the gift of the Holy Spirit be but a poet's dream or a theologian's mental vagary, let us know and say so; but if the power be a reality, and the trouble simply be that we have lost this power, then in the name of our Lord let us seek it till we find it."[107]

By mid-decade came news of a religious awakening in Wales and reports of revival in England and the United States. The *Guardian* showed considerable interest in the progress of the Welsh revival in 1904 and 1905.[108] It reported that no year in the church's history had seen so many and such impressive revivals as those during the previous twelve months. The editor admitted that the revival had not spread to Canada, but nevertheless remained confident that the methods used in Wales would bring the same results in Canada.[109] And in 1905 Reuben A. Torrey, superintendent of Moody Bible Institute, complied by bringing a revival to Toronto.

The *Guardian* introduced Torrey as one whose recent success in Britain, part of a world tour, had been unprecedented since Moody and Sankey.[110] The paper endorsed and promoted the Torrey revival. Over 37,000 copies of a special issue of the *Guardian* circulated to mark the occasion. Torrey's work in Canada was initially declared a success as reports of revivals came in from all over the country. Never before, said Creighton, had he been able "to report so continuously the triumph of the Gospel in the saving of multitudes of men in all the Conferences and on all the districts in our work."[111]

But, in the midst of celebration, religious leaders began to hear revival news that was disturbing. An American minister, Charles S. MacFarland, had been investigating the impact of Torrey's work in the British Isles. Late in 1905 he published a report which claimed that representatives from every school of thought believed that Torrey's work had been harmful. Torrey's critics were disturbed by his narrow-minded denunciation of those holding different theological views, by the "machinery" of his campaigns, and by his commercialism. Some North American ministers responded by urging churches to withdraw support from Torrey's campaigns.[112] More evidence supporting those sceptical of revivalism came two years later when statistics showed a heavy decrease in Nonconformist membership in Wales. Losses were particularly heavy "in the very region over which the revival swept in such power." (The *Guardian* added that this should not be interpreted as a testimony against the reality of the revival.)[113] Already disturbed by professional evangelism, Methodism called more urgently for a "new evangelism" district from professional revivalism.

To add insult to injury, there was the apparently effective use by others of practices identified with Methodism. The *Guardian* had observed early on that a characteristic of the Welsh revival was its impact on denominations "not ordinarily affected by such manifestations or disposed to treat them with a friendly eye."[114] Congregationalists, for example, supported the evangelistic work of one of their prominent British ministers, William J. Dawson. His book, *The Evangelistic Note*, drew favourable notices in the Methodist press.[115] Congregationalists were also instrumental in bringing the well-travelled British evangelist "Gipsy" Smith to North America for an extended period.[116]

It was the Presbyterians, however, who many Canadian Methodists feared had taken their place where aggressive evangelism was concerned. In 1901, just prior to the start of negotiations between the Methodists, Presbyterians, and Congregationalists, Salem Bland saw the convergence of evangelistic practices within Methodism and Presbyterianism as a promising sign that federation was possible.[117] He was not the first to draw attention to the adoption of revival practices by other groups; Methodism had for years noted this with pride. What caught Methodists by surprise was the number of occasions when they had little choice but to accept the role of follower, not leader, in organizing evangelistic campaigns.

This became increasingly evident in western Canada, where the Presbyterians adopted the "Chapman plan" to organize evangelistic campaigns.[118] J. Wilbur Chapman devised a system of carefully arranged "simultaneous revivals" after the American Presbyterians appointed him in 1901 to a new committee on evangelism.[119] In 1907 Chapman visited Winnipeg at the request of the Presbyterian churches there.[120] In 1909, some of Canada's most prominent Presbyterians worked with him in southwestern Alberta and British Columbia, one of several Canadian campaigns that year. W.D. Reid (pastor of one of Montreal's largest churches and later a leader of the pacifist movement), T.B. Kilpatrick (professor at Manitoba College and later Toronto's Knox college), and C.W. Gordon (also known as novelist "Ralph Connor" and a prominent figure in the social gospel movement) joined with Chapman's own evangelists and singers. A report to the *Guardian* commented that it had "more than once been remarked upon that the Presbyterian Church in the West seems to be taking the place of the Methodists as the evangelistic denomination."[121]

Disappointed that the Methodist church had not been responsible for the religious awakening in the west, the *Guardian* put the best face on the situation by noting the co-operative spirit of Methodist ministers during the campaign.[122] But the matter did not end there. A letter to the editor from H.G. Cairns questioned whether it could be said that Methodism even had an evangelistic policy. He recounted the frustrations of trying to work with the Presbyterians. Their General Assembly committee wanted, and was given, full control over the plans, since the Methodists had no similar group with which to negotiate. Local Methodist ministers were invited to join the work and accepted the places assigned to them. Cairns regretted that the effort had not been under joint control.[123] In another letter he added, "I am not jealous of our Presbyterian friends and their new birth in evangelistic zeal, but I am jealous for the retention of our place, our traditional and rightful place in the van of evangelistic work."[124] Repeated calls came for Methodism to regain its rightful place.

But a critical juncture had been reached. A shift could be detected in the plans for evangelistic campaigns. In one western town the revival was organized along the lines of the "Chapman plan" and linked to a visit from J.G. Shearer of the Presbyterian Social and Moral Reform Department[125] and Methodism's own S.D. Chown. The reporter to the *Guardian* described this as a different form of evangelism. It was perceived as "new evangelism" and some at first feared a confrontation (which apparently never materialized) between the "old school" methods and the "sane and scientific evangelism" of Shearer and Chown.[126] Soon campaigns such as this where social reform was expressly linked to evangelistic work became more common. In trying to revitalize their evangelical heritage in this way, Methodists like Chown prepared the way for acceptance of the social gospel, presenting it as an "evangelistic" movement enhanced by a scientific spirit.

Whereas, in the nineteenth century, the statistical success of their evangelism had assured Methodists of the soundness of their theology, the less than reassuring statistics of the early twentieth century did not inspire that same theological confidence. Canadian Methodism searched for a "new evangelism" at a time when others were engaged in a quest for a "new theology," a label enveloping a wide variety of new ideas and a familiar term to *Guardian* readers. Reservations about the revival tradition of "the fathers" were tied for some to questions about old theological assumptions.

In the ensuing theological conversation, many shared the concerns of the respected biblical scholar, Franz Delitzsch (with whom George Workman had studied in Germany). Referring to "a deep gulf" between the old and new theology, Delitzsch feared that the traditional distinctions between "nature" and "grace" had vanished; everything had become "nature." Consequently, there was no room for forgiveness, regeneration, or sanctification – all important aspects of religious experience as understood by Methodism. His opposition to the "new theology," according to the *Guardian*, stemmed from his experience of having seen "miracles of grace" as a youth in Germany, rather than from his learned research.[127]

The impact of higher criticism on evangelism was also problematic. L.W. Munhall, an American Methodist evangelist, created a stir in the *Guardian* after his scathing attacks on the teaching of higher criticism.[128] One of the most interesting of the exchanges on the subject came from C.S. Eby. He saw Munhall as exemplifying the weaknesses of professional evangelism when compared with Methodism's own revivalist tradition. Evangelism, said Eby, was becoming a "superficial hodge-podge of theology, with many an alien mixture which Wesley repudiated and fought against" instead of solid teaching. To this was added "the veriest lollipop doggeral mated to music of jingle," substituted for Wesley's glorious old hymns.

Eby called for a return to the old paths of "true Wesleyan evangelistic enterprise." His models were the Palmers and two leaders of the Holiness Association, John Inskip and William McDonald.

Quite unlike them, Munhall had brought with him to Vancouver what Eby described as "such a conglomerate of Plymouthism, Premillennarianism, broken-down Methodism and Munhallism, that I sat astonished." Against Munhall's methods and his view of verbal inspiration, Eby defended what many would have thought an odd pair – the "old paths" of Wesley and modern biblical scholarship.[129] And by and large, the leaders of Canadian Methodism shared this positive, if not always enthusiastic, attitude towards modern biblical scholarship.

As the new century began there was no firm line between support for revivalism and openness to theological innovation. The *Guardian* published many articles that expressed forward-looking opinions; yet it was quick to defend revivalism against criticism of biblical scholars interviewed by the secular newspapers. "Let them compare the achievements of their vaunted erudition, with the marvellous results of Moody's labors, or Torrey's labors; and they will find their littleness in startling contrast with the grandeur of the soul-saving evangelists God has honored" was the *Guardian's* retort.[130]

The importance which Canadian Methodists continued to attach to successful evangelism is helpful in analysing their different responses to two forms of "new theology" in the first decade of the twentieth century. Attention focused primarily on two of its proponents: R.J. Campbell, whose book *The New Theology* was distributed in Canada in 1907, and George Jackson, who found himself in the middle of a controversy over biblical criticism shortly after his arrival from Britain in 1906.

The New Theology was an immediate sensation in Britain and North America. It went through five editions in less than a month and made R.J. Campbell, an already well known Congregationalist minister, "the most talked of man in England."[131] Initially Campbell's book received a favourable review in the *Guardian* from Ernest Thomas, who presented Campbell as "an earnest evangelistic preacher, with a vital experience of God in Christ."[132] But in the same issue W.B. Creighton took exception to Thomas's review in a lengthy editorial that is strikingly negative, given the support which progressivism enjoyed under his editorship.[133]

A second review of the book following its release in Canada described the "new theology" as "a bitterly disappointing and empty thing." It contended that what Campbell claimed his theology could do was already being attempted, to a degree successfully, by the orthodox churches.[134] A news item a few months later noted that Campbell was no longer influential in the Free Churches; his engagements had been cancelled because of an "instinctive feeling that the gospel Mr. Campbell preaches is not the gospel that can save the world."[135] Despite Creighton's own growing involvement with the social gospel movement, in which Campbell was also active, editorial opinion of Campbell's "new theology" changed little. The *Guardian* predicted that his visit to the United States would likely embarrass some Congregational churches, for his views were "far from popular";[136] his theology was neither constructive nor destructive, but "simply vaporous."[137]

In striking contrast was Canadian Methodism's response to a concurrent event. George Jackson, a British Methodist minister, arrived in Canada in the fall of 1906. Within two years has was embroiled in a controversy over higher criticism. Unlike the earlier case of George Workman, this one was accompanied by widespread popular interest. And unlike the reception of R.J. Campbell's "new theology," Jackson's ideas attracted widespread official support within Canadian Methodism. Looking behind and beyond the actual confrontation of 1909, we can see that the Jackson affair involved more than a skirmish over the academic freedom of higher critics, though that was certainly at issue. Just as significant for Methodism was the solution which his approach to evangelism offered as a way around their problems with revivalism.

George Jackson visited Canada on more than one occasion before moving to Toronto in 1906. He was introduced to Canadian Methodists on his 1902 speaking tour as an "evangelist," not a biblical scholar, because of his involvement with British Methodism's city mission work. The *Guardian* highlighted his evangelistic work as head of Edinburgh's Central Mission, inspired by Hughes's city mission in London.[138] Speaking across the country before several Conferences, Jackson called for the restoration of Methodism's "partially lost evangelistic ideal" which he felt had been obscured by the pastor and the teacher. Reporters described him as "an evangelist of high order" who believed that Christian education should not be substituted for conversion.[139] The following year, Jackson visited Toronto en route to a speaking engagement at a Northfield, Massachusetts student conference.[140] Again the *Guardian*'s report of the event connected Jackson's approach to evangelism with Hughes's commitment to the old spirit, if not the old methods, of British Methodism. This evangelism, said the editor, had restored Methodism's pristine ideals, rekindled its pristine enthusiams for souls, and "set it to aggressive and practical work."[141]

Jackson's wife, Annie, credited Hughes and his city mission with having had a profound impact on her husband.[142] This innovative approach to evangelism, she confirms, caught the interest of several

Canadian Methodists who played an instrumental role in inviting Jackson to Canada. A letter from R.P. Bowles (who succeeded Burwash as President and later as Chancellor of Victoria University) from which she quoted recalled the events which led up to Jackson's seven-year stay in Canada: "The background was that the evangelistic work of the Church, and particularly its preaching was not what it should be. The feeling prevailed that the intellectual and cultural life of the people had advanced beyond the prevailing type of preaching. A reaction was setting in."[143] Aware of the work of the Forward Movement in Britain, Bowles and others were convinced Canadian Methodism needed to adopt this type of evangelism. Consequently, in 1905 a teaching position at Victoria University was offered to Jackson. Because of his commitment to preaching, he turned down the offer, but a year later accepted a call to become the associate minister at Toronto's Sherbourne Street church. Victoria's Board of Regents eventually persuaded him to join the faculty as professor of English Bible, a position which he accepted in 1909.

Even before he began teaching, Jackson found himself in trouble after the local newspapers printed excerpts from an address on Genesis which he had given to the YMCA.[144] Tom Sinclair-Faulkner suggests that the resulting controversy was resolved by *dividing* the theory of biblical criticism from the practice of piety and insisting the latter have priority.[145] Yet for Methodist theology, "theory" had always been *derived* from its practice of piety; Methodism had traditionally recognized the priority of piety. The outcome of the controversy was therefore predictable. George Jackson seems to have recognized this. His approach to the Bible was intimately related to (not divided from) his concern for piety. His fear was that traditional piety and the old methods of cultivating it were in danger of becoming irrelevant in the modern world. There was a need to forge a new kind of evangelism.

Initially those who expected a conventional approach to evangelism from Jackson were not disappointed. One of his first sermons in Toronto, preached at the Metropolitan church, called evangelization of the masses the first work of the church. If the church failed here, he insisted, it failed in its most important purpose. Soul-saving, he reminded the congregation, was their primary responsibility. He warned, "If we give up the brave and fervent spirit of evangelization we tear up our charter."[146] This reiterated statements from his recently published *The Old Methodism and the New*, where he had stated that "Methodists ought to care for Christian ethics; we ought to care much more than we do for Christian theology; but it is for men, for dying men who need the gospel of the grace of God, for whom we must care supremely ... We may still go on discussing 'questions of the hour,' and feeding the souls of the hungry with little, half-baked expositions of great social problems, but [without aggressive evangelism] our work will be done."[147]

Jackson himself recognized that his proposals varied at significant points from what he called "the old Methodism." Before coming to Canada he had intentionally drawn the attention of those who invited him to *The Old Methodism and the New*, hoping thereby to avoid misunderstandings. Dedicated to the memory of Hugh Price Hughes, to whom he credited "the revival in our midst of the only kind of evangelism by which England can be won and held for Christ,"[148] the book made it clear that even in matters as fundamental as conversion, the older expressions of Methodism were true still – but with a difference.[149]

Jackson's critics soon realized that their disagreement with him went beyond his use of higher criticism. One of the numerous letters sent to General Superintendent Albert Carman (Jackson's most prominent detractor) arrived from Edinburgh, where Jackson had worked just before coming to Canada. Word had spread that Carman was mistreating a man who had done such magnificent evangelistic work in Scotland. But the correspondent informed Carman that he was sceptical about the "conversions" at Jackson's Edinburgh mission.[150] A Sherbourne Street church member expressed similar reservations when interviewed by the *Toronto Star*. Recalling that Jackson's chief claim to distinction had been his evangelistic work, board member Thomas Jones told the reporter that "the first year he was, on the whole, satisfactory, although many of us thought that he might have gone farther with his Sunday evening after services. We would have been better pleased had he extended invitations to penitents, asking them to stand up and declare their surrender to religion. We did not expect him to do so every night, but we wanted the evangelical forms at intervals." When the matter was brought up at Sherbourne Street's quarterly meetings, nothing was done. Then what the *Star* called "a more serious objection" was raised when Jackson described modern revival songs as as "skim-milk hymnology" – even going so far as to criticize the "Glory Song" used by Torrey in the recent revival![151]

Some were unhappy with Jackson's approach to evangelism, but others found through his ministry a way of affirming their Methodist heritage. His influence was widespread, although probably not to the extent that Chancellor Bowles suggested when he wrote to Annie Jackson that her husband's published sermons were in almost every Canadian minister's library.[152] But Jackson's sermons presented a "new evangelism" that blazed new paths and opened doors that took some Methodists where even Jackson might have been reluctant to go. The impact of his "new evangelism" on Canadian Methodism has been overlooked as a significant early expression of the social gospel movement. In one important study, for example, the term "new evangelism" is used in connection with the activities of the 1920s, leaving the impression that it was an outgrowth of, rather than a contributor to, social Christianity.[153]

George Jackson's work in Canada illustrates how the concept of evangelism broadened. Innovations were linked to traditional ideas and practices so as to make them acceptable alternatives to older approaches to piety. The linking of old and new was evident in other areas of denominational life as well. A striking feature of Creighton's early editorship is the frequent introduction of controversial subjects juxtaposed the next week – or sometimes in the same issue – by a toned-down discussion of the issue presented in more traditional terms. For instance a 1908 article by Ernest Thomas announced that "we are all social reformers now. We have passed beyond the stage at which we speak of saving souls."[154] The next issue featured an editorial explaining that this meant only "saving souls" in the narrow sense. The church's chief aim was to still to save souls "by bringing their inner life into conformity with God." Even the church's social mission, had to be done by that means. In words that could just as easily have been George Jackson's, the editoral continued: "And if the time ever comes when the mere work of social reconstruction, no matter on how high a plane that work may be conceived, becomes overshadowingly important in the thought of the church, then will she cease to be the great, Divine, life-giving institution that her Divine Lord intended her to be, and become one of the common things of earth."[155] Whether this was a disingenuous ploy to keep most readers happy, or whether it merely reflected ambivalence in the minds of the leaders of the denomination, it was characteristic of the approach to the subject of "souls or the social order" in the first decade of the twentieth century.

S.D. Chown, a social gospeller who ventured into "new evangelism" with like-minded Presbyterians, communicated in a similar fashion. He was adept at phrasing his concerns in terms that even those who might not share his social views could appreciate. When the anticipated revival came, he assured readers, "the old doctrine of individual conversion" would be insisted on as strenuously as ever; but, he added, it would have "a widened area of application."[156] But by 1910 he was ready to concede that things would never be as they once had been. Speaking of those who were "crying for the old-time revival, with the old-time manifestations, when the old-time conditions are gone," he continued, "the old-time power we must have, or we are hopelessly lost, but the new-time application of that power is the great need of our day. One cannot but feel for the dear brethren who stand with tearful eye, pleading with sinners to come to Jesus, before congregations which, when tested, profess to the last man, woman and child, to be converted. The question is 'What are they converted to?'"[157]

Symbolic of the transition within Methodism in the early twentieth century was the breakup in 1910 of the Crossley and Hunter team (due to the poor health of the latter) after twenty-six years of evangelistic work. It was in a sense a portent of things to come. Accompanying Methodism's "coming revival" was a gospel and a model of the religious life that differed from both the nascent fundamentalism of many professional evangelists and, just as significantly, the revivalist piety that Methodism had done so much to propagate. The metamorphosis of evangelism corresponded to a broader exchange of cultural presuppositions; the reorganization of religious life was only part of a larger pattern. The twentieth century heralded a new age to serve; for many the "old paths" were no longer a sure way to the Kingdom of God.

CHAPTER FOUR

"A Charge to Keep ... to Serve the Present Age": Towards a New Model of Piety

And may we not expect that our religion will become less individualistic as we come to realize that we must not only "save our never never dying soul," but also "serve the present age." J.S. Woodsworth

No idea is more than a half truth unless it contains its own opposite, and is expanded by its own denial or qualification. Northrop Frye[1]

At the turn of the century two Albert Carmans, father and son, each expressed the dilemma then facing the Methodist Church. Albert A. Carman, the son, published in 1900 a fictional account of a ministerial candidate's struggle to come to terms with religious tradition in *The Preparation of Ryerson Embury*. We first meet the hero at a revival meeting resisting group pressure to experience an old-time conversion.[2] The book's publication coincided with the efforts of the other Carman, then General Superintendent of the Methodist Church, to promote revivals as part of the Twentieth Century Forward Movement. Ironically, the elder Carman was no more successful in procuring a nation-wide awakening than was the local church in the younger Carman's novel in converting Embury. By the end of the novel the young man had become a labour reformer; by the end of the Forward Movement campaign the direction the Methodist Church would take was much less clear.

Methodists were finding it increasingly difficult to ignore speculation that they were somehow losing their talent to evangelize – what they had considered the very secret of their success. The problem was not entirely new. Religious life not being quite up to the standards of "the fathers" had long been a complaint. Canadian Methodism had undergone considerable modification in an effort to

deal with this situation, whether real or perceived. Apathy, afflu-
ence, expansion, and urbanization were among the factors which
triggered the demise of saddle-bag preachers, camp meetings, and
protracted meetings. In their place were mothers, Sunday school
teachers, settled ministers, and professional revivalists.

While methods changed, the model of piety throughout that century remained much the same, connected as it was to the denomination's revivalist past. But by the turn of the century there were
signs of change here as well. After 1898 the annual statistics showed
that Methodism was not keeping pace with the growth of other
denominations, notably the Presbyterians. In the analysis which
followed, even key aspects of Methodism's traditional piety came
under scrutiny. The reservations voiced by W.B. Creighton, S.D.
Chown, and those who supported George Jackson indicated that
more than a modification of methods best suited to procuring conversion was underway.

Once initiated, Methodism's search for a "new evangelism" became more than a desire to recapture the glories of past revivals.
Uneasiness with the traditional revivalist model of piety evoked
responses ranging from toleration to outright rejection. Methodist
leaders configured a new model of piety in the years leading up to
the formation of the United Church in 1925; thus in this new understanding of the Christian life the influence of early twentieth-
century progressivism was a criticial component. Each facet of traditional Methodist piety – the conversion experience, behaviour, the
expression of religious ideas, and associational forms – was affected
by this development.

In the first case, a reinterpretation of the conversion experience
was underway by the turn of the century and was evident in the
denominational publications and the remarks of prominent leaders.
Methodists had long recognized that the level of emotion accompanying conversion might vary. Indeed, more "solemn" conversions
helped to deflect the charges of excessive emotionalism levelled
against Methodists. Yet those dissatisfied with the approach to religious experience that had developed under the influence of revivalism found little support for or evidence of an alternative
understanding of religious initiation.

However, as the twentieth century progressed, some men and
women began to speak of their religious life without reference to a
conversion experience. Even some who had earlier claimed such an
experience recast the events to make it less dramatic and significant.
H.A. Massey, the wealthy and influential Methodist entrepreneur,
is a case in point. At Massey's funeral in 1896, James Allen, pastor

of Toronto's Metropolitan Church, told those gathered that Massey had always spoken of having experienced conversion at the age of fifteen. That year he persuaded his father to hold special services in their home and helped the pastor to invite neighbours to the meeting. At these revival services a "new emotional experience of peace and joy came into his soul." But now Allen suggested that Massey was taught to believe this was conversion. Allen revealed that just before Massey died, the two of them had realized that conversion had actually taken place much earlier. Contrary to what Massey had believed since he was fifteen, he had obtained in that adolescent experience a "clearer view of Christ," not conversion. Allen continued, "It seems strange that a quiet, consistent life, earnest devotion to duty, calm enjoyment of the public and private means of grace, faithfulness and love in reproving sin, earnestness and success in working for the salvation of others – it seems strange that these should not be regarded as evidences of conversion on account of youth and the absence of vivid emotion."[3]

In explaining his decision to leave pastoral ministry to head the Department of Temperance and Moral Reform, S.D. Chown also reinterpreted his conversion experience. Building the Kingdom of God was the true purpose of the church, he now maintained, and only in the effort to establish the Kingdom would there come "outpourings of revival power giving us numerical increases equal to the days of our fathers."[4] Chown connected the change of emphasis from "revival" to "the Kingdom" to his own spiritual journey. He recounted how, during a conversation with "Bro. Bland of Ottawa" (probably Salem), he had realized for the first time that his own conversion had pointed towards moral reform as the mission of his life: "I thought I had been converted by passing through profound sorrow for sin ending in the clear witness of the Spirit to my forgiveness accompanied by abounding joy. At least that is the way in which I wished to be converted and the way in which I have tried to persuade myself I was converted."

A revised account of Chown's conversion emphasized a determination to do God's will, rather than an emotional experience. His religious experience, he reported, had really been more like the conversions he was observing among contemporary youth. Their motivation was more likely to be a desire to do good rather than to repent and be forgiven for past sins. He defended this, asking, "And who shall say they are not as soundly converted to God as were their fathers though they have not passed through the same convulsive or cataclysmic experiences ... Let us therefore not be pessimistic but believe that God is really saving souls in the midst of us in the persons of our young people who are gladly laying themselves upon the altar of God for the service of humanity."[5]

Not only were there claims of earlier and less emotional conversions; in some cases any conversion experience at all was denied. William Hincks (whose criticism of "explosive" evangelism was instrumental in persuading Toronto Methodists to organize "Decision Days" in the Sunday schools as an alternative to revival services)[6] was disturbed at this new development. Writing his autobiography in 1939 and 1940, he described attending a meeting where one of the speakers (unnamed), a minister for over fifty years, had been "laughing to scorn his own conversion to Christ." A puzzled Hincks wrote: "now he says [his early conversion] was all a delusion at the beginning of his spiritual career. How in the name of decency did he get to be ordained?"[7]

In the twentieth century, an increasing number of Methodists evidently had no conversion experience to reinterpret or repudiate. The clergy reflected this trend, and what they presented in the pulpit was critical, as denominational leaders had long been aware. As one *Guardian* editorial put it: "Pulpit teaching that exalts forms, rites, and sacerdotal functions, or that which consists largely of semi-scientific speculation, is never accompanied by converting power. If the teaching of the pulpit does not present plainly and pointedly that it is the privilege of the people to be converted, and possess peace and joy through believing, what is not taught from the pulpit is not likely to be realized as the experience of the hearers."[8] A significant change in traditional piety was inevitable, the editor claimed, if the spiritual guides no longer presented it as a model of the religious life.

Relating the experience of conversion and call had long been part of the ritual of Methodism's annual ordination service. In the reception service testimonies of the 1880s and 1890s, the ordinands often placed the godly mother alongside the soul-winning preacher as the instrumental figure in their conversion. This coincided with greater interest in child evangelism. But by the early decades of the twentieth century the trend was towards testimonies devoid of a definite conversion experience whether led by mother or anyone else.

Evidence of such a shift appeared in different regions at different times. As late as 1909, the *Guardian's* report of the meeting of Toronto Conference stated that all the young men had "paid tribute to the influence of a Christian home, and especially the prayers of a mother." The paper also noted that "the impetus of revival services in inducing the hesitating soul to take a decided stand was strikingly emphasized, and its blessings apparent in the experiences told."[9] A year later, the report referred to "the holy influences of Christian parents, and the family altar, consecrated pastors and revival services, and the sanctifying and inspiring blessings of Victoria College and her professors." Those attending apparently approved, and they "called out many a hearty 'Amen'" in response to the testimonies.[10]

Other Conferences had begun to hear quite different testimonies. The reporter who attended the 1911 British Columbia Conference noted the variety of experiences among the four candidates for ordination. It was the one patterned most closely after the traditional experience of revivalistic piety that drew his most negative comment: he remarked that "through the nature of the emphasis put upon conversion, [he] came to desire to be bad in order to be good, and so instead of being shepherded, found his goal at last – the pity of it – via the way of sin."[11] In a striking reversal, this conversion experience was viewed not as a delivery from sin, but as a contributor to it. Another candidate's conversion had come as a "purpose in life," while for a third it was "a matter of growth." The fourth person mentioned no conversion, but referred to his home and his parents' prayers. Such variety became commonplace and acceptable. By 1924, the reporter from the Montreal Conference commented that while "a former age might have questioned the absence of the cataclysmatic which it desiderated so greatly in the conversion and calls of redeeming grace," they should "have no qualms so long as the Spirit has accomplished his work, let the calling come how it will."[12]

Developments outside Canadian Methodism validated the concept of the variety of religious experience. Among the most important of these were the new directions taken in religious education. The educational implications of Horace Bushnell's views on nurturing religious experience have rightly been credited with drawing attention to the spiritual status of children within the Protestant churches of North America in the mid-nineteenth century. Changes taking place in religious education at the turn of the century have received less attention. The scientific methods of disciplines which influenced religious education at this time may have had more far-reaching implications for Methodism than generally recognized.

Developments in the psychology of religion with its scientific approach to religious experience in general and to conversion in particular are a case in point. George Coe and William James were pioneers in this field and their views were widely publicized in Canada.[13] Coe explicitly linked his interest in the psychology of religion to his own background: he was a Methodist minister's son who had expected, but failed to experience, a dramatic conversion.[14]

The Spiritual Life, a study of the dynamics of religious transformation, was one of the first attempts to look at personality differences as a variable in the type of conversion experienced.[15] Coe's interest in the "naturalness" of religion was one that he shared with other early twentieth-century modernists.[16]

The *Guardian* was immediately impressed by Coe's statistical work showing that most conversions came during adolescence and used the results of Coe's research to criticize apathy towards conversion of children.[17] Referring to the unerring law of averages and statistics that showed "plainly and conclusively what may be termed conversion-expectation," the *Guardian* urged leaders who worked with young people not to ignore the opportunities of this psychological moment.[18] A later editorial discussed Coe's idea that cultivated impulses led to a spiritual change of character and life "as naturally and inevitably as the physical changes which accompany adolescence."[19]

In 1908 denominational opposition to Coe's research forced his resignation from Northwestern University in Evanston, Illinois, then a Methodist institution. The *Guardian* agreed with Coe's opponents that he should leave if he no longer accepted the "fundamental doctrine" of the Methodist church.[20] Coe found more hospitable surroundings in New York at Union Theological Seminary. He continued to be widely read in and beyond Methodist circles. His highly influential views on religious experience, which challenged Methodism's traditional approach to conversion, accompanied the new sense of professionalism which characterized religious education in the early twentieth century.[21]

William James was another psychologist of religion whose work was influential. So fascinated was he with religious experience (and conversion in particular) that he remarked to a friend, "You will class me as a Methodist, *minus* a Savior."[22] The title of his best-known book, *The Varieties of Religious Experience*, published in 1902, communicated his basic assumption about religious experience – its diversity. Canadians figured in its pages. The Canadian psychologist R. Maurice Bucke represented something called "cosmic consciousness,"[23] while a charismatic New Light preacher from Nova Scotia, Henry Alline, was a prime example of "the sick soul."[24] The division of persons of wide-ranging religious experiences into two classes, the healthy-minded and the sick souls, became the most widely popularized aspect of James's work.

We can only speculate on the response of Methodists, brought up to view a powerful conversion as a positive virtue, to this scientific study. Some who had referred with a degree of satisfaction to psychological research in condemning excesses within the holiness movement[25] suddenly found similar studies striking closer to home. Those already critical of revivals as outdated or ineffective were now joined by those who viewed them as psychologically dangerous. Critics of revivals now had the weight of science behind them. Those who had failed to experience an old-time conversion must have been tremendously relieved to have escaped the "sick soul" category. Those who had already claimed conversion may perhaps be forgiven for refashioning their experience, or at least being reluctant to share its details with others. Though all the blame for the downfall of the class meeting cannot be assigned to scientific research, such studies likely hastened its demise. The new psychology certainly raised questions regarding the fitness of those who testified to a definite conversion experience – the ones who had played a crucial role in the success of the class. Little wonder that those desiring spiritual fellowship quickly regrouped to engage in more "wholesome" activities like Bible study or social service!

The influence of the psychology of religion on the practice of piety deserves a more in-depth study than is possible here. The sources do suggest a link between the new psychology and the changes taking place within Methodism in Canada at this time. The discussions of the definiteness of the conversion experience reflect a growing uneasiness. S.T. Bartlett's letter to Nathanael Burwash in 1907 on behalf of the Sunday School and Epworth League Department referred to "an idea re: our children growing in popularity, that ought to be corrected – viz. that they [children] do not need to be converted. 'Culture' is taking the place of conversion."[26] Burwash's response to Bartlett's request for a statement for the *Epworth Era* reaffirmed the importance of a definite experience of religion. He replied that "one of the most distinctive characteristics of Methodism from the beginning has been the definiteness of her religious experience. 'Ye must be born again' has been her watch word received from the lips of the Savior himself, emphasized by the experience of John Wesley himself, and forming the very heart of his evangelistic preaching." Though decision, instruction, and consecration were necessary, the denomination would fall short of "the high water mark of Methodism" unless every child in the church knew by personal experience that his or her sins were forgiven. He concluded that he would rather "fall back on the old fashioned revival methods imperfect and unsatisfactory as they sometimes were than fall into a method which failed to reach the fullness of the Christian's privilege."[27]

Burwash was a busy man at the 1910 General Conference. The champion of church union and the defender of teaching of higher criticism at Methodist theological colleges also presented his concerns about conversion. In what was described by the *Guardian* as likely the Conference's most effective address, Burwash observed that class meeting participants were becoming less introspective about their religious experience. An exact description or a precise recollection of the details of religious development was not the most important thing, he admitted, but he did feel that Methodists should be able to point to the "permanent form" and results of their religious experience. His description of the religious life differed significantly from what Coe and James proposed. Still essential to his understanding of religious experience were the stages of guilt after recognition of sin, repentance, and the witness of the Spirit as the marks of "Gospel regeneration," without which there was "no normal spiritual life." He attributed Methodism's achievements to the power of this approach to piety; when Methodism no longer preached conversion, he believed it would fail in its most important task, though it might continue to do important ethical, educational, and missionary work.[28]

Though many Canadian Methodists shared the progressivist confidence in science and generally applauded the scientific spirit of the "new evangelism" of the Department of Evangelism and Social Service, applying the scientific method to religious experience was another matter. Reservations were expressed in surprising quarters. S.D. Chown, whose understanding of the "new evangelism" was significantly influenced by the social sciences, spoke on a number of occasions about unforeseen implications of the new psychology. Assessing the impact of George Coe's first book nearly twenty-five years after its publication, Chown credited it with stimulating child evangelism. But it had also left the impression, he feared, that adult conversion was almost hopeless – notwithstanding the examples of St Paul, Augustine, Luther, and Wesley.[29] Had Coe confused the supernatural with physical or psychological laws, thus reducing Christianity to a naturalistic process? The assumption that followed – that children could become adult Christians without experiencing any spiritual crisis – was an idea which Chown described as futile, damaging, dangerous, and subversive of evangelical Christianity.[30] In the same address, however, Chown's new understanding of his own religious experience was apparent in his references to conversion as sacrificial service and the pursuit of a high ideal;[31] absent were the guilt, repentance, and witness of the Spirit so prominent in nineteenth-century conversion accounts.

Chown also recognized the significance of William James's understanding of conversion. James saw conversion as a normal adolescent phenomenon, an aspect of a child's growth to maturity. A useless view was this in producing a better life in a sin-sick soul, Chown argued, for it made evangelism impossible:

You can see at once how contrary all this is to the faith of our fathers which won them their signal soul-saving triumphs. Our old conception of evangelism is turned topsy turvey if conversion is only a fortuitous, kaleidoscopic rearrangement of the elements of our subliminal consciousness without any necessary intervention of divine power. It would be amazing if soul-saving power should accompany the preaching of men obsessed with these ideas, or take place in churches dominated by laymen holding such views ... How the anathemas of the fathers would righteously descend upon his [James's] conception of instantaneous conversion.[32]

By 1912 the works of psychologists of religion were, said Chown, being "quoted and read by our men so as to become their atmosphere."[33] While the challenge of evolution had once posed a thorny intellectual problem, the new psychology threatened to create a moral and spiritual dilemma. He assessed the impact as widespread, for the "catch words and phrases of the new psychology had found entrance into the pulpit, were reechoed by the pew, and caught up by the indeterminate person we call the man on the street."[34] Conversion was belittled even in church, as Chown discovered at one meeting where "an amused titter ran round the crowded congregation" at the mere mention of the word.[35] When Chown viewed the situation in 1930 he conceded that the idea of "salvation by psychology" had supplanted conversion.[36]

If Chown wondered how the psychological approach to religion had become so pervasive, he had only to look to his own denominational paper. The *Guardian* was instrumental in spreading these new ideas. By the end of the First World War, editorials and articles reflecting the methods of scholars like Coe and James were commonplace. Creighton overcame the reluctance to abandon older forms of evangelism that had characterized his earliest editorials on the subject. Now he confidently told his readers that "we must face the fact that what we call conversion, meaning by that usually a very marked, and even violent, change in the spiritual condition, is and must be rather misleading in the case of nearly all of those children of praying homes whose acceptance of Christ dates back to very tender years."[37]

A definite crisis conversion was neither normal nor desirable and to insist that adults experience it was to ask for a psychological impossibility. Religion was not an unnatural or mysterious thing and should not be made to seem so.[38] Although Methodists need not discard conversion, they must, he insisted, recognize that God works in many ways: "because there are no religious thunderings and earthquakes in the child's experience it is none the less true that the Spirit of God is working, and what we may call 'natural' means may be just as effective and even more appropriate, than what we call 'supernatural.'"[39]

Creighton's ideas did not win overnight acceptance among *Guardian* readers or the church at large. But his forthright articles in the paper that claimed to speak for the denomination and his replies (occasionally quite acerbic) to letters critical of his views indicate his confidence that a significant number of persons, some of them influential, were backing him. His re-elections at General Conference would seem to bear this out; he remained editor of the *Guardian* until 1925 when he became the first editor of the United Church's *New Outlook*.

Conversion had traditionally been understood by Methodists as a normative experience. Viewing it as an expression of childhood and adolescent abnormality triggered other changes in the approach to piety. Traditionally the conversion experience had been linked to an ethic centred on what was variously called the pursuit of holiness, sanctification, or Christian perfection. Canadian Methodists were thus concerned with both experience and behaviour. Behaviour was often narrowly interpreted as preoccupation with what an individual could not do, but it also lent support to involvement in reform activities that were for many an introduction to the ideas of the social gospel.

Prescriptions for personal and public behaviour underwent significant modification in the late Victorian period. After more than a decade of debate, the 1910 General Conference dropped the controversial "footnote" listing drinking, card-playing, dancing, and theatre attendance among forbidden activities for Methodists. There was a new emphasis on "educated Christian conscience," rather than specific rules, as the guide to morality. Implicit in the resolution of "the amusements issue" was the realization that Methodism was no longer a small "society" like the one formed by Wesley. Rules governing personal behaviour could not be enforced among its large membership.[40] Recognition of the diversity of religious practice paralleled acknowledgment of the varieties of religious experience.

To educate the Christian conscience on public issues, the denomination promoted publications and sponsored lectures. These coincided with a heightened awareness of social problems associated with the social gospel movement. Studies of the social gospel in Canada note that Methodism played a prominent role in the movement, providing it with leadership and official support.[41] Methodism's enthusiasm for the movement raises a number of questions. How profound was Methodism's response to the social gospel movement? If it was more than superficial, how did Methodism appropriate presuppositions that, on the surface, seem antithetical to the assumptions of its revivalist tradition? Did Methodist involvement affect the practice of piety within the denomination?

Historians tend to use the term "social gospel" very loosely to encompass a wide variety of responses to social issues. It is often mistakenly identified as being coterminous with "liberal theology"; some who were liberal in their theology held conservative social views.[42] The social gospel movement is frequently tied to talk of "establishing the Kingdom of God," although that by itself was no novelty. H. Richard Niebuhr has shown that in the United States the ideal of establishing the Kingdom had long been operative.[43] Some evangelists (Crossley and Hunter among them) used this imagery to speak not only of entering a Kingdom in heaven but of building one on earth as well.[44] And Methodism throughout the nineteenth century was at the forefront of a variety of movements for political and social reform. What, then, was different at the turn of the century?

William R. Hutchison refers to a distinction that has become an influential assumption in discussions of the social gospel. The phrase "social gospel," he observes, is sometimes taken out of its historical context and made a generic equivalent of "religious social reform." The latter includes the activities of orthodox Calvinists, revivalists, and religious conservatives who were engaged in crusades for temperance, peace, antislavery, mission work, and reform of social vices. The novelty of the social gospel movement (and its difference from "religious social reform"), according to Hutchison, lies in its contention that "social salvation precedes individual salvation both temporally and in importance." Attributing to social reform a status that was equal to (and not derived from) individual salvation was, he maintains, a move quite distinct in theory from what evangelicals generally could support. It was this theoretical elevation of social salvation that made the social gospel a distinctive movement.[45]

Hutchison's appeal for a more rigorous analysis of the social gospel movement raises some interesting questions about Methodism's involvement in it. Other than the name, what was "new" about the social gospel? How did Methodism's support differ from its earlier involvement in social reform? Hutchison's narrower definition changes the picture of Canadian Methodism's prominence in the movement; if it is applied, only the most radical, many of whom left the church, would qualify as social gospellers. The transposition of "individual" and "social" salvation which Hutchison sees as characteristic of the social gospel would have entailed a drastic reorientation for Methodism. Is there evidence of this reorientation, or is the approach to reform in basic continuity with Methodism's long-standing interest in social issues? Raising these questions is not to deny that turn-of-the-century Methodism was undergoing change. It is, rather, to ask whether the assumed displacement of "individual salvation" by "salvation of the social order" adequately indicates the nature of that change, particularly in the period before the First World War.

A commitment to applying religion to everyday life was characteristic of Methodism from its beginnings; this was not incompatible with piety but an integral part of it. Consequently, involvement in such social causes as temperance and educational reform had long been a characteristic Methodist concern. E.H. Dewart was only one of the many stalwart supporters of special revival services and the holiness movement who also advocated a close connection between piety and public life. Religious observance was futile and fruitless, he wrote, if it did not result in "more unselfish sympathy for human want and suffering, and more complete consecration to God's service."[46] He saw the separation of religion and lived experience as a dangerous tendency.

Dewart's approach to relating religion and social reform was typical of his own day and was not uncommon well into the twentieth century. In fact, in the pre-war period it is difficult to find much support in the Methodist press for placing (to borrow Hutchison's definition of the social gospel) concern for the salvation of society ahead of, either temporally or in importance, the salvation of the individual. Dewart urged Christians to become interested and involved in social and economic affairs never doubting the proper order: Christian principles, even if embodied in laws, could only be implemented when those principles were first "enthroned in the hearts of the people." Following Christ's example, ministers were to care for humanity "chiefly by so presenting the truth to the conscience so as to make men better and holier, rather than by altering the machinery of civil society."[47] The "new religious socialism" was thereby condemned because it gave no answer to the question, "What must I do to be saved?" Social problems might indeed be solved if all were as unselfish as angels and as self-sacrificing as Christ, but that proposition was of no practical value unless the means of effecting such a transformation were shown. The implication of socialism was that acts of self-sacrifice were conditions rather than the results of salvation – a view Dewart dismissed as thinly disguised Unitarianism.[48]

Dewart's successors at the *Guardian* took a similar position. They praised concern with ethics and the application of the principles of social science while insisting on the priority of conversion. As one editor put it, the most important task was "to get men and women, as our fathers used to say – and as Christ said – converted, for if men and women get truly converted, all the vexed questions of the world – individual, social, industrial, political – would find perfect and speedy solution."[49] When W.B. Creighton was formally named as editor of the *Guardian* in 1906 there was no immediate evidence of a new understanding of how to implement social change. Support for reform was stated in stronger and more frequent terms than previously. Editorials suggested that if the Kingdom was to come, political participation was sometimes as important as attending prayer service, teaching Sunday school, or giving to the church.[50] Readers were warned about the consequences of separating religion from everyday life.[51] However, this by itself was hardly enough to constitute a social gospel.

Creighton realized that he was living in an age that judged religion by its achievements. Men and women demanded a religion of action. To them the niceties of theological speculation were "simply an unknown tongue" and the findings of the higher critics of "meagre interest." "The religion that cleanses the city slums, purifies the politics of a state, or transforms the barbarous customs of a heathen nation" was "the real and only type of religion that is worth considering." Creighton had no quarrel with this. But when he noted the danger of so emphasizing what a person did as to lose sight of what that person was, he was not as divorced from Dewart as some would suggest.[52]

That individual transformation preceded social transformation seemed evident to Creighton in 1908. He called for a more self-sacrificing interest in social issues, but added:

we could not imagine anything more fatal to the high interests that the church is supposed to serve than that she should get the notion that the be-all and end-all of her existence was social reconstruction. For suppose that the whole socialistic programme were worked out ... the great problems that Christianity has before her might still be unsolved. From the standpoint of the church, the really important field of reform is in the hearts of men and women. It is changed men rather than changed conditions that she seeks.[53]

Jesus spoke of inaugurating the Kingdom of God, Creighton wrote in 1912, but efforts to set up the Kingdom externally were futile if it had not been experienced internally.[54]

Official pronouncements issued by the denomination before the war shared many of these assumptions about social change. It is difficult to find a Methodist proposal that presents social reform as separate from, let alone taking precedence over, the salvation of individuals. Yet some historians maintain that by 1906 there was an official acceptance of the principles of the social gospel by Canadian Methodism. One historian suggests that though the social gospel was still in the process of formation by 1914, it "was leading Methodists from a traditional premillenialism [sic] aimed at individual salvation in an afterlife to modern postmillenial [sic] ideas and activities aimed at saving society now." Committee reports accepted after 1906 by the General Conference were "virtually proclamations of the social gospel," although such concerns "by no means dominated the Church by 1914."[55]

However, these reports still focused on the role of the regenerated person in social reform. The 1906 report of the Committee on Sociological Questions, regarded by some as a significant indicator of Methodism's official acceptance of the social gospel, is a case in point. It reads in part: "We hold that the work of the church is to set up the kingdom of God among men, which we understand to be a social order founded on the principles of the Gospel – the Golden Rule, the Sermon on the Mount – and made possible through the regeneration of men's lives."[56] The addition of urban ills to the list of older and largely rural social concerns made the reports longer – but the remedy was not strikingly different.

The First World War galvanized the forces of progressivism in Canada. It lent a new sense of urgency to their discussions. At the 1918 General Conference, the Methodist Church issued what Richard Allen has described as "the most radical statement of social objectives ever delivered by a national church body in Canada."[57] He notes that the Conference's rejection of the capitalist system was accompanied by a shift in "the evangelical emphasis on changing society by changing individual minds or spirits." The committee explained that this assumption had been abandoned in the face of "moral perils inherent in the system of production for profits." The system, rather than the individual, needed to be changed.[58]

Less radical in expression but far-reaching in implication were the changes made in the ritual expressions of denominational life. In anticipation of church union, Methodists brought their membership practices more in line with Presbyterians in 1918. The expectation of a definite experience of conversion as the prerequisite for membership was no longer highlighted – a significant step in this direction. Questions for ordination candidates were revised. They were now asked about "a vital Christian experience" rather than a conversion experience. There was no reference to "the witness of the Spirit."[59] The *Guardian* editorial discussing these changes rightly called the gathering "epoch-making" – a new day and a new spirit. "The world is being turned upside down," it announced, "and many of the old ideas which governed us in the past are being subjected to such scrutiny as they were never called to face before. Particularly in connection with theological and social matters are we face to face with the matter of drastic reconstruction, and thinking men are everywhere keenly alive to a new atmosphere and a new mental environment."[60] In what seems to be an about-face, Creighton dismissed the idea that saving souls would make the world right as "pious twaddle" and "positively vicious."[61]

The social gospel now had the attention of those formulating church policy, but its impact at the local level was "obscured in the underbrush in the valleys of church life" notes Richard Allen.[62] Still, the committee which formulated the radical report thought it inconceivable that the people would reject it. The report presupposed "as Jesus did, that the normal human spirit will respond more readily to the call to service than to the lure of private gain."[63] The importance of Christian service had long been emphasized in Methodist circles. However, a call to personal service, rather than (and not explicitly linked to) personal regeneration, represents an important shift in the Methodist model of piety. Even where it did not blossom into a full-blown social gospel, the emphasis on service created a new and symphathetic ethos. It made possible an endorsement of social gospel principles.

Looking for the change that Methodism was undergoing in the pre-war period only along lines of "souls" or "the social order" may not adequately convey the nature of the transition. If social change were still individualistic in concept, then what may have been shifting was what "salvation" of the individual entailed. It can be argued that instead of (or at least alongside of) a shift towards a more organic conceptualization of social change which discounted the salvation of the individual a new view of the religious life was emerging. It was, however, different in significant ways from the piety that had been shaped and formed by Methodism's past ties to revivalism.

Even so, the disjunction between revivalist piety and the progressivist piety of the social gospel was not as complete as some have suggested. Links to revivalist piety were not entirely missing. A sense of continuity with the old slogan "saved for service" remained. And while the impulse to live a life of holiness did not by itself constitute a social gospel, the doctrine of Christian perfection – what Wesley had called Methodism's grand depositum – served as a vehicle by which some prominent progressives appropriated and preached the social gospel message while still claiming loyalty to the Methodist tradition.

The holiness movement's emphasis on Christian perfection had divided Methodists in the 1890s. During that decade their leaders made their disapproval of supporters of Ralph Horner and Nelson Burns unmistakably clear. Even the Keswick movement came under a cloud of suspicion because of its connections to a theory of salvation and a view of history regarded as questionable. By the end of the decade references to the holiness movement in the columns of the *Guardian* were few and generally uncomplimentary.[64] But while Canadian Methodism officially distanced itself from the movement, its major doctrine could not be so easily dismissed. Instead of simply repudiating the doctrine of Christian perfection, some proposed to reinterpret it. In doing so, many Methodists distanced themselves from the holiness movement and its emphasis of the experience of holiness and moved closer to proponents of social Christianity who urged the practice of holiness in social relationships.[65]

Among those who followed this path was C.S. Eby. A Canadian Methodist minister, a former missionary, and a literary contributor to the holiness movement,[66] he had grave concerns about the Methodist tradition. He saw "a fading away of the heritage of what Wesley called 'our Depositum'" – Christian perfection. He deplored the inability to translate the doctrine and experience of holiness into modern terms. As a consequence holiness had "degenerated into the badge of cranks, or the experience of the few." Critical of the handling of the holiness movement by the leaders of Canadian Methodism, he recalled that "when ignorant zeal in Canada ran off on two different tangents [probably a reference to Horner and Burns], church organ [*Christian Guardian*] and officials were helpless and the subject was largely dropped." He saw a different and more effective exposition of holiness in England where it undergirded a return to Wesley's practical work. The city mission work of Hugh Price Hughes exemplified for Eby an appropriation of Wesley's doctrine of Christian perfection well suited to the modern situation.[67] His own solution was to organize a Socialist church in Toronto in 1909.

Another admirer of Hughes was Ernest Thomas, a strong supporter of social reform who worked in Hughes's West London Mission before coming to Canada. Considered one of the finest of the social gospel leaders,[68] his keen mind was intrigued by new ideas. His diverse activities included attendance at the Queen's Alumni Conferences and involvement with the faculty of the theologically innovative University of Chicago.[69] Thomas, although thoroughly acquainted with a number of ways of articulating social concern, saw Wesley's language of Christian perfection as one manner of presenting social Christianity. The essence of scriptural holiness as he understood it was "a life transformed in all its relations and activities, resulting from a change of spirit by adopting the Christian thought and temper." As such it resonated with the concerns of social Christianity.[70] His account of the radical pronouncements of the 1918 Conference demonstrated that connection. He noted that "one report after another harked back to the sources. The primitive mission of Methodism to spread holiness throughout the land in all its organized forms, and its central doctrine that Christianity is simply love made perfect in personal life and organized society, were reasserted and re-interpreted. Thus in one report after another the old gospel was re-stated in terms suited to present aims."[71]

S.D. Chown's assumptions about social Christianity also involved reinterpretation of Wesley's doctrine of holiness. One historian suggests that Chown's social thought reveals his indebtedness to philosophical idealism and demonstrates "the complete substitution of sociological concerns for theological ones."[72] But a careful examination of his sermons and addresses suggests that at least outside his college lecture circuit he was also easily able to translate the principles of social Christianity into the Methodist vernacular by speaking of Christian perfection. Chown deplored the excesses of the holiness movement, yet regretted that its "deep spiritual significance" had been overlooked. Spiritual life was thereby impoverished.[73] Like Eby and Thomas, he found it necessary to reinterpret Christian perfection as practical holiness; like them he credited Hugh Price Hughes with setting out in his two books (*Social Christianity* and *The Philanthropy of God*) the Methodist response to the problems at the turn of the century.[74]

For Chown, holiness was the test of conversion, not a separate "blessing" or experience: it was the Christian's behaviour manifested after conversion.[75] To make entire sanctification a distinctive spiritual crisis (a mid-nineteenth-century development, he insisted) resulted in the doctrine being "lost in labyrinths of metaphysical subtlety and mystical experience and ... confined to persons of a peculiar spiritual temperament."[76] For Chown, holiness referred to "wholeness of life" and embraced business, politics, and international relationships within the "sphere of personal responsibility and personal piety." This Chown called "enlightened holiness."[77]

This more comprehensive type of holiness virtually replaced conversion as the basis of Methodist piety. Chown often defined conversion as development of "character," whereas character had previously been viewed as one of the results of conversion. Sanctification as "service" was a dominant theme in Chown's preaching. Social service and catholicity, "the vital creed of Wesley" which for a time had been obscured by emphasizing instantaneous conversion, was now coming to fruition in the church union negotiations.[78] Considering the matter of children having definite spiritual crises, Chown believed "they need to come to Christ definitely in the spirit of sacrificial service. They need to face the cross, and submit to it in trust for Divine help, to take it up and carry it." This, said Chown, was conversion.[79]

In the 1920s, Chown linked the decline of revival to a new emphasis on the nobility of enlisting in Christian service rather than the need to forsake sin. Service now was the fundamental concern and individual regeneration a by-product – a reversal of revivalism's presentation of conversion and sanctification. Chown realized that his own preaching had contributed to what he described as a failure to discriminate clearly between social service and evangelism. He admitted that under the direction of the General Conference his work in the Department of Evangelism and Social Service was largely responsible for this development.[80]

Speaking in terms of Christian perfection was not the only way that Methodists expressed their views on social issues. But it was one way of linking present concerns with their heritage. Creighton referred to an old Methodist phrase, "full salvation," in proposing that religion reach the whole life of the individual to become an even fuller salvation than "the fathers" dreamed of in the past. "To them the term [full salvation] implied freedom from sin, as they understood it, or even 'perfect love,' as they interpreted it. But 'perfect love' to-day must be a much more energetic and wide-sweeping thing than forty years ago. It must touch and transform all our business and social relations."[81] "Full salvation," once a description of Methodism's dual emphasis on the experiences of conversion and sanctification, now became a plea for the principles of progressivism.

Religious experience and behaviour were not the only facets of piety to undergo change. Influenced as well was Methodism's theology, its articulation of religious ideas. In discussing theological transitions within Methodism, Robert Chiles argues that because liberalism dominated the theology of American Methodism in the first third of the twentieth century, Methodism had "much more in common with the theology current in other denominations than it did with its own heritage." Lacking a sense of identity, Methodism was "even more susceptible than other denominations to reconstruction under the criteria of liberalism."[82] Yet there is reason to suspect precisely the opposite. Methodism may indeed have been going through an identity crisis at the turn of the century, but in liberalism, one can argue, it found an approach to theology that fitted quite comfortably with its own tradition.

The leaders of Canadian Methodism regarded their theology as one derived in part from religious experience. The handling of controversy reflected that approach, sometimes lending an air of oversimplification to what were perplexing issues for other groups. The *Guardian's* comment on discussions about future probation of the dead, an issue which deeply divided the American Board of Foreign Missions in the 1880s, illustrates a quite typical reaction. The editor approved what he considered a "victory" for orthodoxy, but put the matter in Methodist perspective by remarking that "the solution of this difficulty created by the New Theology is to be found not in speculation about dead pagans but in doing our duty to living pagans."[83]

Methodist progressives did not dispute the theological significance of experience, especially when a more rationalistic approach was proposed as an alternative. Chown, dismissing the importance of philosophical idealism for theology, declared that "Hegelianism, constructing religion out of purely mental processes, has had its day."[84] In his official sermon to the 1914 General Conference, he cited the attempt "to graft German intellectualism upon the tree of practical mysticism which John Wesley planted" as causing problems in ministerial training. Arguing that practical mysticism resented "the domination of a finely-drawn intellectualism," he continued: "We do not need philosophy to commend or enforce our theology. It comes to us direct from revelation and experience."[85]

As the nineteenth century drew to a close, Methodism became more aware that its experiential approach to theology was not unique. The extent to which all branches of the church stressed experience, character, and conduct rather than creeds and dogmas pleasantly surprised Dewart. This, he reminded readers, was familiar to Methodists, for they had always given "greater prominence to the personal experience of pardon and sanctification, than to the belief of dogmas, however sound and scriptural these dogmas may be."[86] But he feared that a tendency to rely too heavily on experience might develop and found it curious that some who had sneered at the spiritual experiences of Methodists, dismissing them as enthusiastic fancies, were now magnifying the evidence of Christian experience in an effort to render external revelation unnecessary.[87] What had been two distinct theological systems, revivalism and nineteenth-century liberalism, converged at this point.[88]

In terms of theological method, Methodism did not simply adopt a completely new approach to theology. Familiar assumptions regarding the symbiotic relationship of religious life and doctrine prevailed. So it is not surprising that a period which reassessed the experience of conversion and the implications of holiness precipitated doctrinal reformulation. Looking at theological reconstruction in the early twentieth century suggests that the presentation of religious ideas was indeed affected. This relationship between experience and theology is illustrated by the spiritual journey of J.S. Woodsworth in *Following the Gleam*, what he called "a modern pilgrim's progress." Woodsworth's theological perplexity during his preparation for the ministry triggered a decision to leave the ordained ministry of the Methodist church after years of doubting his own suitability for it. As he was coming to this decision, religious experience was for him, as for Methodists in the past, linked to how he presented his actions and ideas.

A troubled Woodsworth wrote to his old theology professor with whom he had studied at Victoria College in 1902, confident that if anyone could help, it would be Burwash. His letter left no doubt that Wesley's answers to many questions differed from his own.[89] Burwash's reply apparently did not resolve his theological difficulties, for a few months later he arrived at the Annual Conference with a letter of resignation in his pocket.[90] But the committee that examined him did not accept his resignation, an outcome which Ramsay Cook describes as "truly astonishing." Perhaps, as Cook argues, this can be attributed to the "almost total disarray" of Protestant doctrine in Canadian Methodism as a result of the inroads made by theological liberalism. Or perhaps the committee saw before them a promising young pastor (by no means the first to have had a "crisis of faith") who with patience and time might find a way of dealing with religious doubt. Whatever the reasoning, that year and again in 1907 he was persuaded by senior ministers to reconsider. His resignation was not accepted until 1918, and only then, as he explained it, because of "the much more serious question of unorthodoxy in economics and politics."[91]

Woodsworth believed that the theological issues which began to trouble him soon after ordination stemmed in part from his reflection on what he had learned at Victoria College and Oxford University.[92]

But perplexity over Methodism's articles of faith was not the entire problem. For him the "root of the difficulty" lay elsewhere: the "matter of personal experience." His religious experience had not been "what among Methodists is considered normal. From earliest childhood, I was taught the love of God, and have endeavored to be a follower of Jesus. My experience has determined my theology, and my theology my attitude toward the Discipline. And all three, according to our standards, are un-Methodistical." He believed that Burwash's definition of conversion as "one experimental crisis of religious life, from which a consciously new life dated its beginning" was still widely accepted. Woodsworth could not testify to such an experience, nor did he expect to be made "perfect in love" in this life.[93] Experience, the ground of assurance for Burwash, led Woodsworth in quite another direction.

Because he was unable to claim the experience of Methodist "orthodoxy," Woodsworth sought ways to reinterpret his Christian faith. He was by no means alone in this quest. But not all concurred with his decision to leave the Methodist church. Many remained and took on the task of theological reconstruction. They developed a new theological vocabulary which accompanied the shift of emphasis from "a definite conversion from sin" to "a definite commitment to service." Reference to "the witness of the Spirit" virtually disappeared while new prominence was given to the idea of "sacrificial service," a theme central to the emerging model of piety. Methodist progressives also mingled intellectually with others who linked sacrificial service with religious experience and shared their assumption that experience was an important component of theological method. In doing so they became participants in the lively theological conversation going on in centres of theological education in Canada and the United States.[94]

Union Theological Seminary and the University of Chicago were among the institutions involved in this exchange. Canadian Methodist leaders were familiar with the views of such theological educators as William Rainey Harper, the founder of the University of Chicago, whose articles appeared in the *Canadian Methodist Quarterly*. Publications from the American Institute of Sacred Literature, which he helped to found, were used by some chapters of the Canadian Methodist Epworth Leagues.[95] By 1908, works by other University of Chicago professors were listed as prescribed texts for probationers in the Methodist ministry – and a growing cause for concern among some. One student who dropped out of the probationers' course explained to Burwash that after he had been baptized with the Holy Spirit, he became aware of the troubling nature of the editorials in the *Guardian* and some of his textbooks. Books by Ernest Dewitt Burton and Shailer Mathews, both University of Chicago professors, were particularly upsetting. Disturbed by their radical ideas, the young man decided he "would not dare go on with such a course of study."[96]

Several influential Canadian Methodists either attended or taught at the University of Chicago before returning to Canada, among them H.B. Sharman.[97] A declared agnostic by the age of nineteen, Sharman found himself unable to reconcile claims of science with the religious instruction given him by his devout parents. Excited by the prospect of tangling with those who held Christian beliefs, he attended one of H.T. Crossley's revival services hoping for an opportunity to challenge him. To his surprise, it was the evangelist who challenged him as he implored the audience to test the statements of Jesus. Every one, he claimed, could be proved as surely as laboratory experiments.

And so began Sharman's fascination with the biblical records of the life of Jesus. While teaching science in Manitoba and Ontario he developed his own method of Bible study and research. The annual Bible study conferences in Northfield, Massachusetts, started by D.L. Moody in 1886, offered him still another context to pursue his study of the New Testament. At Northfield he met John R. Mott, chairman of the Student Volunteer Movement's executive committee, and at his invitation became Corresponding Secretary of the SVM in 1893. He combined this position after 1896 with that of Bible Study Secretary of the Student Department of the International YMCA. He eventually resigned from these organizations when he realized that their assumptions about the Bible were incompatible with his own, which were being shaped by biblical criticism. His love of biblical studies took him in 1900 to the University of Chicago, where he spent six years as a student and three as a teacher. Unpersuaded that he would find academic freedom even at a theological school notorious for its liberal views, he declined a permanent position there. He returned to Ontario and made a financial success of the Metal Culvert Company which he had established during his 1908 summer vacation. By 1915 he had the financial independence to devote his time to helping students understand the life of Jesus. Three years later he published a collection of Bible studies, *Jesus in the Records*. Widely used by the Student Christian Movement, the book made a considerable impact on religion in Canadian universities.

The theological influence of the liberalism of "the Chicago School" was also felt in western Canada. William Creighton Graham, a transplanted Methodist from Ontario, taught at the University of Chicago from 1926 to 1938 after completing doctoral studies there. But, disillusioned by Chicago's academic politics, he accepted the invitation to become Principal of United College in Winnipeg, where he decisively shaped the life of the college until his retirement in 1955.[98]

At least part of the University of Chicago's appeal was the empiricism of its theological method. Reviewing a book by Douglas Clyde Macintosh (a Canadian Baptist graduate of the University of Chicago), Lorne Pierce alluded to this connection. While he thought Methodists might question the author's empirical method and many of his conclusions, he was pleased that Macintosh was sending readers "back to the origin of all theology, back to practical religious experience."[99] There was also an affinity between Methodism's emphasis on sacrificial service and the same theme in Shailer Mathews's theology, particularly in his interpretation of the Atonement.[100]

Sacrificial service and involvement in public life as an expression of religious commitment provided common ground for an approach to theology geographically closer to home: the philosophical idealism of the Presbyterian colleges. Was idealism's influence as profound within Canadian Methodism as in Presbyterianism? Was it appropriated in the same way? These are questions that can only be answered with comparative studies of theological education in Canada. What can be said is that a new chapter began in 1892 when Victoria College acted on the decision formally approved by the General Council in 1886 and moved from Cobourg to federate with the University of Toronto. Methodist and Presbyterian ministerial candidates now studied on the same campus and took classes with professors from denominations other than their own, some of them proponents of philosophical idealism.[101]

But not all who looked for a reconciliation between tradition and modernity followed the paths blazed by J.S. Woodsworth, the empiricists, and the idealists. The pulpit afforded some ministers an opportunity to communicate the social and intellectual implications of modernity in other ways, as Salem Bland's biography of James Henderson suggests. The warm reception which Henderson met as he made his way from his first pastoral charge in the backwoods of the Belleville district to Methodism's most prestigious churches is a reminder that preachers of progressive theology did not always meet with resistance, as we sometimes assume. Henderson's popularity is particularly noteworthy, since Bland presents his story as a microcosm of the life of the Methodist church as it moved from revivalism to progressivism.

Setting the stage for Henderson's early ministry, Bland recalled as the most outstanding feature of Methodism between 1850 and

1880 its expectation of "a vivid personal experience of a great spiritual change." In those days, as Bland remembered them, few made their way into the Methodist fold "except through the very narrow door of a conscious conversion."[102] Bland repeated the typical Methodist interpretation of Wesley's distinctive theological contribution: shifting the basis for assurance of salvation from doctrinal correctness or sacerdotalism to experience. This marked a "change of first importance in the history of Christianity ... in its worth and power quite co-ordinate with that re-discovery of the autonomy of the soul that is the glory of the Protestant Reformation."[103] He credited the emphasis on a personal experience and communion with God as the chief reason why Methodists had been unsurpassed and rarely equalled in their devotion to missions and social reform. Their involvement in the temperance movement, described by Bland as "the most distinctive social reform movement of our day," was a case in point.[104]

James Henderson knew Methodism's revivalist tradition well. His family joined a Methodist church in Scotland after revival services conducted by E.P. Hammond.[105] After the family moved to Canada, young James was recruited by a Methodist minister who had heard of his involvement in revival services and mission work in Glasgow.[106] In 1871 he was accepted as a candidate for the ministry and became a circuit-rider who, "still under the influence of a revival ... brought into his work the methods which he had found so convincing in his own experience."[107]

The Henderson that Bland first met in the mid-1870s was a man who "constantly bubbled over with theological speculation." (Bland, a teenager at the time, sometimes regarded this tendency with disapproval!)[108] Henderson was an avid reader and his eclectic taste in books included the works of Darwin, Huxley, and Tyndall. He found no inherent conflict between science and religion.[109] After 1877 he entered what he called "a new era in the style and substance of my preaching" with the discovery of the sermons of William Ellery Channing, Frederick William Robertson, and Henry Ward Beecher. Meanwhile he continued to hold revival services. He remembered as one of the highlights of his ministry the meetings in Cookshire which were "so revolutionary that an outstanding politician wrote urging me to desist and close the doors of our church for a season as such a revival threatened to smash his party."[110]

Soon Henderson was preaching that revelation was progressive, that is, not confined to the events recorded in the Bible.[111] His sermons from the 1890s also reflect the same interest in the social implications of Christianity evidenced in the Methodist press of the time. Summaries of his sermons with such titles as "Christ as a

Revolutionist," "The Present Distress," and "The Coming Social Crisis" appeared in the Toronto and Montreal daily newspapers. Bland presented Henderson as a mediator between the evangelical tradition and contemporary thought and gave a clue to his success in that role: "it must never be forgotten," noted Bland, "that these sociological addresses were only occasional expositions, borne along on the tide of full and rich evangelical preaching."[112] No other Methodist pulpit that Bland could think of presented such a full and many-sided gospel, and he doubted whether there was a preacher in Canada in the 1890s who was so boldly and frankly sociological.[113] And yet Henderson met with no significant disapproval.

Henderson was identified with Methodism's progressive wing and had resolved upon coming to Toronto in the 1890s to strike a balance by conciliating old and new. As he watched the theological pendulum over his long career, he feared the loss of that delicate balance, detecting near the end of his life an extreme swing towards new ideas. "God save us from converting the pulpit into a rostrum for the discussion of economic nostrums and sociologic quackeries!" he wrote to a friend. Replacing the spiritual pulpit with a sociological one inverted the divine order, for "the spiritual always leads to the sociological: we cannot say that the sociological leads to the spiritual." He was convinced that Wesley's assumption that Christianity impinged on all aspects of life, including the social, still provided the strongest basis for social action. "I do not say we must preach just as Wesley did," he wrote, "but I say we must preach the same old Gospel in terms of the evangelical thinker today."[114]

Henderson himself grappled with that old Gospel. His series of sermons on life after death packed the Dominion Church in Ottawa, where he was pastor between 1907 and 1911. Thousands, according to one newspaper report, arrived too late to find a seat. In these sermons he rejected the idea of a "material hell," a departure, he admitted, from Wesley and early Methodism; in its place he described a "moral hell."[115] In his presentation of life after death we see flashes of the progressivist understanding of religion. "Character is heaven," he insisted, and "character is hell" – "heaven" and "hell" were not references to places. Salvation was experienced as God lifted the soul out of one condition of character and put it into another condition of character; but that was not to say that God lifted the soul from one place to another. Heaven and hell were present in this world, and would be found in the world to come only if taken there by us.[116]

The First World War gave to questions of death and future life a new sense of urgency. Preaching a sermon on "Death and the Soldiers' Eternal Fate" at Timothy Eaton Memorial Church in 1916, Henderson told of a mother who had written him following her son's death on the front. The son had made no profession of religion and had seldom gone to church. If the teachings of Methodism were true, she feared he was unsaved. Henderson assured his listeners: "If such a mother is here tonight, let me tell her (and those who are not prepared for this, do not listen) you have just to listen for a minute to the beating of your own heart – for we interpret God's heart through our own – you have just to listen to the voice that speaks through the instincts of your own motherhood, to be assured that no Church, no creed, no minister, no book has any authority to say that your son is not saved, or is eternally lost." The contrary was more likely the case, since the son had laid down his life for God, for freedom, and for country. "I do not take the position," he continued, "that his death is accepted as an atonement, but I do say that the very fact that he lived as he lived, that he died as he died, show that he, consciously or unconsciously, united himself in spirit with the Christ who died on the tree and whose whole life was a sacrifice for others."[117]

Bland saw Henderson as one of the first to feel the spirit of a new day in Methodism, one of the first to yield to it, and one of the most influential in advancing it in Canada.[118] Henderson had mediated a new theology, guiding Methodism to a tolerant and peaceful acceptance of new ways of social and theological thinking. He believed that without the genial and open-minded atmosphere which Henderson helped to create, the radical intellectual crusaders would have experienced more difficulties.[119] Apparently Henderson never lost the evangelistic warmth and passion of his early ministry. Admired as "enthusiastic philosopher, ardent humanist, and passionate evangelist," he allayed resentment and disarmed opposition.[120]

In John Wesley such Methodists discovered a model for reconciling evangelicalism and modernity, for his was a faith that was "fixed at the centre, and free at the circumference."[121] As long as Methodism was true to the spirit of its founder, Henderson was confident that it would not attach more importance to a creed than to Christ. He was part of a tradition that granted him "all manner of personal freedom, and one within whose broad and general statements I can develop a creed which is vitally and really my own."[122] There was much to ponder in new ways of expressing religious ideas, but Wesley remained the exemplar of a piety that did not preclude an openness to explore them. Echoes of Wesley's willingness to have fellowship with a person whose theology differed from his – if the "heart" was "right" – bolstered support for such theological reinterpretation. The essence of religion was an "orthodoxy of the heart." Progress was marked not by correctness of theology, but by the devotion of a person's life. "If the heart is right," *Guardian* editor Creighton concluded, "we can safely leave the correcting of theology to time and the Spirit of God."[123]

Finally, changes were evident in the ways of cultivating piety. The class meeting and work with children were indicators of this transition. They were portents of the denomination's reconsideration (and, for some, repudiation) of the type of evangelism that claimed a revivalist lineage. With a cloud of suspicion surrounding a definite conversion experience, the main feature of the class meeting – sharing accounts of that experience – became increasingly irrelevant. The fluctuation in attendance throughout the nineteenth century had generally been attributed to attitudinal problems such as apathy or guilt over sin. But the statistics presented at the first General Conferences of the twentieth century made it obvious that the problem went deeper. A special committee formed to look into the problem reported that Methodism had received 25,822 new members between 1902 and 1906, but 1,180 class leaders had resigned.[124] Many now dared to consider alternatives to the class meeting.

The impulse to create new organizations not only reflected a change in the approach to cultivating piety, but likely hastened the process of that change. Scrutinizing testimonies of religious experience had been an essential part of class meeting, a weekly reminder of the type of experience that Methodism considered "normative." Conformity was difficult to resist. Those who were gaining an appreciation of the variety of religious experience now assumed that they had been *taught* to expect a particular type of experience, one which for some had failed to materialize.

As Edward Burwash considered Nathanael Burwash's accomplishments after his death in 1918, he counted his father's work as class leader among them. He knew of many congregations where the traditional methods of his father still persisted: a member would give an account of his or her present religious experience and Burwash would comment, his objective to correct errors and point the way to "higher attainment." But "with the greater objectivity of modern church life centred round the ideas of practical Christian activity, organization and service," Edward observed older subjective methods falling "somewhat into the background."[125] Sherbourne Street church in Toronto typified this transition, announcing in the *Guardian* in 1918 that its quarterly board had abolished the class meeting. This decision "may have a wide effect when thoroughly understood," the report stated, adding that "they propose to do away with the name 'class-meeting' and give it something connected with social service. It is hoped by this means many who have not attended the class will be induced to come."[126]

The work with children also reflected these changing assumptions. Though many nineteenth-century Methodists were convinced of the importance of nurturing children in the faith, their view of "nurture" usually involved a definite, though not always dramatic, conversion experience for the child.[127] Those who favoured Horace Bushnell's model of Christian education, where children remembered no time when they were not Christians, admitted late in the century that their church did not exemplify it. The method of receiving children as members did not take into account the experience of those who might never need converting.[128]

The new religious education specialists soon entered into the debate. At the beginning of the twentieth century no college and few churches employed a religious education worker. By 1923 there were over a thousand employed, a dramatic change which Ernest Thomas credited to George Coe, William Rainey Harper, and Henry F. Cope, a member of the Religious Education Society.[129] At Methodism's major theological college, Frederick W. Langford, secretary of Methodism's Education Department, became professor of Religious Pedagogy in 1919. Just two years earlier he had had trouble volunteering his services to teach a course in religious education at Victoria College.[130]

A more "natural" understanding of religious experience saw it as of a piece with everyday life. Though W.B. Creighton suspected that the majority of those reading the *Guardian* in 1919 still did not share his opinion, he increasingly favoured this new approach. Singing, praying, and Bible reading did not appeal to the average boy, said Creighton, and he doubted that God had ever intended it to. Rather, the "religion of the boy" should be "a religion of the out-of-doors rather than of the church, a religion of the football field rather than of the orthodox prayer meeting; a religion of good fellowship and the frankest kind of speech, a religion with a maximum of work and a minimum of rest."[131] Along similar lines, Frank H. Langford, head of the Board of Religious Education, expressed in 1921 his satisfaction with the spiritual life of young people in their mid-teens. His opinion was that it had never been better. However, in keeping with the recognition of the variety of religious experience, he described their religious life as "expressing itself in ways that were almost unknown to their fathers and mothers."[132]

The recognition that the emerging model of piety differed from the traditional revivalist type in more than the methods of evangelism became more pronounced in the 1920s. Methodism could no longer put off finding what one correspondent to the *Guardian* called "a new standard of sainthood." He continued, "The Christian citizen is really the highest type of Christian ... The normal Christian is the man of the world – of *this* world, *God's* world – who lives the full human life by the grace of God."[133]

The *Guardian* admitted that it seemed impossible to do some things as well as "our fathers" had. But that recognition brought optimism as well as sadness. Accompanying the loss of the old piety was "a vision of what the gospel must do for the world that the fathers did not have." As for the mission of the church, it was "not to repeat the successes of our fathers, and to do our work as they did theirs." Twentieth-century Methodists were to be innovators, not imitators: they were "to blaze out a new path ... in the new world which the years have evolved." The familiar words of one of Charles Wesley's hymns, "A Charge to Keep," which spoke of serving the present age, echoed with the *Guardian's* prediction: "If the church of to-day is willing to serve its day and generation to the full glory of God, it will learn how to do it with splendid effectiveness."[134]

Advocating a progressivist approach to the religious life was not without its problems. One of the most immediate was the task of devising a new strategy for evangelism. Understandable confusion accompagnied the new use of religious language which appropriating Wesley in a different guise entailed. The lingering presence of a model of piety shaped by Wesley's Aldersgate conversion experience remained, as did a yearning for the methods of evangelism which had accompanied North American revivalism. Yet in seeking to revitalize Christianity in Canada by offering an alternative approach to piety, the spiritual guides of twentieth-century Methodism were convinced that they were preserving the spirit, if not the letter, of Methodism no less than those who looked to the past to defend more familiar ways.

CHAPTER FIVE

The Fragmentation of Evangelicalism and the Transformation of Tradition

Every young and growing people has to meet, at moments, the problem of its destiny... The fathers are dead; the prophets are silent; the questions are new, and have no answer but in time... the past gives no clue to the future. The fathers, where are they? and the prophets, do they live forever? We are ourselves the fathers! We are ourselves the prophets!

John Hay, 1902

We can no longer treat life as something that has trickled down to us... [We] have to substitute purpose for tradition; and that is I believe, the profoundest change that has ever taken place in human history.

Walter Lippmann, 1914[1]

At the 1914 General Conference, General Superintendents Albert Carman and S.D. Chown concluded their message to the assembly by addressing the subject of evangelism. Chown told those gathered that God had led Methodists "beyond the time when revivals might be started to save the Church from disintegration, or put a spiritual insurance policy upon careless souls. No amount of earnestness will put life into old shibboleths when God has spoken to His children that they go forward... The old battle-cries do not now inspire. There is no magic in words which do not contain a message, and there is no message unless it meet a felt need of the day."[2]

How then was Methodism to meet the "felt need of the day"? The "old shibboleths" and "old battle-cries" had given Methodism its distinctive identity. They were also part of the common language of the evangelical consensus which dominated nineteenth-century North American religion. Once the power of these words was gone, a recognition of a fragmentation of evangelicalism and a reorganization of agencies related to it soon followed. Out of that old consensus emerged new and coexisting approaches to the Christian life.

Methodism in Canada soon found its identity as part of a new social consensus that one scholar describes as a "broad capitalist-socialist, reformer-revolutionary, intellectual consensus... forming the common soil of modern liberalism." Techno-economic change did not develop insidiously behind people's backs and over their heads; people actively engaged in the transformation of their basic activities and ideas about the world.[3] At first Canadian Methodists watched from a distance the progress of events in the United States and Europe. In the early decades of the twentieth century they experienced those transitions themselves; their own values were tested. Progressivist assumptions about prosperity, professionalism, voluntarism, interventionism, and science converged to shape twentieth-century religion in important ways.

The self-denial of Methodism's nineteenth-century ethic fitted uneasily with the assumptions of a "culture of abundance."[4] The expectation and enjoyment of prosperity – perhaps as much as wartime despair – prompted a reassessment of older values. Canadian Methodists living at the turn of the century were numbered among those who experienced a momentous change in lifestyle. Witold Rybczynski's study of the concept of "home" divides the history of physical amenities into two major phases: all the years before 1890, and the three following decades. If this sounds outlandish, he says, it is worth remembering that such "modern" devices as central heating, indoor plumbing, running hot and cold water, electric light and power, and elevators were unavailable before 1890, but were well known by 1920.[5]

What Rybczynski describes as "a great technological divide" associated with the "democratization of comfort" coincided with the oft-expressed yearning of the time to feel "at home" in the world.[6] Some women proposed to make the world more homelike by turning old notions of "true womanhood" and domesticity inside out. Those who joined the Woman's Christian Temperance Union took up the cause of reform of public life in the name of "home protection." Their observation of women whose lives were ruined by the drinking habits of others demonstrated the social nature of sin – the message of social gospel preachers. They recognized the organic and associative nature of social relationships and the interweaving of home, community, and nation. Their moral imaginations were expanded by the realization of the shortcomings of an ethic that focused only on self-control, for men (at least) were not able to control themselves.[7]

Other champions of reform shared their willingness to intervene in public and even personal affairs to bring about moral and social change. Reform-minded journalists, urban affairs specialists, and voluntary associations (many of them church-related) succeeded in changing the design of Canadian cities.[8] Together they implemented a radically new approach to social problems: the bureaucratic method founded on the science of statistics. Specialists "dedicated to the twin ideals of economy and efficiency" promised to uplift and improve the world – an essentially secular goal but "defined within a Christian context and jumbled together in the drive for social reconstruction."[9] A confidence in statistical methods was shared by many identified with the social gospel movement and was evident in denominationally sponsored studies such as the social service surveys conducted jointly by Canadian Methodists and Presbyterians.[10]

While the successful implementation of much of the progressivist agenda is sometimes seen as the triumph of the collectivist ideal, a strong sense of individualism persisted. Even on the prairies complex technological and operational methods became associated with an individualism which one historian says "would have done business leaders proud." As the twentieth century unfolded, new attitudes succeeded the earlier co-operative ethos; firm social stratification replaced egalitarianism.[11]

Twentieth-century individualism was tempered by the recogition of the interconnectedness of life – and perhaps disturbed by that realization. Preoccupation with psychological well-being paralleled interest in social reconstruction and was, suggests one historian, derived in part from it. Paul Boyer argues that the impact of involvement in social reform was most profoundly felt at the individual, not the civic or societal, level. Many resolved a spiritual crisis through social service as their engagement restored a sense of Christian community, provided emotional exhilaration, and expanded the potential for intimacy.[12] Recognizing the importance of "saving society" did not end concern for "cure of souls" of individuals. Psychological insights put new demands on professional ministers.[13] Interest in both physical and psychological health was widespread in Methodist circles. The social gospel's emphasis on "muscular Christianity" and the Woman's Christian Temperance Movement's keen interest in scientific temperance, health, and heredity are but two examples of the linking of religion and health by progressive Methodists.[14]

This rapprochement between religion and culture also affected the relationship of clergy and laity. New "authorities" created by the communications revolution challenged the role of the minister and in some cases set a different agenda.[15] Ministry was redefined as a "service vocation," notes William McGuire King, involving service to and on behalf of the world rather than opposition to it. This "ministry" was one in which the laity were participants as volunteers in auxiliary organizations. Methodist denominational structures took full advantage of this spirit of voluntarism and enveloped the youth work, missionary funding, moral reform, and social service spawned by it. Auxiliary organizations, King suggests, helped to break down older revivalist assumptions about the relationship between church and society, proposing instead the creation of a Christian civilization. The emphasis of the auxiliary societies on professionalism, education, vocation, and social service ensured a ready reception for theological liberalism and the social gospel at the popular level.[16] Religious activity took on a new form that fitted the associative temper of the times.[17]

Those who aspired to build a Christian civilization looked far beyond Canada and whole-heartedly supported world missions. The interest in evangelizing the world for Christ so evident in the last decades of the nineteenth century continued in the twentieth. The enthusiam had a transforming effect on missionary work. Between 1900 and 1925 financial support quadrupled. By the time of church union the Methodist Woman's Missionary Society, organized in 1881, reported 122,134 members and a budget of more than $400,000. Its auxiliaries were by then supporting over a third of the denomination's missionaries sent overseas as doctors, nurses, teachers, and secretaries.[18] Young people and university students were also ardent supporters of missions. Frederick C. Stephenson's Young People's Forward Movement was officially endorsed by the Methodist church in 1898 and soon raised over $3 million for missions. University students supported the cause through involvement in the Student Volunteer Movement and the Student Christian Movement.[19]

Perhaps wishing not to be outdone, businessmen from Canada and the United States met in New York in 1906 to launch a movement of their own. But unlike the women and young people, the Laymen's Missionary Movement decided not to raise its own funds. Instead its members proposed to lend their expertise to make denominational fund-raising campaigns more "efficient." The interdenominational Canadian Laymen's Missionary Movement was formed in 1907 with strong leadership from such well-known Methodists as Newton Wesley Rowell, Joseph Flavelle, and H.H. Fudger.

From the outset the Laymen's Missionary Movement reflected the assumptions of its leading advocates. So confident was the movement of the superiority of Anglo-Saxon civilization that evangelizing "the heathen" seemed little more than a matter of putting missionaries, churches, schools, and hospitals in place. It was a technical problem that needed only the proper system of planning and execution to be solved. (Many of the same laymen were strong supporters of union who argued that denominational barriers hampered the efficiency of Christian agencies at home as well as overseas.) Although enthusiasm waned after the war, repercussions were felt long after the movement's heyday. A long-lasting alliance had been forged between laymen and a new generation of young clergy. Several young Methodists were drawn into administration of missionary work through the Laymen's Missionary Movement, among them Jesse Arnup and James Endicott. They held influential positions in the United Church and in the decades after church union infused the new denomination with the expansionist assumptions characteristic of the Laymen's Missionary Movement.[20]

Caught up in a technological and ideological revolution, progressives were persuaded that the future held unlimited possibilities. Little wonder that the piety of progressivism exuded a confidence that the Kingdom of God was at hand and might be brought nearer by the intervention of Christian reformers at home and missionaries abroad. Such faith in progress was an old idea, but coupled with it was a new impatience with the past. Progressives assumed that the future, not the past, held the keys to the Kingdom. As the spirit of Methodism became redefined as the spirit of progressivism, much was borrowed from the revivalist past. However, a reluctance to acknowledge those connections reflected progressivism's ambivalence towards tradition.

How then were Methodists to serve this "present age"? Membership statistics signalled serious problems. The Presbyterians surpassed them in numbers and by 1923 they had fallen behind the Church of England to become the third largest Protestant group in Canada. Although between 1901 and 1921 Methodism grew by 26 per cent, Baptists grew 32 per cent, Presbyterians 67 per cent, and Anglicans 106 per cent. The *Guardian* commented that the statistics did "not tell the whole story" – but gave no clues to what the rest of the story was.[21] One significant factor was immigration. In those two decades population mushroomed, but large numbers of those immigrants were members of non-Methodist churches and not inclined to change their religious affiliation. However, that was little consolation at the time.

Revivalism, once the pride of a rapidly growing denomination, suffered a reversal. There were now some who saw it is a contributing factor to Methodism's drop in membership. W.B. Creighton reminded readers that for years he had deplored the preoccupation with statistics that led "by hook or by crook" to doubling, tripling, and quadrupling the membership. Now, he chided, the church was having to face the fact that those increases had not been "real." "A made-to-order revival, with an up-to-the-minute revivalist, has swept some hundreds of 'converts' into the Church, and we have 'numbered the people' with great rejoicing, only to find that after one year, or two, or three, the Church was just where it was before, and where it would remain until another 'revival' came along and swept the same people again into the Church."[22] Statistics now supported the arguments of those who no longer saw revivalism as the most effective approach to evangelism.

Methodists suddenly faced difficult questions about their identity, the answers to which left them confused though not institutionally divided. Had "the fathers" given them a less "usable past" than they had supposed? With tradition linked so strongly to a particular approach to evangelism, what happened once old methods and assumptions were left behind? What of Methodist piety? Revivalism and the piety shaped by it were considered the tradition of "the fathers." Methodists were guided in their spiritual journeys by a particular way of becoming, being, and remaining Christian. A definite experience of conversion, validation of that experience by the "witness of the Spirit," and the ever-problematic "Christian perfection" were stages of the normative religious life. Now a new pattern of piety, profoundly influenced by progressivism, was emerging.

Those who practised this progressivist piety recognized the importance of the natural as well as the supernatural understanding of religious experience. Their behaviour was guided by the educated conscience of the individual and the principle of sacrificial service identified with the social gospel. They welcomed the theological reformulation of religious ideas and proposed modified associational forms. Not all Methodists adopted this approach to piety. Yet when compared with the alternatives, even the social gospel and liberal theology, which the progressives were offering as a "truer" interpretation of the Methodist tradition, looked increasingly attractive.

Canada's evangelical consensus, for decades showing signs of strain, proved unable to withstand these pressures.[23] The developing fissures were apparent in the discussions of evangelism during and after the 1910 General Conference. Dissatisfaction with popular evangelistic practices was voiced by a number of delegates, including Nathanael Burwash. While still insisting on the importance of a definite religious experience, Burwash was less convinced of the wisdom of depending on revival campaign conversions. Burwash's letter to his wife described what happened when the matter came before the General Conference's evangelism committee. "I was led to speak earnestly on the futility of a big conventional effort to get up a revival and to propose a more deeply spiritual method," he wrote. "It carried all the best men of the Committee and some who were ready to fight the College to the death [on higher criticism] said openly that this was new light on our position to them and that they were with us."[24]

The evangelism committee's report incorporated Burwash's well-known convictions on the subject: "the importance of a clear and definite experience of the witness of the Spirit by the renewing of the Holy Ghost" and the admonition to "preach the doctrine of Christian perfection and seek to be living witnesses to its reality."[25] Acting on the committee's recommendation, the General Conference appointed a standing Committee on Evangelism. Named as one of the members, W.B. Creighton remarked after its first session that never in Methodist history had there been a more remarkable and significant meeting. It was unanimously agreed that, for the present, evangelism would be carried on quietly through individual churches and individual members, not by large evangelistic campaigns. The oft-repeated phrase "the revival we had been looking for had already come" summed up the spirit of the meeting, for the Spirit had given "a new vision of opportunity for service."[26]

Articles and editorials in the *Guardian* soon reflected the tone of the 1910 deliberations. When the American evangelistic team of J. Wilbur Chapman and his singing partner Charles Alexander arrived in Toronto a few months later, the response of the paper was restrained. Although the *Guardian* admitted that the campaign had undoubtedly improved religious life in the city, it noted that the number of conversions did not meet expectations. Chapman himself seemed disappointed.[27] Even more striking were the responses to the questionnaire which Creighton sent to the ministers of the Methodist churches in Toronto. Over two-thirds of the respondents reported that Chapman's services had added practically no new members. There was no noticeable improvement in either "spiritual tone" or church attendance. The meetings had little influence on the community. Some even believed the campaign had a negative impact and criticisms were numerous.[28]

Revivalism was not just a Canadian problem, as Methodists discovered when the denomination's Ecumenical Conference was held in Toronto in 1911. One delegate who credited the old message and methods of revival for the large increase in membership in his branch of Methodism was quickly challenged. Creighton agreed with those who contended that the old methods no longer produced the same results. They seemed "to fall pointless and dead," and "to have lost all their virtue." It was "slowly coming to be recognized that the normal conversion should be that of which no memory exists."[29]

Session delegates dealing with evangelism set out an agenda which differed in important respects from those of the past. They discouraged the expectation of a cataclysmic conversion and advocated the use of methods that suited the child as well as the adult. Every evangelist was to be a social reformer, dealing with social as well as individual needs. Young people were to be trained to Christianize culture. New ways of cultivating piety were badly needed, they felt, to combat the "apathy and singular sterility" which had resulted from professional peripatetic evangelism. They urged that a distinction be made between evangelism (which assumed constant soul-saving) and revivalism (which assumed periodic).[30]

More attention to the social mission of the church was soon evident in the *Guardian*. When evangelist Billy Sunday opposed social gospel leader Washington Gladden, Creighton quickly sided with Gladden.[31] Editorials which urged local churches to become centres for social reconstruction in their neighbourhoods became more commonplace. Creighton publicly expressed reservations upon learning of plans for a four-week evangelistic campaign at a well-known Methodist church. He wondered whether a higher interest would not be served "if that fine body of Christian men and women would give that month up to a social study of their own neighborhood with the idea of social reconstruction, instead of upon themselves."[32]

The new anti-revival tone of the *Guardian* surprised even some who hoped to broaden the task of evangelism. C.E. Bland (Salem's brother) had been instrumental in initiating the discussion about evangelism at the 1910 General Conference. He was dismayed that Creighton seemed to suggest that revival services were no longer a worthwhile method of social reconstruction. Bland believed this to be a new departure for the official paper of Methodism.[33] But Creighton was unrepentant. He remained vocal in his scepticism about revivalism, and even sharpened his criticism after the war. Noting that formerly it had been "like interfering with the Ark of God to criticize the methods of an evangelist," he credited the war with sparking a new spirit of independence which had led the church to pursue new methods of evangelism.[34]

This new spirit of independence did not, however, translate immediately into new membership terms. Old ideas and practices were stubbornly resistant to change in some areas, even after the war. R. Edis Fairbairn, a frequent contributor to the *Guardian* from his pastoral charges in the Maritimes and Newfoundland, wrote in 1923 of his frustration with loyalty to old customs.[35] Men and women had never been more fitted for Christian service by "sympathy with Christian ideals and cultivated powers," yet the membership barrier made it difficult for them to become fully involved in the work of the church. In each of his pastoral charges, "fit and proper persons" had declined church membership because they misunderstood the qualifications. They assumed that only those who had been "converted" or "born again" were eligible for membership in a Methodist church. To complicate matters, their expectation was inconsistent with Methodism's program of religious education, which no longer presented that type of conversion as normative.

The popular view of church membership, which saw conversion as its prerequisite, was neither biblical nor Wesleyan in Fairbairn's view. The gospels did not present faith as being contingent on affirmation of a dogmatic formula or attainment of a particular experience. Faith was linked to a decision to follow Christ; religious experience came after, as the person engaged in service. The assumption that conversion was prerequisite distorted the picture of early Methodism as well, for Wesley had required of members only "a desire to flee from the wrath to come." Methodism had veered from this principle in practice; there was no mention of conversion in membership vows or the communion service. Fairbairn concluded that Methodists had become victimized by the damaging influence of revivalism: it was a "vicious tradition."

In 1923 Fairbairn's ideas were still controversial and, by his own admission, provoked resentment in some quarters. His recommendation that the church hold an inquiry on the matter was met with suspicion. But he was not alone in raising questions about the status of the "non-professing." One Ontario minister proposed that consecration, rather than conversion, be emphasized for the "non-professing," those claiming no conversion experience. He estimated that these persons represented the larger part of an average congregation.[36] His suggestion drew angry responses from several *Guardian* readers. One wrote that he was thankful that few ministers would have had the audacity to write such an article, and few readers would believe it.[37] Creighton, however, defended the article as "practical and exceedingly helpful."[38] Criticism of the paper continued, with some readers going so far as to inform Creighton of their prayers that he might "become a Christian." His critics no longer represented Methodism's "common faith," he retorted, and a new day was bringing a more tolerant spirit.[39]

What appeared to Creighton to be a "common faith" must have appeared fragmented to others. Frustration was heightened when regeneration of society was added to regeneration of the individual, for it seemed as though the mission of the church had somehow changed. Rural areas felt unanticipated repercussions from the emphasis on social service and the "new evangelism" of social regeneration. A reader identifying himself as "H.A. Seed" commended the church's growing concern for the social problems of the city, but insisted that the old revivalist ways were still effective in rural areas. "City manners and methods," he warned, seemed to spread "to the remotest corners of our rural districts, where they are anything but applicable."[40]

Confusion and alienation accompanied Methodism's attempts to distance itself from revivalism, feelings similar to those which in other denominations attracted the disenchanted to the fundamentalist movement. Fundamentalism drew the interest of Presbyterians and Baptists, but was not as appealing to Methodists. Fundamentalists obviously had little in common with Methodist progressives. But even for those who thought of themselves as traditional Methodists fundamentalism held only limited appeal, for their assumptions about the religious life differed significantly. Defenders of the old ways of Methodist revivalism may have been unhappy with the implications of a "new evangelism," but they found little comfort in the company of fundamentalists. Like the Plymouth Brethren, whose ideas had helped to shape the movement, those in fundamentalist circles still talked of conversion and Christian holiness. To traditional Methodists, these words carried a different message: conversion was first and foremost an *experience* of repentance and forgiveness which "the witness of the Spirit" (not an affirmation of the correctness of biblical texts) validated. It was not primarily a *belief* about salvation. Holiness could refer to an experience or to behaviour but in either case Methodists saw it as involving possibilities for personal and social progress that were incompatible with a premillennialist view of the world. A theology based on believing biblical propositions did not share Methodism's confidence that an authentic religious experience to which the witness of the Holy Spirit attested ensured an "orthodoxy of the heart" in harmony with biblical principles.

New publications and associations surfaced to defend "the fundamentals" of the faith. Fundamentalists insisted that evangelicals had always believed these "fundamentals," including a complicated premillennial theory of the history of God's dealings with humanity and a particular approach to biblical authority. From a Methodist perpective both seemed of more recent origin than fundamentalists were willing to admit. Canadian Methodist publications had long rejected the dispensationalism of the Plymouth Brethren[41] and were suspicious of the defence of biblical authority which usually accompanied it – the "inerrancy of the original autographs."[42]

If fledgling fundamentalism had been unappealing to nineteenth-century Methodists, the full-blown variety of those who took modernists to task was even more repugnant to progressives in the early twentieth century. They raised new questions about the movement and its dispensational view of history after a premillennial conference was held in Chicago early in 1914.[43] Conference speakers denounced those who refused to refer to the second coming of Christ in their terms, sparking a debate in the *Guardian* over whether premillennialism was a Methodist doctrine.[44] Creighton first tried to suppress the discussion. His policy changed a few months later when the dispensationalists used the outbreak of the war to corroborate their views about the end of the world. War, they said, was a count-down to the "new dispensation." This idea perturbed Creighton, for he feared Christians would lose faith in reforming society and confine their efforts to regenerating individuals. Not even the war would destroy civilization, for God was active in the world. Indeed, he was confident that the war would help to usher in an era where another war would be almost impossible.[45]

Though information disseminated from Methodism's Toronto headquarters was unsympathetic to dispensationalism, the *Guardian* discovered that the *Sunday School Times*, a publication widely used by Methodist Sunday school teachers, was not so discriminating. In 1918, an editorial called the war the greatest battle in the history of the world and outlined a sequence of events that would soon follow. Creighton deplored the article's premillennial tone, for it left the impression that there would be a personal reign of Christ over a reborn world.[46] He took a harsher line two years later, contending that "certain peculiarities of doctrine" that the *Sunday School Times* had recently developed made it "at best, an unreliable guide to Christian people."[47] He urged pastors and Sunday school officers to decide whether they wanted their scholars "to imbibe the doctrines of this new cult" with its claim that the doctrines of the second coming and interpretation of Scripture were essential to Christian character and work. The Scofield Bible and other "innocent-looking helps" also had their source in this group, which by 1920 was circulating "The Fundamentals" as its articles of faith and supporting seminaries patterned after Moody Bible Institute.[48]

Conflict between denominational leaders who rejected premillennialism and prominent professional evangelists was inevitable. Differences over premillennialism led the *Guardian* to reverse itself on persons it had earlier praised. Commenting on a feud between the

University of Chicago's Shailer Mathews and Moody Bible Institute's Reuben Torrey, Creighton described Mathews as one whose "ability and scholarship are beyond question, and his moral character above reproach," but sounded a little less certain about Torrey, who was "also supposed to be a godly man."[49] Moody's school in Chicago, applauded in the 1890s for its training program for workers at city missions, was now criticized as the parent of a chain of schools that had adopted its premillennialist creed.[50]

The dispensationalism of professional evangelists provided additional ammunition for those who wanted to replace revivalism with religious education. J.H. Philp, an Ottawa minister, felt there was still too much preaching about conversion and not enough said about nurture. "Today the comparative futility and narrowness of this Protestant evangelism is being forced home upon us," he declared. "The victorious life of faith is linked to a superstition taken over from early days as to the end of the world and a bodily return of Jesus. The cure of all the unrest to-day – social and economic – lies in the imminent end of all such things in the re-appearance of the Christ. What a futile remedy! A confession of impotence."[51] Even the apostle Paul's conversion did not deter Philp from condemning fundamentalist evangelism; Paul was a clear case of William James's sick soul – an adult with a troubled heart and conscience. Christian nurture, not conversion appeals stemming from fear of the imminent end of the world, had to become the "preeminent method of evangelism" if the church was to have an assured future.

In the twentieth-century realignment of Protestantism, it was the fundamentalists who claimed to be the true heirs to the nineteenth-century evangelical tradition. The holiness and pentecostal sects, which were to some extent influenced by nascent fundamentalism,[52] also laid claim to the evangelical tradition. And so, with nineteenth-century revivalism identified with early twentieth-century fundamentalism, a good part of Methodist "tradition" was now claimed by sectors of Protestantism with whom they had clashed in the past. Though Methodism remained remarkably united during the fundamentalist-modernist debates, they were not entirely unaffected by the resulting tensions. They were left at times confused about their identity and ambivalent about their relationship to what seemed to be a new movement with an old and familiar name: evangelical Protestantism.

Opposition to fundamentalism was spearheaded by social gospel sympathizers. Responding to requests for information on dispensationalism, the Department of Evangelism and Social Service issued a series of pamphlets in 1922 and 1923.[53] As one of the pamphlets observed, the doctrine of the new birth was "being applied to the world's need as to the individual soul" with social Christianity's belief that the world could be made anew. The pamphlet's proposals for "saving the world" were analogous to approaches to conversion of the individual. One plan presented in positive terms corresponded to the emerging model of piety within Methodism with its affirmation of the natural and gradual development of spirituality. "Some look for the emergence of new motives during the gradual transformation of the present order," it observed. "They believe that spiritual views of life are even now operative and will speedily operate yet more effectively... In th[e] rule of the spirit of Jesus they see the coming of Christ. By the operation in all the activities and relations of life of this spirit the world, they think, will be saved." On the other hand, the approach of the premillennialists was unflatteringly likened to the revolution expected by supporters of "economic determinism," a not too veiled reference to the recent Russian Revolution.

Decades earlier, E.H. Dewart's *Broken Reeds* had rejected the teachings of the Plymouth Brethren. To him they smacked of a perverse form of Calvinism – there was no room for free will. Now half a century later there were echoes of these older concerns of "limited atonement." The Department of Evangelism and Social Service's pamphlets objected to the dispensationalist idea that "a few will be saved" and "these few will form the new order." Charging that the fundamentalists' objective was "redemption, not by conversion or by sanctification, but by the revolutionary compulsion of unwilling subjects," the pamphlet cited Torrey and Scofield's references to "Kaiser Jesus" and to Christ "reigning with a rod of iron." They also criticized Moody Bible Institute and the *Sunday School Times*. The Department feared that moderate reformers like themselves were in danger of extinction because of the polarization of the "revolutionary" approaches of fundamentalists and radical socialists."

The people in the pews could hardly be blamed if they were puzzled by this maze of nomenclature. Following the visit of American evangelist C.S. Price, a report to the *Guardian* suggested that Methodist opinion of the campaign was mixed. Some thought the old doctrines were emphasized; others asked whether Methodism had ever preached premillennialism or adopted a literalist interpretation of the Bible.[54] Both sides were right. For some this growing identification of fundamentalism with revivalism eased the way to reinterpretation of the Methodist tradition. It made it easier for Methodists to cut old ties, to distance themselves from fundamentalism's less appealing approach to piety. Others were simply bewildered, unable to profess an experience of the old-time religion, uncomfortable with the new social evangelism, and unattracted to the fundamentalists who now claimed to be the evangelicals.

Yet the fragmentation of revivalist piety is only part of the picture. Expressions of concern over the growing divergence of alternative approaches to piety were mixed with discussions of a new experiment in co-operation. The changes taking place within evangelical Protestantism made it at times both easier and more difficult for Methodists to contribute to the unification of traditions to which church union aspired. Church union was presented to them as the blending of old traditions to create one that was new. Methodists gave their whole-hearted support to this endeavour at a time when it was becoming difficult to claim important parts of their own past. Union negotiations raised uneasiness about their identity. How could they ensure that this "new tradition" would carry something of the old when Methodism's contribution to it was generally discussed in such terms as "enthusiasm," "aggressive evangelism," "spirituality" – all of them linked to a nineteenth-century past that sometimes seemed more distant than Calvin's sixteenth century?

Methodism's interest in interdenominational co-operation did not begin with the union negotiations that were launched in 1902. The divisiveness which sometimes accompanied revivalism has obscured the possibilities for grander ventures of co-operation envisaged by some involved in evangelistic campaigns. Revivals both promoted and popularized union by demonstrating its practicality. After the Methodist union of 1884, attention was directed to the more ambitious proposal of an interdenominational merger. Revivalism entered the picture immediately. A discussion of the possibilities of a Protestant federation in an 1885 issue of the *Canadian Methodist Magazine* noted that though Methodism's historical connections were with the Church of England, its "spiritual affinities" were much closer to Presbyterianism. The two denominations had joined for revival services in more than one western town "with the happiest of results." This sentiment became more commonplace after the Crossley and Hunter evangelistic team made the "union revival" their trademark.[55] Presbyterians were strong supporters of revivals in western Canada, rivalling Methodism for leadership in "aggressive evangelism."

A revivalist piety set the tone for Nathanael Burwash's presentation of church union to the various branches of Methodism which gathered from all over the world for the 1911 Ecumenical Conference. God, he explained, had been preparing the churches for union for over fifty years. He reminded them that the beginning of the ecumenical movement dated back to the mid-century revivals – the Fulton Street prayer-meeting in New York, the Ulster revivals, the work of Moody and Sankey, and mission work in India.[56] Burwash recalled how in the days before union revivals, "Methodists thought Presbyterians without much religion and Presbyterians thought Methodists ignorant and fanatical." Union revivals brought their religious world views together for at least a few weeks each year. In cities, towns, and villages, a week of united prayer "was only the beginning of a revival, lasting for weeks, multiplying the converts in all our churches. I remember one Scotch Presbyterian Church in which in one winter the communicants were multiplied from five hundred to a thousand souls. The old dividing dogmas were forgotten by us all as our hearts were quickened and filled with the central vital truths of the common gospel."[57]

Burwash anticipated some objection to union because of the lingering loyalty to Methodism's revivalist piety. Speaking to those who feared the loss of the denomination's "qualities and atmosphere," he agreed that Methodism's "emphasis upon a definite religious experience of salvation by faith" was "the characteristic quality of Methodism from the beginning." But, he asked, "is not this experience the fundamental thing to-day with a Congregational Moody, with a Presbyterian Drummond as well as with a Methodist Sankey or Hugh Price Hughes to-day? Believe me, brethren, this it is which we are all setting before us as the end of our united efforts for Canada to-day; and while that is the case we shall not get far away from the essential quality of Methodism."[58] He assured them that individual responsibility, the influence of the Holy Spirit, Christian perfection, and the testimony of experience would all be retained – and even enhanced – in the proposed union.[59]

Revivals were, of course, only one of the contexts in which Methodists worked with other denominations. With the organization of federated theological colleges in Toronto, Montreal, and later Winnipeg, the classroom provided a new forum for discussion and co-operation. Writing in 1894, a few years after Victoria College relocated in Toronto, Burwash called the denominational schools "a divine leaven of unity," and noted how the move had changed the approach to "polemical theology."[60] The spirit of unity was fostered outside the classrooms as well, in city mission work, missionary societies, and Bible study groups. But for some theological students, according to one graduate, it was a shared evangelical piety that provided a basis for such co-operation.[61]

This young Methodist preacher recalled for *Guardian* readers how he had been met upon arrival in Toronto in 1888 by members of the YMCA prayer group. At the first meeting, he listened as one of the students "fairly launched into a red-hot confession of the most scriptural kind of conversion, such as have caused the attendants of many a Methodist class-meeting to shout, praise God, and weep for joy." At the close of the meeting, he approached the young man expecting to meet a Methodist. Much to his surprise, he found instead a student from Wycliffe. Amazed, he asked himself, "What! Could there be such real conversions, such Scriptural testimonies in the Church of England?" After talking further with his new friend he discovered that "there was a great similarity in our spiritual experience, apart from little local surroundings, and in the words used in expressing our spiritual progress. We were one in heart and in the salvation of Jesus Christ."

Denominational exclusiveness was undoubtedly challenged as theological students encountered philosophical idealism and other new intellectual currents which cast traditional doctrine in a different light. But even those who continued to think in more traditional terms saw the advantages of church union. The aforementioned theological student described his first pastoral charge, where he was forced to compete with the very denominations to which his Bible study friends belonged. The spirit of co-operation disappeared. He was dismayed to learn that "in a very short time our ardor for the pure Gospel was chilled, and the clear light of brotherly charity was clouded. We felt that we were dragged down to the level of hedgehogs, compelled to raise our petty little theological bristles." Similar experiences were likely instrumental in the grooming of other unionists.

A revivalist piety shared with persons from other denominations made it easier for some to adjust to denominational differences. As Nathanael Burwash addressed the 1911 Ecumenical Conference, he expressed the sentiments of many – perhaps even most – Canadian Methodists. But ironically the men whose names he evoked in that address – Moody, Sankey, Drummond, and Hughes – all had died by 1911. Taking their place were Methodists, Presbyterians, and Congregationalists committed to the assumptions of a "new evangelism" anxious to distance itself from identification with revivalism. The Methodist church that decided to negotiate for union in 1902 was significantly different in its assumptions about evangelism from the Methodist church that became part of the United Church in 1925.

Methodists in search of a "new evangelism" now joined with Presbyterians like T.B. Kilpatrick of Toronto's Knox College. He spoke in 1911 of the "end of the old type of revivalism which had been so great a hindrance to evangelism." He linked that development to D.L. Moody, whom he praised for bringing evangelism "nearer to the New Testament type than it had been since the Reformation."[62] For liberal evangelicals, Kilpatrick among them, Moody's legacy was not found in the fundamentalism that came to be associated with Moody's Bible Institute; it was carried by the city mission workers trained at the school in the 1890s and the missionaries inspired by Moody and the Student Volunteer Movement to seek "the evangelization of the world in our generation."

Perhaps Methodists can be be excused if Moody's name was less revered among them. If indeed he had put an end to "the old type of revivalism," it had been, after all, Methodist revivalism. They were also able to find in their own founder a model for social involvement and missionary activity: John Wesley was no longer merely a revivalist but a social reformer with the world as his parish. It was Wesley, not Moody, whom Methodists credited with having inspired them to join Presbyterians and Congregationalists in the "new evangelism." Watching other denominations incorporate what he saw as Methodist practices, Ernest Thomas observed:

If scriptural holiness and its application to the whole life of the nation is the programme of Methodism, that programme is no longer the peculiarity of our communion. And seeing that the crown is not to be taken from us of having helped to bring other churches to that same ambition, we need not fear that the essential mission of Methodism will be imperilled by any possible form of union with the other bodies who have already in large measure accepted our aims.[63]

But as union drew closer it was not always easy to find a distinctive place for the supposedly ubiquitous "Methodist spirit." Kilpatrick, for example, viewed revivalism as distinct from (and even a hindrance to) evangelism.[64] With revivalism under a cloud, it proved difficult to convince the other uniting parties that there was substance as well as "spirit" in the Methodist tradition. There was a growing pessimism about the prospects of preserving elements of the Methodist past. An Ottawa minister, Robert Milliken, recounted how at the beginning of the union negotiations he had heard a prominent Presbyterian minister outlining the heritage of the two groups. From Presbyterianism came the strengthened ideals and heroism growing out of past persecutions. Coming from Methodism, with its beginnings in an evangelical revival, the speaker expected religious emotion.

Milliken thought he detected in that address signs that Presbyterians found in Methodism an insignificant or even undesirable tradition. There was, he remarked, "no mistaking [the speaker's] inference that the preaching and teaching of Methodism was directed mainly towards the production and cultivation of this emotional fervor as the most essential element in the religious life and experience. Not much strength expected from that heritage."[65] Still, Milliken admitted that a narrow conception of piety, linked and limited to an emotional conversion experience, had dogged Methodism. Indeed it was now a principle hindrance. Vital as "emotion" was to religion, it was not Wesley's only message.

The Department of Evangelism and Social Service also recognized the problems inherent in identifying the Methodist tradition with nineteenth-century methods "so intimately related to some peculiarities of that century that as the century fades the specific activity becomes less effective" – a very convoluted reference to revivalism. The Department conceded that the thought forms and patterns of the scores of thousands of persons who remained "Victorian" had to have a place, and yet emphasized that the task of evangelism was different than in Moody's day. The Victorian age had passed away.[66]

If one looks for "Methodism" only in terms of its nineteenth-century manifestations one could argue, as some have, that it simply disappeared with the creation of the United Church of Canada.[67] However, to do so overlooks the way that the Methodist tradition itself, as least as reflected in its piety, was in a process of transformation at the time of the union negotiations. Methodism made a significant contribution to the United Church in more than just its numbers. Among its most important contributions was the long-standing commitment to both evangelism and social service which it carried into union. However, the proper relationship between the two was already under scrutiny. In an era of increasing specialization, the old marriage of evangelism and social service with its give and take would grow increasingly difficult to hold together as the century progressed.[68] Some signs of the alienation which has since resulted in their virtual separation were already present before union. And as the pace of change accelerated in the twentieth century, a church committed to "serving the present age" risked being condemned to cultural irrelevancy if it was unable to move as quickly as the times.

New ways of understanding religious experience, new opportunities for Christian service, and an openness to innovative approaches to theology helped prepare Methodism, and later the United Church, to take a leading role in a new alignment of denominations. Gone was the old evangelical consensus and in its place were new patterns of Protestant denominational alliance, one which we commonly identify as evangelical or fundamentalist, the other as mainline or ecumenical. Methodism's transformed piety provided a new model for the religious life which would become just as characteristic of mainstream Protestantism as revivalistic piety had been of nineteenth-century evangelicalism.

In the shaping of Protestantism in Canada this was no small thing. It framed one of the major responses to the issues raised by fundamentalists and progressives. Although most Methodists had little patience for the intricacies of the fundamentalists' approach to the Bible, they could understand the liberalism of a modernist like Harry Emerson Fosdick. Fosdick once told S.D. Chown that he was doing what Methodism had always done – taking the teaching of the Bible and putting it into the language of the people. Chown was simply following old Methodist principles when he defended Fosdick, saying, "What he believes in is not a set of doctrines without any of the elasticity of Christian liberty, but concentration upon the doctrines which are of value because they are reproducible in the experience of a Christian man."[69]

And then there is the quotation which Creighton cited to answer the question, "What is Christian faith?" "It is not an opinion," he replied, "or any number of opinions, be they ever so true... We do not lay the stress of our religion on any opinions, right or wrong, neither do we begin, nor willingly join in, any dispute concerning them. The weight of all religion rests on holiness of heart and life." Creighton maintained that this sounded like something Fosdick might say, and some would call him a heretic for it. The "heretic" in this case, however, he identified as John Wesley.[70]

Epilogue

... perishing is the initiation of becoming. How the past perishes is how the future becomes.   Alfred North Whitehead[1]

The transformation of Canadian Methodism which has been examined here took place as part of a major realignment within North American Protestantism. This new configuration was visible by 1925. It signalled the end of the evangelical consensus which Methodist revivalism had done much to shape. Encompassing more than the time and place that one became a Christian, revivalism had coloured the understanding of how religion was to be experienced, practised, articulated, and cultivated. The repercussions of the realignment were felt in various ways. Many denominations soon found themselves caught up in doctrinal controversies. Yet Methodism, which arguably stood to lose as much as anyone, given the extent to which its tradition in North America was intertwined with its revivalist past, was relatively free of open controversy.

But doctrine and polity were not the only manifestations of religious change in this period. Methodism in Canada underwent a reorientation less visible, but no less fundamental, than that experienced by other major denominations. Its way of presenting the religious life underwent a transformation, out of which emerged a new conception of piety. This was, in part, an effort to find new words to express the old gospel – "to serve the present age," as Charles Wesley had put it. Also involved was a process of distancing the denomination from a type of evangelism that used the old words to preach (what seemed to Methodists) a new gospel.

The growing tendency to identify revivalism with fundamentalism relocated many of Methodism's traditional symbols and rituals to a presentation of the religious life which was foreign to its members in many respects. For some the accompanying sense of loss was acute and still lingers. For Methodists like the Beecham family of Hybla, Ontario, near Peterborough, the transition was difficult. Their congregation, formerly the Zion Methodist Mission in the Bay of Quinte Conference, experienced the repercussions of the developments which this study has described. Many across Canada rejoiced in the theological convergence that made church union possible. But John Beecham now remembers it a different way. Son of a charter member of the congregation founded in 1886 and present on the Sunday that church union was announced, he later remarked, "When the Methodists got as dry as the Presbyterians they went together."

There was little opposition to church union in Hybla, but no real enthusiasm for it. Meanwhile the congregation treasured and sought to preserve the tradition which had shaped its religious identity. This proved to be no easy task, and the area became fertile ground for new denominations and organizations associated with the fundamentalist movement. Evidence of the old ambivalence to groups such as the Plymouth Brethren and the Pentecostals surfaced to complicate matters. A young man converted in a Zion Church evangelistic meeting in 1925 later helped to organize a Plymouth Brethren Gospel Hall in the community. Despite their alienation from the United Church, the Beechams refused to join. Asked by his daughter about that decision, John Beecham replied, "If you had known your Methodist grandfather as I knew him, you wouldn't need to ask that question. He wouldn't go with the Brethren!" She recalls her grandfather, Walter Beecham, many times saying, "The Brethren say, 'Once saved always saved.' They keep preaching eternal security. I tell you they don't know what they're talking about! A man has to repent of his sins. To just get right down on his knees and ask forgiveness to be right with the Lord." Questions about the relationship of infant baptism, conversion, and church membership remained troublesome. The child born to John and Mae Beecham in 1927 was baptized; the child born ten years later was not.[2]

Fundamentalism was not simply a preservation of what nineteenth-century evangelicalism had represented – nor were the progressives so far away from it as is sometimes claimed. In the new presentation of piety, there was much continuity, which facilitated its appropriation at the popular level. For many, the possibilites for "transformation" now expanded beyond the conversion of the individual and included society as well. Progressivism still promised twentieth-century Methodists what revivalism had promised their spiritual forebears: a way of changing individuals and institutions. The emphasis on service incorporated much of the thrust of the ethical ideal of Christian perfection. As for theology, there were points of connection between old and new because of the premium which both placed on experience. New associational forms sought, like the older ones, to cultivate this new understanding of the religious life.

So for all the talk of leaving the revivalism of "the fathers" behind, the past continued to challenge and inform Canadian Methodism. That this was the case should not be surprising, for in a sense revivalism had itself represented a transformation of the "Wesleyan tradition" just as momentous. As Sidney Mead has pointed out, God's purpose in raising up the "Preachers called Methodist" as explained at the 1784 Christmas Conference was "To reform the continent, and to spread scriptural holiness over these lands." Some distinction, says Mead, was intended between the two. Just thirty-two years later, that distinction had faded. Bishop McKendree, a frontier revivalist, declared that the purpose of Methodism was to reform the continent by spreading scriptural holiness. Methodists assumed that if a person was saved and sanctified, then fundamental social change would inevitably follow. Mead suggests that for nineteenth-century Methodists, the securing of "conversions" in conjunction with "the perfecting of the saints" was equated with, and even took the place of, responsibility for society.[3] In Canada a century later, a new twist had been added to that traditional slogan. More and more Methodists became convinced that the mission of Methodism was to spread scriptural holiness by reforming the nation.

That transition in the most dominant of the traditions which comprised nineteenth-century evangelical Protestantism was only one of the indications that a critical juncture had been reached. The revivalist spirituality of one century was eclipsed in the next, and in its place were new patterns of piety which, while owing much to it, seemed at once alike and different. Edward Shils has a pictorial analogy that is helpful in suggesting the way that change and continuity mingled in that process. Likening traditions to raindrops on a window pane, he describes how a wavering stream of water comes into contact with another stream moving at a different angle. For a brief moment, they fuse into a single stream, then break again in different directions, each carrying something of the stream from which it broke away.[4] In Canada, revivalism provided an opportunity, however brief, for diverse traditions to come together under the banner of evangelicalism. When they again diverged, Canadian Methodism found that its tradition had become part of new streams, and part of new approaches to religious life and practice within Canadian Protestantism.

Appendix

Census Figures, 1871–1921

Year	Total Pop.	Methodist	Presbyterian	Anglican	Baptist	Roman Catholic
PRINCE EDWARD ISLAND						
1871	94,021					
1881	108,891	13,485 (12.4%)	33,835 (31.1%)	7,192 (6.6%)	6,236 (5.7%)	47,115 (43.2%)
1891	109,078	13,596 (12.5%)	33,072 (30.3%)	6,646 (6.1%)	6,265 (5.7%)	47,837 (43.9%)
1901	103,259	13,402 (13.0%)	30,750 (29.8%)	5,976 (5.8%)	5,905 (5.7%)	45,796 (44.4%)
1911	93,728	12,209 (13.0%)	27,509 (29.3%)	4,939 (5.3%)	5,372 (5.7%)	41,994 (44.8%)
1921	88,615	11,408 (12.9%)	25,945 (29.3%)	5,057 (5.7%)	5,316 (6.0%)	39,312 (44.4%)
NOVA SCOTIA						
1871	387,800	40,871 (10.5%)	103,539 (26.7%)	55,124 (14.2%)	73,558 (19.0%)	102,001 (26.3%)
1881	440,572	50,811 (11.5%)	112,488 (25.6%)	60,255 (13.7%)	83,761 (19.0%)	117,487 (26.7%)
1891	450,396	54,195 (12.0%)	108,952 (24.2%)	64,410 (14.3%)	83,122 (18.4%)	122,452 (27.2%)
1901	459,574	57,490 (12.5%)	106,381 (23.1%)	66,107 (14.9%)	83,241 (18.1%)	129,578 (28.2%)
1911	492,338	57,606 (11.7%)	109,560 (22.3%)	75,315 (15.3%)	83,854 (17.0%)	144,991 (29.4%)
1921	523,837	59,069 (11.3%)	109,860 (21.0%)	85,604 (16.3%)	86,833 (16.6%)	160,872 (30.7%)
NEW BRUNSWICK						
1871	285,594	29,856 (10.5%)	38,852 (13.6%)	45,481 (15.9%)	70,598 (24.7%)	96,016 (33.6%)
1881	321,233	34,514 (10.7%)	42,888 (13.4%)	46,768 (14.6%)	81,092 (25.2%)	109,091 (34.0%)
1891	321,263	35,504 (11.1%)	40,639 (12.6%)	43,095 (13.4%)	79,649 (24.8%)	115,961 (36.1%)
1901	331,120	35,973 (10.9%)	39,496 (11.9%)	42,005 (12.7%)	80,874 (24.4%)	125,698 (38.0%)
1911	351,889	34,558 (9.8%)	39,207 (11.1%)	42,864 (12.2%)	82,106 (23.3%)	144,889 (41.2%)
1921	387,876	34,872 (9.0%)	41,277 (10.6%)	47,020 (12.1%)	86,254 (22.2%)	170,531 (44.0%)

QUEBEC

Year						
1871	1,191,516	34,100 (2.9%)	46,165 (3.9%)	62,449 (5.2%)	8,690 (0.7%)	1,019,850 (85.6%)
1881	1,359,027	39,221 (2.9%)	50,097 (3.7%)	68,797 (5.1%)	8,853 (0.7%)	1,170,718 (86.1%)
1891	1,488,535	39,544 (2.7%)	52,673 (3.5%)	75,472 (5.1%)	7,991 (0.5%)	1,291,709 (86.8%)
1901	1,648,898	42,014 (2.5%)	58,013 (3.5%)	81,630 (5.0%)	8,483 (0.5%)	1,429,260 (86.7%)
1911	2,002,712	42,646 (2.1%)	64,132 (3.2%)	103,812 (5.2%)	9,258 (0.5%)	1,724,693 (86.1%)
1921	2,361,199	41,884 (1.8%)	73,748 (3.1%)	121,967 (5.2%)	9,257 (0.4%)	2,023,993 (85.7%)

ONTARIO

Year						
1871	1,620,851	462,264 (28.5%)	356,442 (22.0%)	330,995 (20.4%)	86,723 (5.4%)	274,162 (16.9%)
1881	1,923,922	591,503 (30.7%)	417,749 (21.7%)	366,539 (19.0%)	106,680 (5.5%)	320,839 (16.7%)
1891	2,114,321	654,033 (30.9%)	453,147 (21.4%)	385,999 (18.3%)	106,047 (5.0%)	358,300 (16.9%)
1901	2,182,947	666,388 (30.5%)	477,386 (21.9%)	368,191 (16.9%)	117,819 (5.4%)	390,304 (17.9%)
1911	2,523,274	671,755 (26.6%)	524,605 (20.8%)	492,435 (19.5%)	132,809 (5.3%)	486,157 (19.2%)
1921	2,933,662	685,463 (23.4%)	613,532 (20.9%)	648,883 (22.1%)	148,634 (5.1%)	576,178 (19.6%)

MANITOBA

Year						
1881	65,954	9,470 (14.4%)	14,292 (21.7%)	14,297 (21.7%)	9,449 (14.3%)	12,246 (18.6%)
1891	152,506	28,437 (18.6%)	39,001 (25.6%)	30,852 (20.2%)	16,112 (10.6%)	20,571 (13.5%)
1901	255,211	49,936 (19.6%)	65,348 (25.6%)	44,923 (17.6%)	9,168 (3.6%)	35,672 (14.0%)
1911	455,614	68,412 (15.0%)	103,661 (22.8%)	88,807 (19.5%)	14,003 (3.1%)	74,480 (16.3%)
1921	610,118	71,200 (11.7%)	138,201 (22.7%)	121,309 (19.9%)	13,652 (2.2%)	105,394 (17.3%)

SASKATCHEWAN

Year						
1901	91,279	12,028 (13.2%)	16,232 (17.8%)	15,996 (17.5%)	2,416 (2.6%)	17,651 (19.3%)
1911	492,432	78,325 (15.9%)	96,564 (19.6%)	75,342 (15.3%)	18,371 (3.7%)	90,092 (18.3%)
1921	757,510	100,851 (13.3%)	162,165 (21.4%)	116,224 (15.3%)	23,696 (3.1%)	147,342 (19.5%)

Census Figures, 1871–1921

Year	Total Pop.	Methodist	Presbyterian	Anglican	Baptist	Roman Catholic
ALBERTA						
1901	73,022	10,125 (13.9%)	11,597 (15.9%)	9,634 (12.8%)	3,010 (4.1%)	15,464 (21.2%)
1911	374,663	61,844 (16.5%)	66,344 (17.7%)	55,602 (14.8%)	19,491 (5.2%)	61,902 (16.5%)
1921	588,454	89,723 (15.2%)	120,991 (20.6%)	98,395 (16.7%)	27,829 (4.7%)	97,432 (16.6%)
BRITISH COLUMBIA						
1871	36,247					
1881	49,459	3,516 (7.1%)	4,095 (8.3%)	7,804 (15.8%)	434 (0.9%)	10,043 (20.3%)
1891	98,173	14,298 (14.6%)	15,284 (15.6%)	23,619 (24.1%)	3,098 (3.2%)	20,843 (21.2%)
1901	178,657	25,047 (14.0%)	34,081 (19.1%)	40,996 (22.9%)	6,506 (3.6%)	33,639 (18.8%)
1911	392,480	52,132 (13.3%)	82,125 (20.9%)	100,952 (25.7%)	17,228 (4.4%)	58,397 (14.9%)
1921	524,582	64,810 (12.4%)	123,022 (23.5%)	160,978 (30.7%)	20,158 (3.8%)	63,980 (12.2%)
CANADA						
1871	3,689,257	567,091 (15.4%)	544,998 (14.8%)	494,049 (13.4%)	245,805 (6.7%)	1,492,029 (40.4%)
1881	4,324,810	742,981 (17.2%)	676,165 (15.6%)	574,818 (13.3%)	296,525 (6.9%)	1,791,982 (41.4%)
1891	4,833,239	847,765 (17.5%)	755,326 (15.6%)	646,059 (13.4%)	303,839 (6.3%)	1,992,017 (41.2%)
1901	5,371,315	916,886 (17.1%)	842,442 (15.7%)	681,494 (12.7%)	318,005 (5.9%)	2,229,600 (41.5%)
1911	7,206,643	1,079,892 (15.0%)	1,115,324 (15.5%)	1,043,017 (14.5%)	382,666 (5.3%)	2,833,041 (39.3%)
1921	8,788,483	1,159,458 (13.2%)	1,409,407 (16.0%)	1,407,994 (16.0%)	421,731 (4.8%)	3,389,636 (38.6%)

Source: 1871 figures from *Census of Canada,* 1871, 246–9
1881 figures from *Census of Canada,* 1881, vol. 1, 202–8
1891, 1901, 1911, and 1921 figures from *Census of Canada,* 1921, 568–9

Notes

CG   Christian Guardian
CMM   Canadian Methodist Magazine
CMMR Canadian Methodist Magazine and Review
CMQ   Canadian Methodist Quarterly
UCA   United Church of Canada Archives

INTRODUCTION

1 Whitehead, *Adventures of Ideas*, 7.
2 Bland, "The Real Jesus: Christianity from a New Point of View or; Is the World Ready for the Christianity of Jesus?," Bland Papers, file 552. The clipping is unidentified, but 20 January 1922 is handwritten on the copy. Ironically, in the 1870s Salem's father, Henry Flesher Bland, was leader of a group whose position on the "moral status" of children raised questions about the importance of conversion; see Semple, "The Nurture and Admonition of the Lord," 162.
3 On the polarization within Protestantism, see Marsden, *Fundamentalism and American Culture*; Marty, *Righteous Empire*, especially 177–87; and Jean Padberg Miller, "Souls or the Social Order."
4 Leonard I. Sweet, ed., *The Evangelical Tradition in America*, 70–3.
5 Notwithstanding the merits of the work on Methodist revivalism done by Canadian historians, the assumption of declension operates in a way that obscures revivalism's continuing importance for defining Methodist identity in the late nineteenth century; see for example the approach to the subject taken by Brooks and Semple.
6 Brauer, "Conversion" and "Revivalism and Millenarianism in America."

7 Brauer, "Conversion," 229–33. The stages he notes are indifference; consciousness of sinfulness; growth in spiritual understanding; changes in attitudes and behaviour thought by some to be conversion but only increasing anxiety; the conversion experience itself; a feeling of having been born anew; and, finally, a compulsion towards transformation of self and society through a process of sanctification.

8 Ibid., 234–43.

9 Brauer, "Revivalism and Millenarianism in America," 147–8; "Conversion," 242–3.

10 Shils, *Tradition* and his essay on tradition in *Center and Periphery*. I have found Shils's work to be very suggestive; his approach shaped several of the questions that I put to my source material and thus underlies the research in ways that are difficult to document. For this definition of tradition, see Shils, *Center and Periphery*, 183.

11 Shils, *Tradition*, 34.

12 Ibid., 27.

13 Ibid., 213–15.

14 Ibid., 15.

15 Ibid., 46.

16 McKillop, "John Watson and the Idealist Legacy," 73.

17 McKillop, *A Disciplined Intelligence*, 224–8. On the importance of idealism, see Fraser, "Theology and the Social Gospel among Canadian Presbyterians," 35–46. For the thesis that sociology displaced theology see Cook, *The Regenerators*.

18 Clifford, "The Impact of the Presbyterian Controversy over Church Union on the Methodist Church in Canada," 19 notes that the problem of how various groups appropriated union is one which requires more research.

19 For intellectual changes, see McKillop, *A Disciplined Intelligence*. In *The Social Passion*, Allen deals with the changing social conditions in Canada as background for his work on the social gospel movement. Keith Markell deals largely with external changes of the period examined in "Canadian Protestantism against the Background of Urbanization and Industrialization in the Period from 1885 to 1914" as do Magney, "The Methodist Church and the National Gospel" and Brooks, "The Uniqueness of Western Canadian Methodism."

CHAPTER ONE

1 John Wesley's advice to preachers from *The Doctrines and Discipline of the Methodist Episcopal Church in America* (1798), 59 and a verse from a Methodist song cited in Carroll, *Case and His Cotemporaries*, 2:434.

2 Playter, *The History of Methodism in Canada*, 25–6.

3 See statistical tables appended.

4 General Conference, *Centennial of Canadian Methodism*, 12.

5 Carroll's *Case and His Cotemporaries* is the most notable example. On the role of revivalism in establishing Methodism as a major Protestant denomination, see Clark, *Church and Sect in Canada*; also see Grant, *A Profusion of Spires*, 54–67; 104–17; 165–9. On early American Methodism, including an excellent discussion of the itinerant ministry, see Hatch, *The Democratization of American Christianity*.

6 Stevens, *Life and Times of Nathan Bangs*, 136–7.

7 Carroll, *Case and His Cotemporaries*, 1:22.

8 Ibid., 5:234.

9 Nathanael Burwash, "Life and Labors of Nathanael Burwash," Burwash Papers, box 28/622–37, 3. Carroll's *Case and His Cotemporaries* contains numerous similar accounts.

10 Richey, *A Memoir of the Late Rev. William Black*, 18–28.

11 Clark, *Church and Sect in Canada*, 56–63. On Freeborn Garrettson, see Rawlyk, *Wrapped Up in God*, 55–75.

12 French, *Parsons and Politics*, 65–7. Maritime Methodists may have been anxious to avoid being confused with some of the New Light Baptist antinomians whose excesses discredited revivalism; see Bell's introduction to *New Light Baptist Journals of James Manning and James Innes*.

13 French, *Parsons and Politics*, 202.

14 Clark, *Church and Sect in Canada*, 240–3.

15 Reid, *Mount Allison University*, 38–41.

16 Young, *Manitoba Memories*, 11. Riddell, *Methodism in the Middle West*, 81–2 describes Young's ministry as "fittingly representative of the spirit, the purpose, and the methods exhibited by the early Methodist ministers in the Middle West as elsewhere."

17 Young, *Manitoba Memories*, 339.

18 James Woodsworth, *Thirty Years in the Canadian North-West*, 113–14.

19 Riddell, *Methodism in the Middle West*, 128.

20 Withrow, *Barbara Heck*, 140–8, 152–66, 211.

21 For illustrations of conference revivals see Carroll, *Case and His Cotemporaries*, 2:61, 87; on camp meetings see Arthur Kewley, "Camp Meetings in Early Methodism" and "Mass Evangelism in Upper Canada before 1830."

22 The term is often used to describe the period between the Great Awakening and the publication of Horace Bushnell's *Christian Nurture* in 1847; for example see Goen, "The 'Methodist Age' in American Church History," 562–72. Hudson argues that the period extended to the First World War; see "The Methodist Age in America," 3–15. For a similar characterization of Canadian religious life in this period, see French, "The Evangelical Creed in Canada," 18.

23 For a critical review of revivalism from the perspective of a German Reformed theologian whose piety was sacramental in form, see Nevin, *The Anxious Bench*. In the nineteenth century, "evangelical" was redefined to distinguish those who emphasized the centrality of personal religion from those whose Christianity had a more sacramental focus; see Dayton, "Whither Evangelicalism," 143–7 and "The Social and Political Conservatism of Modern American Evangelicalism," 73–4.

24 See French, "The People Called Methodists in Canada," 77 on "the Methodist mind."

25 Several scholars have commented on the impact of revivalism on Wesley's movement. After delineating the central features of the "Methodist age," Goen comments that he leaves it to the professional Methodists to argue how far Wesley would own this as authentic Methodism; see "The 'Methodist Age' in American Church History," 563. Chiles, *Theological Transition in American Methodism*, 19 defines Wesley's theology as "not simply evangelical Arminianism or Anglicanism in earnest," which he says may be a minority position within Wesley's tradition. The question in this study is not Wesley per se, but how he was understood in the last quarter of the nineteenth century; evangelical Arminianism was more than a minority position in Canada at that time.

26 On Burwash, see Van Die, *An Evangelical Mind*.

27 Burwash, "Life," Burwash Papers, box 28/622–37, 4–5.

28 Ibid., 6.

29 Ibid., 7.

30 Semple, "The Decline of Revival in Nineteenth Century Central-Canadian Methodism" and "The Impact of Urbanization on the Methodist Church in Central Canada" associates the decline of revival with nurture of children. He argues that by the latter half of the century revivals had essentially ceased to have a significant influence on the development of Methodism. I am suggesting that revivalism continued to play a role in shaping the responses of Methodism after 1884.

31 Hammond, "The Reality of Revivals," 113 suggests that even many who are converted "in some profound experiential sense" have likely learned their faith as part of their general social experience rather than in "a precisely defined revival atmosphere."

32 Burwash, "Sixty Years of Canadian Methodism," Burwash Papers, box 19/498, 8. In this 1910 address, Burwash again relates his conversion experience in detail.

33 Burwash, "Life," Burwash Papers, box 28/622–37, 8–9.

34 Ibid., 9.

35 Carroll, *Case and His Cotemporaries*, 5:81, 109, 134, 158–9, 167–8. On the impact of Caughey's revivals, see Bush, "James Caughey, Phoebe and Walter Palmer and the Methodist Revival Experience in Canada West"; Bush, "The Reverend James Caughey and Wesleyan Methodist Revivalism in Canada West," 231–50; and Carwardine, *Transatlantic Revivalism*, especially 102–33.

36 General Conference, *Centennial of Canadian Methodism*, 312.

37 Burwash, "Life," Burwash Papers, box 28/622–37, 10.

38 General Conference, *Centennial of Canadian Methodism*, 312.

39 See Bush and Carwardine for a discussion of the role of the laity during the mid-century revivals, as well as Scott, *From Office to Profession* on the concomitant changes in the concept of ministry.

40 Burwash, "Life," Burwash Papers, box 28/622–37, 49.

41 Ibid., 52.

42 S.D. Chown, "My Life," Chown Papers, box 16/455–8, 6–7.

43 Ibid., 11.

44 Ibid., 19.

45 Letter to C.T. Scott, [undated draft], Burwash Papers, box 8/114.

46 Letter to the editor from Ernest Thomas, "Higher Criticism and the Revivalists," *CG*, 17 January 1906, 20.

47 Boylan, "Evangelical Womanhood in the Nineteenth Century," 66–7, 76.

48 Whiteley, "Called to a More Suitable Mission."

49 "Revivals," *CG*, 2 December 1885, 760.

50 Young People's Department, "Revivals," *CG*, 9 January 1895, 23.

51 For example, in the 1885 issues of the *Guardian*, approximately 415 of 482 obituaries referred to a specific conversion experience. Of the 67 notices where no definite experience was mentioned, the person was usually described as "a member of the church," "one who loved God," or one who had "consecrated" his or her life. Interestingly, a large number of the latter were born early in the nineteenth century. In 32 cases, a conversion was mentioned where no birth date was noted. "Our Righteous Dead" is particularly interesting in the issues published before 1895. After that time, the new editor, in an effort to deal with a backlog of long notices, implemented a strict policy limiting the length of the obituaries. The biographical sketches in *Case and His Cotemporaries* usually include the specific year of the itinerant's conversion and often noted a particular revival.

52 On the holiness movement in Canada, see Aikens, "Christian Perfection in Four Representative Canadian Methodists" and "Christian Perfection in Central Canadian Methodism 1828–1884."

53 On Palmer's "altar theology," see White, *The Beauty of Holiness*, 22–3. For the Palmers' work in Canada, see 239, 244. The places in New

Brunswick are wrongly located in Nebraska ("NB") in the appendices. Also see Bush and Carwardine on the Palmers in Canada.

54 Burwash gives an account of this phase of his religious development in "Life," Burwash Papers, box 28/622–37, 25–6, 62 and "Sixty Years of Canadian Methodism," Burwash Papers, box 19/498, 14–17, 32–3.

55 "Sixty Years of Canadian Methodism," Burwash Papers, box 19/498, 14 and "Life," Burwash Papers, box 28/622–37, 26.

56 Burwash, "Life," Burwash Papers, box 28/622–37, 62.

57 Burwash, "Sixty Years of Canadian Methodism," Burwash Papers, box 19/498, 33.

58 Letter to the editor from J.C. Stevenson, CG, 28 January 1885, 51–2.

59 "An Explanation," CG, 5 February 1902, 81. Part of the controversy involved the procedure by which the "footnote" was added to the Discipline. Salem Bland charged that the vote to append it was taken when only 100 of the 280 delegates remained. He believed that the General Conference was not aware of its inclusion in the larger report; it had thus been smuggled in. See his letter to the editor, CG, 5 February 1902, 82; also letters from S.J. Shorey, CG, 12 March 1902, 162 and 9 April 1902, 232.

60 Temperance was often on the agenda of holiness camp meetings. On the Second Great Awakening and reform, see Smith-Rosenberg, "Women and Religious Revivals" in Leonard I. Sweet, ed., The Evangelical Tradition in America, 199–256; Timothy L. Smith, Revivalism and Social Reform, 133–4, 164–8; and Dayton, Discovering an Evangelical Heritage. On the early history of the temperance movement in Canada, see Barron, "The American Origins of the Temperance Movement in Ontario," 131–50; Clemens, "Taste Not; Touch Not; Handle Not," 142–60; Garland and Talman, "Pioneer Drinking Habits and the Rise of Temperance Agitation in Upper Canada Prior to 1840," 171–93; Arndt, Prohibition in Canada.

61 Miller, "Unfermented Wine on the Lord's Table," 3–13 documents the discussion in the church courts and describes the role of the Woman's Christian Temperance Union in changing communion practices in local churches.

62 Chown, "My Life," Chown Papers, box 16/455–8, 39.

63 On Annie McClung, see obituaries in New Outlook, 8 September 1926. For Nellie L. McClung on revivals, see McClung, Clearing in the West, 293–300. On the work of women as evangelists see Whiteley, "Modest, Unaffected and Thoroughly Consecrated."

64 CG, 3 August 1892, 489; also see "Piety and Culture," CG, 11 August 1886, 504 as an example of numerous items related to this theme.

65 "What Are You Doing for Christ?" CG, 12 October 1892, 648.

66 "The Problem of the Hour," CG, 3 August 1892, 489.

67 E.H. Dewart, "Fraternal Address," *CG*, 28 August 1895, 546. Also see "The Spiritual and the Temporal in Preaching," *CG*, 4 November 1891, 696; "The Work of the Christian Church," *CG*, 14 November 1894, 728; "The Office and Work of the Christian Ministry," *CG*, 22 August 1894, 538.

68 Grant, *Profusion of Spires*, 103–12; Prentice et al., *Canadian Women*, 103–5; Boylan, "Evangelical Womanhood in the Nineteenth Century," who notes that "precisely because nineteenth-century women had fewer acceptable avenues to usefulness and activity, religious behavior became a more important means of self-expression for them than it was for men," 76.

69 Runyon, "Wesley and 'Right Experience.'"

70 Timothy L. Smith, "John Wesley and the Wholeness of Scripture," 246–62; Dreyer, "Faith and Experience in the Thought of John Wesley," 12–30; Brantley, *Locke, Wesley, and the Method of English Romanticism*.

71 Burwash, *Wesley's Doctrinal Standards*, xvi.

72 Ibid., 71–2; 172–3; emphasis in source.

73 Dewart, "The Development of Doctrine," 8, 37–8.

74 Ibid., p. 46; also see Burwash, *Wesley's Doctrinal Standards*, vi–vii.

75 For a discussion of this debate see Bebbington, *Evangelicalism in Modern Britain*, 16–17; 27–34; 60–5; 161–2; 171–2.

76 "Arminianism and Calvinism," *CG*, 21 January 1885, 33.

77 T.W. Hall, "Points of Comparison of Methodist Theology with the Theology of Other Churches," *CMQ* 4 (October 1892):356, 359.

78 Albert Carman, "Methodism in Bloom," *CMM* 20, no. 4 (October 1884):370 and "The Church's Working Doctrines," *CMM* 28, no. 1 (July 1888):45–6.

79 Ibid., 48. Also see Albert Carman, "Our Own Centennial," *CG*, 22 January 1890, 57. Even Carman's more liberal successor as General Superintendent continued to connect doctrine to experience and evangelism; see Chown, "The Betrayal of Speech or Accent," Chown Papers, box 4/100, especially 6–8.

80 Burwash's impact on Methodism in this period is considerable. Chown once commented that Burwash's remarks were always "the last and highest word; and when he had spoken, there was none to answer"; see his tribute at the time of Burwash's retirement from the position of President of Victoria University in "Valedictory to Dr. Burwash," *CG*, 22 October 1913, 2.

81 Burwash, "Life," chapter 20a, box 28/622–37, 3. Burwash died before he could complete his autobiography. His own account ends with his pursuit of Christian perfection in the early 1860s; his son continued the work (including the section cited here) using material from his father's papers.

82 Burwash, *Manual of Christian Theology*, vi.

83 Semple, "The Decline of Revival," 1.

84 See as an illustration "The Georgia Evangelists," *CG*, 10 November 1886, 713.

85 Ryerson, *Scriptural Rights of the Members of Christ's Visible Church*; Carroll, *Case and His Cotemporaries*, 5:170–2.

86 Bland, *James Henderson*, 31.

87 Watson, *The Early Methodist Class Meeting*, 134–52 and "Methodist Spirituality," 230–43; Rack, "The Decline of the Class-meeting" 12–21.

88 *CG*, 16 November 1892, 721.

89 "Class-meeting," *CG* 29 December 1880, 412.

90 Chown's conversion, described above, is a good example. Chown continued to value the class meeting or a group with a similar function; see his sermon on the text "Wherefore comfort yourselves together and edify one another," Chown Papers, box 10/252. Years later he advocated a "Fellowship of Christian Experience" explicitly linking it to his own conversion; see *New Outlook*, 28 September 1932, 909.

91 Burwash, "Life," chapter 20b, box 28/622–37, 2.

92 Robert McArthur, "Evangelism," *CMQ* 2 (1890):199; also see W.H. Parr, "What Is the Value of Classes," *CG*, 9 February 1898, 82.

93 J. Wesley Savage, "The Benefits of Class-meetings," *CG*, 7 August 1889, 499.

94 *CG*, 21 January 1885, 34.

95 James Harris, "The Last Decade, What Shall It Bring Forth," *CG*, 29 January 1890, 67; "Class-leaders Convention," *CG*, 23 November 1892, 740; J.J. McLaren, "Class-leaders Conventions,"*CG*, 20 November 1895, 739.

96 Lynn and Wright, *The Big Little School*, 154, 160. On the Sunday school in Canada, see Grant, *Profusion of Spires*, 103–8, 165.

97 Boylan, *Sunday School*, 5. Her research supports the assessment of Lynn and Wright above. She notes that Christian nurture did not quickly displace conversion as the main goal of instruction, and some publications presented both views (as did the *Guardian*); see 147ff.

98 Van Die discusses the controversy over the moral nature of children and church membership, *An Evangelical Mind*, 26–37.

99 "Horace Bushnell," *CG*, 11 August 1880, 252. Methodist John Vincent and his Chautauqua movement may have been more decisive in the long run; see Boylan, *Sunday School*, chapter 5.

100 John Kay, "The Religion of Childhood and Youth: Part I," *CG*, 3 November 1880, 350.

101 John Kay, "The Religion of Childhood and Youth: Part II," *CG*, 10 November 1880, 358.

102 "The Children," *CG*, 15 April 1885, 232.

103 W.J. Waddell, "An Ideal Christian Experience," *CG*, 12 December 1894, 787.

104 On the views of childhood current in this period see Kett, *Rites of Passage*, 117–18.

105 "Our Methodist Young People," *CG*, 28 March 1894, 200. For other examples of discussion in the *Guardian* see G.C. Field, "Relation of Children to the Church," *CG*, 8 July 1891, 419; "The Young People of the Church," *CG*, 18 July 1892, 440; F.G. Lett, "How May We Best Secure the Salvation of the Children in Our Sunday-schools and Congregations?" *CG*, 25 January 1893, 58; and Joseph Deacon, "Of Such Is the Kingdom," *CG*, 16 August 1893, 516.

106 Burwash, *The Relation of Children to the Fall, the Atonement, and the Church*, 26–7. (The emphasis is Burwash's.) Burwash retained this view of conversion alongside his support of higher criticism; see his letter to the editor of the *Epworth Era*, "A Serious Danger," 15 April 1907, Burwash Papers, box 2/25.

107 See Bush for the continuing importance of camp meetings to promote the teaching of holiness; for the Palmers' involvement, see White, *The Beauty of Holiness*, 165–86 and 237–44.

108 Semple, "The Decline of Revival," 8–10, 12–13. On "ordered revivals" see Scott, *From Office to Profession*, 137–8.

109 Salem Bland ["The Observer"], "At Long Last the Church on Her Full Job," UCA microfilm reproduction of Bland Papers, reel 69. The clipping is unidentified, but a reference to the Oxford Group movement suggests a date in the early 1930s.

110 Salem Bland, "After Sixty Years," 15 September 1940, Bland Papers, file 711a, 4.

111 Graves, "Converting Individuals, Converting the World," 3.

112 As examples, see *CG*, 6 February 1884, 45; *CG*, 11 February 1891, 84.

113 *CG*, 15 March 1893, 169. For accounts of the campaign, see *CG*, 1 March 1893, 137 and *CG*, 5 April 1893, 212. The remark linking the end of revival to the demise of Methodism is repeated often; as examples see *CG*, 4 February 1885, 73; *CG*, 21 October 1885, 664; *CMM* 24, no. 3 (September 1886):285.

114 "Revivals," *CG*, 2 December 1885, 760.

115 Ibid.

116 "Shall We Have a General Revival This Year?" *CG*, 7 November 1894, 712. This support for revival is typical of the *Guardian* under Dewart's editorship. For other significant illustrations of his support for revivalism and its relation to the "mission of Methodism," see "The Mission of Methodism," *CG*, 3 February 1884, 52; "Dangers and Duties of Methodism," *CG*, 21 January 1885, 40; "The Mission of Methodism," *CG*, 23 June 1886, 392; "Evangelistic Work," *CG*, 10 January

1894, 24. For a similar approach by another important denominational publication, see "Revivals," *CMM* 23, no. 2 (February
1886):184. This *CMM* editorial illustrates the difficulty of establishing
the identity of the writers of the *CG* editorials. William Withrow was
editor of *CMM* in 1886. When A.C. Courtice was editor of *CG*, an
almost identical editorial appeared in the 1 February 1899 issue. Just
as probable as plagiarism is the possibility that someone else was
temporarily taking over Courtice's editorial responsibilities. Since
such a change was generally not announced in the paper and since
the editorials were unsigned, readers would often be unaware of the
identity of the writer. Though I will often refer to editors by name, it
is difficult to establish their authorship of particular editorials with
absolute certainty.

117 "Methodism," *CG*, 15 August 1888, 520. This is the view of numerous editorial articles in the two decades preceding the formal union
negotiations with the Presbyterians and Congregationalists which began in 1902. For samples of editorials along this line see "Witnessing
and Working," *CG*, 6 October 1880, 318; "How to Promote Revivals,"
CG, 28 January 1885, 49; [untitled editorial], *CG*, 4 March 1885, 129;
[untitled editorial], *CG*, 17 August 1887, 521.

CHAPTER TWO

1 Lewis Carroll, *Through the Looking Glass.*
2 *CG*, 12 October 1887, 647.
3 McLoughlin, *Revivals, Awakenings, and Reform,* 112 and *Modern Revivalism,* 8–13; Timothy L. Smith, *Revivalism and Social Reform,* 8, 80, 88–94.
Smith and McLoughlin agree on this point despite differences in their
explanation of why revivals occur; see Smith, "My Rejection of a Cyclical View of Great Awakenings" and McLoughlin, "Timepieces and
Butterflies," 97–110.
4 Timothy L. Smith, *Revivalism and Social Reform,* 92.
5 For John Nelson Darby's role in both Canada and the United States,
see Sandeen, *The Roots of Fundamentalism,* chapter 3. For the appeal of
the Brethren in Canada, particularly among the Baptists, see Clark,
Church and Sect in Canada, 358–64.
6 Marsden, *Fundamentalism and American Culture,* 46.
7 Sandeen, *The Roots of Fundamentalism,* 163. He suggests that Calvinist
antagonism towards perfectionism may account for this response,
though by itself it would not suffice as an explanation if Methodists
themselves no longer cared for that doctrine (as the holiness movement suggested); cf. 177. Among Canadian "proto-fundamentalists,"
Methodists were also significantly under-represented; see Sawatsky,
"'Looking for that Blessed Hope,'" 98, 168ff.

8 Sandeen, *The Roots of Fundamentalism*, 106
9 Sandeen, "Towards a Historical Interpretation of the Origins of Fundamentalism," 68.
10 Dewart, *Broken Reeds*, 26–8, 34. For a similar treatment of the group by another Methodist pastor, see Strachan, *Wandering Lights*.
11 Dewart, *Broken Reeds*, 4. His identification of the "evangelists" as Brethren, despite their denials, is likely accurate; for example, on F.W. Grant, see Sandeen, *Roots of Fundamentalism*, 80, 238, 289. The places where Dewart says their influence was felt are located between London and Toronto, the same region of Ontario visited by Darby.
12 Dewart, *Broken Reeds*, 4.
13 Ibid., 6.
14 Ibid., 9–11.
15 Ibid., 20.
16 Ibid., 12.
17 Ibid., 24–6. It is not surprising that the biblical inerrancy of Princeton Theology attracted those who proposed this approach to conversion. Sandeen notes that Charles Hodge substituted the doctrine of verbal inspiration of Scripture for the witness of the Spirit referred to in the Westminster Confession; see Sandeen, *Roots of Fundamentalism*, 118–19.
18 Dewart, *Broken Reeds*, 21.
19 Ibid., 31–2.
20 Ibid., 32.
21 For examples of editorials on the subject after 1884, see "Unjust Condemnation," *CG*, 18 February 1885, 104; "Prevalent Plymouth Errors," *CG*, 8 April 1885, 216; "Questionable Theology," *CG*, 17 February 1886, 104; "What Must I Do to Be Saved?" *CG*, 3 March 1886, 136; and "What Must I Do to Be Saved?" *CG*, 3 February 1892, 72.
22 Letter to the editor signed "Watchman," "The Wiles of Plymouthism," *CG*, 2 May 1888, 276.
23 "Pride and Presumptions of Antinomians," *CG*, 1 September 1880, 279.
24 Burwash, *The History of Victoria College*, 466–7.
25 Burwash, *Wesley's Doctrinal Standards* in the introductory notes to Wesley's sermon xvi, "The Means of Grace," 150. Also see xvii.
26 Burwash's introduction to the Canadian edition of Steele, *Antinomianism Revived*, 3–4. Steele's book is concerned primarily with Plymouthism's view of salvation. The last chapter connects dispensationalism to erroneous thinking about personal regeneration.
27 The *Sarnia Observer*'s coverage of local church reaction has been collected in Lindsay Reynolds, "The Great 'Plymouth Brethren' Controversy in South-Western Ontario, 1872–73," uca.
28 *Sarnia Observer*, 7 February 1873, 2.

29 The series was published between March and May, 1873. Duncan's explication of doctrinal errors echoes Methodist concerns and gives an interesting preview of the later divisions within and across evangelical denominations during the fundamentalist controversy. For example, there are interesting references in the final article to Plymouthism's disdain for ordered ministry and theological training. These evangelists also encouraged the laity to administer the Lord's Supper and baptize in the name of the Lord Jesus rather than in the name of the Father, Son, and Holy Ghost; see *Sarnia Observer*, 9 May 1873, 2.

30 "Objections to Methodist Evangelistic Methods," *CG*, 15 February 1888, 104. The objection to the participation of women is a feature of Plymouthism that deserves closer examination. Janette Hassey has examined changes in fundamentalism's attitudes towards women in public ministry in *No Time for Silence*. Methodism was generally more open to the lay leadership of women, particularly those like Phoebe Palmer who were successful in evangelistic work; see White, *The Beauty of Holiness*, especially chapter 7.

31 Dewart, *Broken Reeds*, 33–4.

32 "Antinomianism Revived," *CG*, 1 February 1888, 72. Dewart was surprised that Methodist discussions in the United States rarely made reference to this deviant approach to conversion despite its propagation by some popular evangelists.

33 Letter to the editor from R. Aylesworth, "Plymouthism," *CG*, 15 February 1888, 99.

34 "The Office and Work of Ministry," *CG*, 26 March 1884, 100.

35 Allen, "Salem Bland: The Young Preacher," 86.

36 *CG*, 11 August 1886, 499. Also see Carman's attack on the "namby-pamby style of conversion" (in the same address where he recounts that his own conversion had taken place in a revival meeting) in *CG*, 16 June 1886, 369.

37 Quotations from the *CG* criticizing "evangelists" that are cited by Semple in "The Decline of Revival," 16–17, should be read with this distinction in mind. More than their emotional excesses was at issue, although this was no doubt a concern.

38 Sandeen, *The Roots of Fundamentalism*, 77–8; 101 and especially 177–81.

39 Steele, *Antinomianism Revived*, 22–88, 148–61.

40 "The Christian Conscience," *CG*, 27 February 1889, 136.

41 John R. Strickland, "Wesley's Views on Entire Sanctification," *CG*, 18 October 1893, 659–60, drawing on remarks from William McDonald, president of the National Holiness Association. On the interest in holiness in the late nineteenth century, see Wacker, "The Holy Spirit and the Spirit of the Age in American Protestantism, 1880–1910," 45–62 and Bebbington, *Evangelicalism in Modern Britain*, 151–80.

42 Ross, "Ralph Cecil Horner," 94–103. For Horner's own account of these events, including a lengthy account of his experience of sanctification, see *Ralph C. Horner, Evangelist*.

43 Horner, *Ralph C. Horner, Evangelist*, 46.

44 Ibid., 20.

45 "Montreal Conference," *CG*, 1 June 1887, 345.

46 Ross, "Ralph Cecil Horner," 95–101. The proceedings are described in detail in this article.

47 Horner, *Ralph C. Horner, Evangelist*, 75–6.

48 "Rev. R.C. Horner Case," *CG*, 30 May 1894, 344.

49 "Montreal Conference," *CG*, 6 June 1894, 353.

50 T.G. Williams, "A Needed Exposure," *CG*, 10 May 1893, 291.

51 Nathanael Burwash, "A Book Review by Chancellor Burwash," *CG*, 28 March 1894, 196. Burwash was alarmed that Boland's book had circulated widely among young preachers and he recommended Horner as an antidote, 197.

52 *CG*, 2 October 1895, 630.

53 *CG*, 12 June 1895, 377.

54 For an account of the major strands of the holiness movement (including passing references to Canada), see Dieter, *The Holiness Revival of the Nineteenth Century*. For the controversy over the Canada Holiness Association, see Sawatsky, "'Unholy Contentions about Holiness.'" For Burns's own account of the events, see Truax, ed., *Autobiography of the Late Rev. Nelson Burns*.

55 There are numerous examples of this in Burns's autobiography, of which the following is typical: "I realized that the camp-meeting had revolted against my leadership, and that, therefore, permanent success was impossible." Also see 88, 95, 96, 104, 114, 115, 120.

56 Ibid., 122–3.

57 Ibid., 105–20 is a recitation of the various periodicals and groups which withdrew their support – often with Burns's connection of this with their resulting demise – including the Salvation Army, the band movement, and several branches of the holiness movement. He described Methodism as the "Holiness Creed Movement" because of its emphasis on scriptural holiness.

58 Ibid., 105ff. discusses the fall-out.

59 See "The Witness of the Spirit," *CG*, 4 January 1888, 8; "A Misleading Theory of Divine Guidance," *CG*, 28 August 1889, 552; "A Dangerous Tendency," *CG*, 20 May 1891, 321; *CG*, 1 July 1891, 409; "Dangerous and Misleading Teaching," *CG*, 22 July 1891, 456; "Some Curious Criticisms," *CG*, 19 August 1891, 520; "Mr. Burns on His Defence," *CG*, 1 March 1892, 136.

60 Carman, *The Guiding Eye* and "The Guidance of the Holy Spirit," *CG*, 25 July 1888, 474–5.

61 James Harris, "Scriptural Holiness," *CG*, 25 January 1888, 51. Harris seconded the motion for Burns's expulsion from the ministry; see Truax, ed., *Autobiography of the Late Rev. Nelson Burns*, 118.

62 "Danger Ahead," *CG*, 26 October 1887, 678. For Burns's response, see *CG*, 9 November 1887, 705.

63 *CG*, 7 June 1893, 353. The reporter described the case as "even more grave than that against Rev. Mr. Sifton" – a minister who had been charged with neglect of duty, using drugs which "unfitted him for ministry," and cruel treatment of his wife. See also *CG*, 13 June 1894, 372.

64 "The Trial and Suspension of Rev. A. Truax," *CG*, 7 June 1893, 360.

65 *CG*, 6 June 1894, 361; *CG*, 13 June 1894, 377. For Burns's views on the Bible, see Truax, ed., *Autobiography of the Late Rev. Nelson Burns*, 118: "From my present standpoint, I can only point to it as a venerable curiosity, a kind of souvenir of past ages, and relegated to the shelves of antiquity." On the divinity of Christ, he says he had been "required by the iron logic of investigation to disrobe Jesus of his divinity, leaving him a mere man, battling in the world to introduce Divine guidance as a power or force which was to elevate humanity towards the goal of its perfection," 96.

66 For a discussion of the impact of the Keswick movement and its connection to fundamentalism, see Sandeen, *The Roots of Fundamentalism*, 176–81; Marsden, *Fundamentalism and American Culture*, 77–85, 94–101, 119; Dieter, *The Holiness Revival of the Nineteenth Century*, 187–8; Bebbington, *Evangelicalism in Modern Britain*, 151–80, 217–20. The connection between the Plymouth Brethren and the Keswick movement merits exploration, given their influence on Hannah Whitall Smith; see her autobiography, *The Unselfishness of God and How I Discovered It*, especially 179–80, 190–5, 220, 234–7.

67 Several who had become disillusioned by the Canada Holiness Association's Divine guidance turned to Keswick; one was R.N. Burns (not to be confused with Nelson) in "Visit of the Keswick Brethren," *CG*, 19 April 1893, 244. Also see B. Sherlock, "The Keswick Brethren," *CG*, 24 May 1893, 323.

68 *CG*, 24 January 1894, 5.

69 "Christian Perfection – The Keswick Dispute," *CG*, 19 February 1896, 118.

70 In "Holiness Literature," *CG*, 9 September 1896, 584.

71 "Recent Holiness Movements," *CG*, 7 April 1897, 216. The editorial was a response to a Presbyterian Keswick supporter who had criticized previous holiness movements for failing to secure ethical results because of their emphasis on eradication of sin; this was a not too veiled attack on Wesleyan holiness.

72 "Alleged Opposition to Holiness," *CG*, 2 September 1894, 561. Also
see "Methodists and Holiness," *CG*, 23 May 1894, 326 and "Noisy Dis-
order in Worship Is No Evidence of Holiness," *CG*, 15 August 1894,
520.

73 "Holiness and the Church," *CG*, 17 July 1895, 449.

74 McKillop, *A Disciplined Intelligence*, 139. On responses to evolution in
Canada see Taylor, "The Darwinian Revolution."

75 Ibid., 139–40.

76 One historian who has examined the impact of evolution on Protestant thinking at the turn of the century argues that historians have
restricted their accounts to an analysis of the intellectuals' response to
Darwin because that is all the response there was; see Szasz, *The Divided Mind of Protestant America*, 5. Meyer, "American Intellectuals and
the Victorian Crisis of Faith," 591–2 notes that the public had a tendency to accept the new ideas at a superficial level and remain relatively unchanged by them.

77 Szasz, *The Divided Mind of Protestant America*, 3. On social impact of
Darwinism see Bannister, *Social Darwinism*, Hofstadter, *Social Darwinism in American Thought* and Kaye, *The Social Meaning of Modern Biology*.

78 Szasz, *The Divided Mind of Protestant America*, 8–9. Randall, "The
Changing Impact of Darwin on Philosophy," 126–8 suggests that evolution was a godsend to many religious seekers, and was "speedily
brought to the support of faiths already worked out in the pre-
Darwinian era, especially of the faiths of Romantic idealism." He
points out that idealism had its own version of evolution for which
Darwin was either irrelevant or additional support. This is a reversal
of the relationship which McKillop sees between the two.

79 "Attack and Defence," *CG*, 5 March 1884, 76. Also see William Harri-
son, "Science and Religion," *CMM* 20, no. 5 (November 1884):449–54,
a report of the Montreal meeting of the British Association for the Advancement of Science.

80 "The Rev. Dr. Dallinger on Evolution," *CG*, 4 January 1888, 8.

81 "Evolution," *CG*, 20 January 1892, 40.

82 "Sin – The Evolutionists' View of It," *CG*, 11 September 1895, 584.

83 "Reasonable Faith," *CG*, 14 August 1901, 513.

84 "Dr. Bowne's Lectures on Theism: Theological Conference, Victoria
University," *CG*, 28 November 1900, 754. Warnings of the dangers of
pantheism were, of course, not new. For its links to idealism, see
Erastus I. Badgley, "Pantheism," *CMM* 22, no. 2 (August 1885):151.
Badgley, professor of Logic and Philosophy at Victoria College, was
particularly concerned about the works of Plotinus, Spinoza, and Hegel, noting (as does McKillop) idealism's impact on British philoso-

phy. He also warned against the "organic pantheism" of Darwin, Huxley, and Tyndall, 151–8.

85 John J. Tigert, "Biblical Criticism and the Christian Faith," *CG*, 13 November 1901, 730–1. An earlier editorial had noted the similarities between Kant, Schleiermacher, and Methodism, and urged Methodism to "ever continue to be so filled with spirituality as to be able to harmonize with all trustworthy philosophic thought, and penetrate it with power to save the people," *CG*, 3 January 1900, 8.

86 Salem Bland, "My Intellectual Pilgrimage," UCA microfilm reproduction of Bland Papers, reel 69, 43–4. Eucken was a well-known author and lecturer in his day and winner of the Nobel Prize for Literature in 1908.

87 S.D. Chown, Sermon on text "I am come that they might have life," March, 1912, Chown Papers, box 3/68. For an earlier criticism of idealism, see his report on the Theological Conference held at Victoria College, *CG*, 8 December 1897, 777. Another who noted Eucken's influence is F.W. Wallace (who succeeded Burwash as Dean of Theology). His letter to Burwash during a trip to Germany mentioned that his plans included hearing Harnack, Deissmann, Seeburg, and Kaftan, and reading several of Eucken's works. See F.W. Wallace to Nathanael Burwash, 10 September 1910, Burwash Papers, box 5/60. S.P. Rose also mentions Eucken in his address to the M.E. Church, South conference, printed in *CG*, 20 May 1914, 15. For a different interpretation of Bland and Chown, see McKillop, *A Disciplined Intelligence*, 225–7 and "John Watson and the Idealist Legacy," 84–6.

88 McKillop, "John Watson and the Idealist Legacy," 73.

89 The astonishing interest in its publication is described in Szasz, *The Divided Mind of Protestant America*, 19.

90 The AISL was of considerable importance in Canadian Methodist circles. The Theological Union became affiliated with it in 1890; see *CG*, 23 July 1890, 467. One of AISL's guiding spirits, OT scholar William Rainey Harper (who became the first president of the University of Chicago in 1892), also contributed articles to the *CMQ*; see "Systematic Bible Study," *CMQ* 3 (April 1891):162–71 and "The Rational and the Rationalistic Higher Criticism," *CMQ* 4 (October 1892):427–56. The *Guardian* was also impressed by the numerous summer sessions of the Institute; see *CG*, 17 June 1896, 385.

91 Van Die, "Nathanael Burwash and 'The Conscientious Search for Truth,'" 12, and Gauvreau, "The Taming of History," 332–6. For Burwash's approach to biblical criticism, see Van Die, *An Evangelical Mind*, 102–13.

92 Salem Bland, "Retrospect and Prospect," Bland Papers, file 705. Bland also describes his initial objections to higher criticism in an article on

"Queen's Theological Alumni Conferences in the '90's," *Queen's Review* 4 (October 1930):237–41 in which the importance of higher criticism is again clear (whereas philosophical idealism is mentioned only in passing).

93 Salem Bland, "The Revolution of the Last Forty Years," Bland Papers, file 700, 2–3.

94 Salem Bland, "The Modern View of the Bible," UCA microfilm reproduction of Bland Papers, reel 69, an unidentified clipping.

95 A number of studies have been done on the impact of higher criticism; see Sinclair-Faulkner, "Theory Divided from Practice," 321–43; Moir, *A History of Biblical Studies in Canada*; Boyle, "Higher Criticism and the Struggle for Academic Freedom in Canadian Methodism"; and Prang, *N.W. Rowell*, 70–88.

96 As examples of the exchange *CG*, 2 November 1890, 756, 760; 17 December 1890, 803; 23 December 1891, 808; 18 January 1892, 74.

97 *CG*, 10 March 1897, 146–7. See a similar criticism by Burwash, *CG*, 24 March 1897, 178. Workman continued his criticism of Smith (a leading Canadian literary figure) in *The Old Testament Vindicated as Christianity's Foundation*; Burwash wrote the introduction, and it was highly praised in *CG*, 26 May 1897, 323.

98 George Workman, "To the Board of Regents of Victoria University," 6 January 1892, Burwash Papers, box 8/113. Workman's "orthodoxy" did become an issue in the second phase of the controversy after his dismissal from Montreal's Wesleyan Theological College in 1907.

99 The following is a sampling of the positive presentation of biblical criticism: "Careful Advice," *CG*, 16 June 1897, 376; "The Bible under Higher Criticism," *CG*, 10 January 1900, 24; "Notes and Comments on the Theological Conference at Victoria College," *CG*, 27 November 1901, 760; "Who Will Show Us Any Good," *CG*, 20 August 1902, 529; Rev. Prof. Stewart, "Higher Criticism," *CG*, 11 July 1894, 442. Riddell, *Methodism in the Middle West*, 230 observed that Manitoba was "not seriously disturbed," and credited the trust placed in Old Testament Professor Stewart for the calm reception of the new ideas.

100 S.D. Chown, "Ottawa Address," Chown Papers, box 12/338. The manuscript is undated, but the context is the recent 1910 General Conference.

101 "Misleading Methods of Teaching Error," *CG*, 20 September 1893, 600. Also see "Modern Progress in Theology," *CG*, 25 November 1891, 744.

102 Porter, *The Vertical Mosaic*, 459.

103 Turner, *Without God, Without Creed*, 268.

104 Gilbert, *Religion and Society in Industrial England*, 176–87.

105 Graham, *Greenbank*, 274–81 on Methodism and passim on evangelical Protestantism.

CHAPTER THREE

1 Joseph de Maistre cited in Hirschman, "Reactionary Rhetoric," 70 and J.S. Woodsworth, *My Neighbor*, 26.
2 Hirschman, "Reactionary Rhetoric," 65.
3 Mathews, "The Second Great Awakening as an Organizing Process, 1780–1830," 23–43. Also see McLoughlin, *Revivals, Awakenings, and Reform*, 98–140.
4 In analyses of the relationship between Christianity and culture in this period, it is sometimes suggested that the churches reacted to encroaching secularization by intentionally accommodating their theology to the secular; in doing so, they unwittingly hastened the process they hoped to hold at bay. This underestimates the extent to which all social institutions, both religious and secular, were affected by changes at the turn of the century.
5 Bliss, *Northern Enterprise*, 285–311.
6 MacDougall, *Rural Life in Canada*, 29; see 19–56 for a statistical analysis of "rural depletion." For an interesting discussion of how the patterns of population movement affected women, see Cohen, *Women's Work, Markets, and Economic Development in Nineteenth-Century Canada*, 120–7; also see her statistical tables, 159–70.
7 Bliss, *Northern Enterprise*, 286–7; McCalla, "An Introduction to the Nineteenth-Century Business World," 14–15.
8 Bliss, *Northern Enterprise*, 335–42; for description of a similar transition in the United States, see Chambers, *The Tyranny of Change*, 19–20, 43–72. For a suggestive way of analysing this transition see Sklar, *The Corporate Reconstruction of American Capitalism*, 1–33. Sklar uses the term "corporate" to refer not to the incorporation of property, but rather to the capitalization of the property through negotiable securities and the corresponding separation of ownership and management, with management handling administration by specialized and bureaucratic methods. As such it involves a pervasive process of economic change from a price-competitive market to an administered, controlled market; see 4–5 (footnote 1). Sklar notes the corresponding qualitative changes which distinguish the corporate phase from the urbanization of the preceding period of capitalism; see 26.
9 Chambers, *The Tyranny of Change*, 21–8; Cohen, *Women's Work, Markets, and Economic Development in Nineteenth-Century Canada*, 120–8, 146–51.
10 Rutherford, *The Making of the Canadian Media*, 91. On the impact of advertising on culture, see Lears, "From Salvation to Self-Realization"

and Christopher P. Wilson, "The Rhetoric of Consumption." On the impact of new technology on the home see Margolis, *Mothers and Such*.

11 Sklar, *The Corporate Reconstruction of American Capitalism*, 22–3.

12 Chambers, *The Tyranny of Change*, 106ff. See also Porter, *The Vertical Mosaic*, 35–6, who characterizes the early twentieth century as a prosperous period during which Canadians had difficulty articulating collective goals. For a discussion connecting the middle-class anxiety of the progressive age to the social gospel movement, see Boyer, "*In His Steps*: A Reappraisal," 60–78.

13 "The Old and the New," *CG*, 3 March 1886, 136. Also see "The Methodist Outlook," *CG*, 21 October 1885, 664 and "The Church and the Age," *CG*, 25 January 1888, 56, *CG*, 26 August 1891, 537. Allen, "Salem Bland: The Young Preacher," 76 describes the Methodism of the 1880s as "national in scope, broadening in cultural proportions, and flashing here and there with a new catholicity of spirit." He adds that this "new Methodism" seemed often to be only "the old writ large" since the new was often obscured by counter-trends and the force of the old.

14 Lenhart, "Methodist Piety in an Industrializing Society," has examined the transplanting of rural piety to late-nineteenth-century Chicago, pointing to the incompatibility of its focus of change as emanating from within the individual with the city's view of the arena of change: science, the economy, and the collective unit. See especially chapter 4. Ahlstrom, *A Religious History of the American People*, 743 comments that revivals enabled the churches to reach beyond the circle of personal acquaintances to the anonymous mass of city folk, as well as offering a measure of the excitement of the earlier camp meetings. He notes that revivalism constituted "the single largest response of evangelical Protestantism to the challenge of the urban frontier."

15 Timothy L. Smith, *Revivalism and Social Reform*, chapter 4 passim. To what extent this was the case in Canada is not clear, although visiting evangelists did attract large crowds in the cities.

16 Norwood, "The Shaping of Methodist Ministry," 341. Also see Russell E. Richey, "Evolving Patterns of Methodist Ministry," 20–37.

17 Allen, "Salem Bland: The Young Preacher," 87.

18 Allen (ibid.) says of the Moody meetings: "Half the adult population of Toronto seems to have heard Dwight Moody in his visit to Toronto in 1885, and the [Toronto] *Globe* gave him nine or ten columns of coverage per day."

19 On Jones and Small, see "The Revival in Toronto," *CG*, 20 October 1886, 664 and "The Revival: Shall It Go On?" *CG*, 27 October 1886, 681.

20 "Conferences of the Maritime Provinces," *CG*, 27 July 1887, 394.

21 *CG*, 23 June 1897, 394.
22 Timothy L. Smith, *Revivalism and Social Reform*, 41.
23 Many of these accounts of conversion and call are recorded in the *CG*'s reports of the various Annual Conferences.
24 "Toronto Conference," *CG*, 23 June 1880, 197.
25 "Bay of Quinte Conference," *CG*, 20 June 1906, 10. This is not to suggest that the denominational leaders were unconcerned about education or social position, for clearly this was not the case. It is rather to counter the notion that conversion was either absent or peripheral to late-nineteenth-century Methodism. On the contrary, it continued to be central – at least to the way Methodism presented itself.
26 J. Cooper Antliff, "The True Aim of Preaching," *CMM* 22, no. 4 (October 1885):332–3. On the relation of the offices of pastor and evangelist, see James H. Rigg, "Primitive Methodism and Modern Revivalism," *CG*, 27 May 1885, 322; "Evangelism," *CMQ* 2 (1890):195–205; also see "Aggressive Christianity" *CMM* 22, no. 4 (October 1885):376.
27 "Evangelization Society," *CG*, 25 February 1880, 60.
28 *CG*, 24 March 1880, 94 and *CG*, 14 April 1880, 118.
29 Sam Jones cited in McLoughlin, *Modern Revivalism*, 291.
30 Ibid., 291. See also Weisberger, *They Gathered at the River*, 233–5. For Jones's view of conversion as indicated through his own experience, see Jones and Small, *Sam Jones and Sam Small in Toronto*, 127–45.
31 McLoughlin, *Modern Revivalism*, 282–3. However, he characterizes the reform aspects of Jones's evangelism as "specious and repressive."
32 "The Revival in Toronto," *CG*, 20 October 1886, 664. For Moody's appeal among Presbyterians and Baptists, see *CG*, 6 September 1893, 568 and *CG*, 28 August 1895, 547. The tendency towards Plymouthism in Moody's calls for conversion, as well as his views on holiness and premillennialism, remained points of disagreement between Moody and the Canadian Methodist church, despite praise for his work in general.
33 "Sam Jones in Toronto," *CG*, 13 October 1886, 648.
34 "Method as an Element of Success," *CG*, 17 November 1880, 364. See also a letter to the editor, "Evangelistic Methods," *CG*, 12 December 1888, 787, which blamed this superficiality on the "unsectarian" evangelists, and an editorial "The Modern Evangelist," CG, 29 July 1891, 472.
35 Letter to the editor from A. Browning, "Evangelists and Evangelists," *CG*, 9 December 1896, 794.
36 "Professional Convert Manufacturers," *CG*, 8 December 1897, 770. Also see "Free-lancers," *CG*, 9 December 1891, 771; "Sabbath Evening Revivals," *CG*, 2 March 1898, 130; A. Langford, "Sabbath Evening Re-

vivals," *CG*, 2 March 1898, 136; E. Stephens, "The Penitent Bench and Enquiry Room," *CG*, 5 August 1903, 24.

37 S.P. Rose, "The Passing of the Protracted Meeting," *CG*, 13 May 1896, 306; H.H. Fudger, "The Needs of Toronto Methodism," *CG*, 22 February 1899, 114.

38 See Steele, *Antinomianism Revived*, 5–14. Steele linked the errors of Plymouthism's approach to salvation of the individual to their dispensational view of history.

39 "The Rev. Mr. Parsons on Methodist Revivals," *CG*, 12 October 1887, 646.

40 For the impact of these conferences see Walter Unger, "'Earnestly Contending for the Faith.'"

41 "The Niagara Bible Conference," *CG*, 9 August 1893, 504.

42 "Is It True?" *CG*, 30 September 1896, 625.

43 "The Second Coming of Christ," *CG*, 23 February 1898, 120. See also "Strong Evangelism," *CG*, 13 February 1901, 97, which praised the appointment of Conference evangelists and urged that the work of evangelism not fall into the hands of those "whose doctrinal teaching is gloomy, who do not count this a genuine, glorious and successful dispensation of the Holy Spirit, but an interim period between the first and second advents which will not see the salvation of the world."

44 "Shall We Have a General Revival of Religion This Year?" *CG*, 10 December 1890, 792.

45 Kent, *Holding the Fort*, 325–40.

46 For a discussion of the expansion of the Salvation Army in the last two decades of the nineteenth century, see Moyles, *The Blood and the Fire in Canada* and Clark, *Church and Sect in Canada*, 378–88, 418–22.

47 "The Salvation Army," *CG*, 17 March 1880, 84. Also see "A New Movement," *CG*, 14 April 1880, 116, which describes it as "free from everything that could give offence as being extravagant or uncouth. The work it is accomplishing proves its right to recognition as an evangelizing force."

48 "The Salvation Army," *CG*, 12 May 1880, 148.

49 "The Salvation Army," *CG*, 16 April 1884, 124.

50 Ibid., 124. For other examples of this type of criticism, see *CG* editorials 2 January 1884, 4; 20 February 1884, 60; 4 March 1885, 249; 13 October 1886, 648.

51 "Drift," *CG*, 29 April 1885, 260.

52 "Congregationalists and the Salvation Army," *CG*, 2 April 1884, 111.

53 Allen, "Salem Bland: The Young Preacher," 85–6.

54 The *CG* reported that the editor of Britain's *Methodist Times* had urged such a union, *CG*, 4 March 1885, 136. A year later, a report of C.S. Eby's lecture at Victoria University's Theological Union meeting noted

that he had hinted at forming a "Salvation Army branch," *CG*, 22 December 1886, 803.

55 "Evangelism," *CMM* 24, no. 3 (September 1886):286. For examples of positive assessments of the movement, see *CG*, 25 November, 1885, 739; *CG*, 12 August 1885, 500; *CMM* 20, no. 3 (September 1884):277; Robert McArthur, "Evangelism," *CMQ* 2 (1890):200–1. For reservations, see "Revivals and Revivalists," *CG*, 25 July 1888, 467, where it is criticized as part of the trend towards placing responsibility for revival in the hands of "professionals."

56 W.H. Withrow, "The Epworth League – Objections Met," *CG*, 1 January 1890, 4.

57 "In Darkest England and the Way Out," *CG*, 12 November 1890, 728; "General Booth's Scheme," *CG*, 31 December 1890, 840; "The Salvation Army and Its Leaders," *CG*, 29 October 1890, 696.

58 W.S. Blackstock, "New Departure of the Salvation Army," *CMQ* 3 (1891):95.

59 *CG*, 28 December 1892, 825.

60 "General Booth in Canada" *CG*, 10 October 1894, 641. Dewart also summarized an appreciative article by Charles A. Briggs which described the Army's growth as "the most marvellous ever enjoyed by a religious organization in so short a time"; see "Professor Briggs on General Booth," *CG*, 12 December 1894, 785.

61 "'The Bitter Cry,'" *CG*, 6 February 1884, 44; "Evangelistic Work in Cities in Towns," *CG*, 12 September 1888, 584. On the early history of the city mission movement in North America see Smith Rosenberg, *Religion and the Rise of the American City*.

62 For Hughes's reservations about the Salvation Army, see "City Mission Work," *CG*, 22 February 1888, 120, an editorial comment on an article in the *Methodist Times*. The *Methodist Times* had remarked, "We have all been backing the Army, because we believed it got at the poor, and on the strength of that conviction the Army has received immense amounts of money … Our friends must now look to their laurels."

63 Hughes's influence was widespread in Canada. Both the *CG* and the *CMM* carried reprints of *Methodist Times* editorials. Riddell, *Methodism in the Middle West*, 228 notes that Hughes's published sermons "found their way into the library of many Methodist ministers and gave a new cast to their pulpit utterances." Salem Bland maintained that it was these sermons that "startled the Christian world" and initiated a new type of evangelism; see "Good News for Our Day," 8 January 1927, Bland Papers, file 650. When the editors of Wesley College's student newspaper wanted advice on understanding their "mission"

in Winnipeg, it was to Hughes they wrote; see Allen, "Children of
Prophecy," 17. For an interesting discussion of Hughes that sees his
social Christianity as an extension of traditional Methodism rather
than an established break (as is usually assumed), see Manson, "The
Religious Thought of Hugh Price Hughes." Manson documents the re-
printing of Hughes's writings in Canadian Methodist publications.

64 "The Rev. Hugh Price Hughes and the 'Forward Movement' of English Methodism," *CMM* 28, no. 3 (September 1888):233.

65 "A Great Work," *CG*, 14 November 1888, 728. The report is cited in
Rev. Prof. Stewart, "Home and Foreign Missions," *CMQ* 1 (April
1889):143–4.

66 "Sensational Services – The 'Forward Movement,'" *CG*, 1 January
1890, 8; "The Past Year in English Methodism," *CG*, 22 January 1890,
56; "Forward Movements," *CG*, 5 February 1890, 88.

67 James Woodsworth includes reports on All Peoples' from Nellie Mc-
Clung and his son, J.S. Woodsworth, in *Thirty Years in the Canadian
North-West*, 241–59; also see Emery, "The Methodist Church and the
'European Foreigners' of Winnipeg," 85–100. For activities, see the All
Peoples' Mission report for 1907–8 in appendix 4 of J.S. Woodsworth,
Strangers within Our Gates, 319–41.

68 "The Fred Victor Mission," *CG*, 21 November 1894, 744; "The Fred
Victor Mission," *CG*, 20 February 1895, 120.

69 "A Philanthropic Institution," *CG*, 31 October 1894, 696 makes special
mention of her work. Sheffield had previously contributed a series of
articles entitled "Three Months in the Chicago Bible Institute," *CG*,
8 August–12 September 1894, giving descriptions and high praise for
the Institute. Also see "Trained Lay Workers," *CG*, 1 January 1890, 8
and "A New Ministry for the Masses," *CG*, 17 April 1889, 248–9 on
Moody's program for city workers. It was this aspect of Moody's work
that impressed Salem Bland, who noted the practical evidences of domestic happiness and peace, the charities and philanthropies, and the
social and national service that had issued from his work; see his
"Memorial of Dwight Lyman Moody," 22 December 1899, Bland Papers, file 377. Bland later changed his assessment of Moody's work;
see clipping attached to sermon, "While Moody Preached the Workers
Suffered," [1937].

70 Shaver, "A Partial Report of the Students' Christian Social Union," appendix 4 in J.S. Woodsworth, *Strangers within Our Gates*, 349–53.

71 See Thomas, "Servants of the Church: Canadian Methodist Deaconess
Work, 1890–1926," 371–95.

72 For analysis of the relationship between Methodist revivalism and the
Canadian social reform movement, see chapter 4 below; also see Tim-

othy L. Smith, "The Evangelical Origins of Social Christianity" in *Revivalism and Social Reform*, 148–62 and Gorrell, *The Age of Social Responsibility*.

73 For example, an editorial commending the impact of Hughes's mission on Methodism's attitude to reform was followed by a notice of Lyman Abbott's installation at Plymouth Church, mentioning with a disapproving tone "his loose views on the subject of probation," *CG*, 22 January 1890, 56. For more positive editorials on Abbott see "The Pulpit for Today," *CG*, 15 August 1888, 520 and "The New Reformation," *CG*, 21 November 1888, 745. Washington Gladden was known to Canadian Methodism, but was identified in a review of at least one of his books with a program for personal evangelism. See "Applied Christianity," *CMQ* 2 (April 1890):254–65, a review of Gladden's *Parish Problems*. Chown's review of *Christianity and Socialism*, *CG*, 9 January 1907, 10, stressed Gladden's individualism.

74 "The World's Great Want," *CG*, 22 August 1888, 536 and "The Work of the Christian Church," *CG*, 14 November 1894, 728.

75 Dewart's criticism was directed against secular reformers who emphasized the environment to the exclusion of changed individuals; see "Personal Religion and Work," *CG*, 22 November 1893, 744; also see "The Spiritual and the Temporal in Preaching," *CG*, 4 November 1891, 696.

76 E.A. Stafford, "Christian Socialism," *CMQ* 3 (July 1891):366 insisted that "Christian Socialism will ... reach the goal of an ideal condition of society by the perfecting of the individual"; also see "About Preaching," *CG*, 20 November 1895, 744 and "Environment vs. Life," *CG*, 12 July 1899, 440, where Courtice maintained, "This is the harmony of the universe, the regeneration of society by the regeneration of the individual, the renovation of the nation by the renovation of every citizen."

77 "Toronto Conference," *CG*, 21 June 1899, 389.

78 Albert Carman, "The Gospel of Justice," *CG*, 26 August 1891, 532; also "M.T.S.," "Christian Workers Convention," *CG*, 11 December 1889, 786–7 and the editor's announcement of the convention *CG*, 9 October 1889, 649. Lectures by Graham Taylor, a social gospel leader who later joined Chicago Theological Seminary, were particularly noted.

79 Salem Bland, "The Kingdom of God Realized Only in Individual Regeneration," 1899, Bland Papers, file 356. Support for the primacy of individual regeneration came from other denominational leaders well known in Canadian Methodist circles. For example, "The Church and the Social Movement," *CG*, 12 April 1899, 232 draws attention to an article in the *American Journal of Sociology* by Shailer Mathews, who became a leader of the University of Chicago "modernists." He main-

tained in 1899 that the work of the church must be strictly spiritual, "to produce regenerate men" and to "insist that sin is the cause of social evils." For Mathews's later position, see Hudson, "Walter Rauschenbusch and the New Evangelism," 416–20. At this time Graham Taylor, who like Mathews emphasized sacrificial service, also advised that the church keep out of politics and not be identified with schemes of social reconstruction; his views are cited in "The Social Function of the Church," *CG*, 17 January 1900, 40.

80 Albert Carman, *General Superintendent's Address* (Toronto: William Briggs 1902), 4, 6 warned of Methodism's demise if it failed to evangelize the unconverted masses.

81 Timothy L. Smith, *Revivalism and Social Reform*, 61.

82 "General Conference," *CG*, 28 September 1898, 617. Bland's name was still associated with the resolution two years later; see "General Conference Evangelistic Movement," *CG*, 21 February 1900, 125.

83 Ibid., 126.

84 "The Coming Revival," *CG*, 26 September 1900, 610.

85 See *CG*, 19 April and 26 April 1899. For a description of the campaign implementation in Manitoba, see Riddell, *Methodism in the Middle West*, 251–3.

86 *CG*, 17 October 1900, 658.

87 "Forward into the New Century," *CG*, 2 January 1901, 1.

88 For an intriguing look at the impact of prosperity on the Methodist Church, see Bliss, *A Canadian Millionaire*. He notes that much of the money for this campaign was raised in a few of the large Toronto churches, 10 per cent of it from Sherbourne Street Methodist alone.

89 A similar Methodist campaign in the United States was apparently no more successful. Aiming for twenty million dollars and two million converts, the campaign reached only the financial goal. As 1902 drew to a close, there had been less than one hundred thousand additions to the church (see "Is It Significant?" *CG*, 24 December 1902, 825), though an eleventh-hour campaign on the last four days of the year was quite successful; see *CG*, 28 January 1903, 3.

90 "The Need for Evangelism," *CG*, 11 September 1907, 577.

91 "Our Statistics," *CG*, 30 July 1902, 481. There was also concern over the numbers of Sunday school and Young People's Society members.

92 "Toronto Conference," *CG*, 22 June 1898, 389; "Toronto Conference," *CG*, 21 June 1899, 389; see also "After Revivals: What?" *CG*, 27 March 1901, 193. Ralph Brecker, "Delegate to GC of M.E. Church South," *CG*, 21 May 1902, 322 also discusses this problem of "leakage."

93 "Decrease of Increase," *CG*, 10 August 1898, 497.

94 C.S. Eby, "To the Angel of the Church of Canadian Methodism," *CG*, 20 August 1902, 533.

95 On the planning committee's announcement, see *CG*, 25 March 1903, 5 and the editor's note, 7.

96 Albert Carman, "The Bicentenary Revivalist Movement," *CG*, 5 August 1903, 7.

97 Albert Carman, "The Wesley Bicentenary," *CG*, 22 April 1903, 6.

98 "The Coming Services," *CG*, 23 September 1903, 5.

99 S.D. Chown, "The Place of Fear in Religion," *CG*, 20 January 1897, 34.

100 S.D. Chown, "Service and Salvation," *CG*, 24 October 1900, 681.

101 S.D. Chown, Address to Spiritual Conference, Victoria University, 21 November 1900, Chown Papers, box 11/285, 3.

102 Ibid., 11. Also see Chown's sermon for the Bay of Quinte Conference ordination, 5 June 1904, Chown Papers, box 2/66, 17–19 on the need for an "ethical revival."

103 Ernest Thomas, "Reformation, Revival and Resuscitation," *CG*, 11 November 1903, 8. For a continuation of this series, see *CG*, 4 and 18 November 1903.

104 Letter to the editor from Ernest Thomas, "Higher Critics and the Revivalists," *CG*, 17 January 1906, 20.

105 Ernest Thomas, "Dr. Torrey in Montreal: An Appreciation," *CG*, 22 May 1907, 9. I have come across no studies of Canadian press coverage of revivals, but my impression is that it was generally favourable before that time. For example, in "The Torrey-Alexander Mission," *CG*, 24 January 1906, 3, the editor says coverage by the press had been good. For the crusade for reform among newspaper reporters, see Rutherford, *A Victorian Authority* and *The Making of the Canadian Media*; see also the section on "muckraking" in Hofstadter, *The Age of Reform*, 186ff. On newspaper relationships with the clergy in general, see *A Victorian Authority*, 197–204.

106 Creighton, "My Father and the United Church," 98.

107 "The Revival," *CG*, 9 January 1907, 5–6.

108 "The Remarkable Revival in Wales," *CG*, 18 January 1905, 6 notes its strongly ethical character. There were numerous items on its progress, especially in the February and March issues.

109 "Thanksgiving Retrospect," *CG*, 25 October 1905, 2–3.

110 "Torrey-Alexander Meetings," *CG*, 27 December 1905, 5.

111 "A Harvest of Thanksgiving," *CG*, 21 March 1906, 5. For statistics and more assessments of the Toronto revival, see "What Toronto Pastors Say of the Mission," *CG*, 24 January 1906, 4 (part of a special issue marking the event); "The Close of the Mission," *CG*, 31 January 1906, 4; George B. Davies, "The Great Revival in Toronto," *CG*, 14 February 1906, 9.

112 Hudson, *Religion in America*, 367. Hudson links the incident to the modernist-fundamentalist controversy, noting that Torrey and Dixon (both dispensationalists) responded to this criticism by launching a

counter-attack which culminated in the publication of the *Fundamentals* (which they edited) between 1910 and 1915. See also Marsden, *Fundamentalism and American Culture*, 118–23 and Sandeen, *The Roots of Fundamentalism*, 188–207.

113 "Religious Statistics for Wales," *CG*, 4 March 1908, 4.

114 "If There, Why Not Here?" *CG*, 15 February 1905, 4.

115 "The Evangelistic Note," *CG*, 29 March 1905, 5; "The Evangelistic Note," *CG*, 11 October 1905, 5. On his Toronto visit, see *CG*, 1 November 1905, 4 and 8 November 1905, 5. For his Winnipeg visit, see *Manitoba Free Press*, 16 October 1907, 10 and *CG*, 6 November 1907, 22; 20 November 1907, 23; and 27 November 1907, 4.

116 "A Great Evangelistic Campaign," *CG*, 19 September 1906, 3.

117 Salem Bland, "Some Signs of the Times: A Call to Church Federation," Bland Papers, file 386.

118 "Prairie Provinces – Special Correspondence," *CG*, 17 March 1909, 18.

119 For a description of Chapman's work, see McLoughlin, *Modern Revivalism*, 377–89.

120 "Prairie Provinces," *CG*, 17 March 1909, 18. Kilpatrick had been involved in evangelism for a number of years. An earlier letter named him and William Patrick (better known for his "initiation" of the union negotiations in 1902) in connection with a successful move to adopt the "revival methods which at one time were the exclusive glory of Methodism"; see T.E. Holling, "A Suggestion for the Wesley Bicentenary," *CG*, 25 February 1903, 9. For C.W. Gordon's views on the Chapman plan, see "The Simultaneous Evangelistic Mission in Minnedosa Presbytery," *Presbyterian*, 18 and 25 February 1909.

121 On the British Columbia campaign, see Kilpatrick and Shearer, *The Kootenay Campaign*. For Winnipeg, see "A.S.," "The Chapman Evangelistic Campaign in Winnipeg," *CG*, 18 December 1907, 11. For Toronto, see Gordon V. Thompson, "The Chapman-Alexander Evangelistic Campaign," *CG*, 21 October 1908, 11–12; G.A. Warburton, "The Chapman-Alexander Mission," *CG*, 21 December 1910, 7; and "The Chapman-Alexander Mission," 6. The most critical response to "simultaneous campaigns" came from the Maritimes; see report of the Maritime correspondent, *CG*, 9 March 1910, 22 and report of "Simultaneous Evangelistic Campaign in St. John, N.B.," *CG*, 16 March 1910, 22, which warned that "a reaction against all outside, special agencies is taking possession of the thoughtful." An article titled "Maritime Provinces," *CG*, 28 February 1912, 27 referred to a "revulsion of feeling" for outside evangelists, because of meagre results.

122 "Evangelizing Canadians," *CG*, 12 May 1909, 5.

123 H.G. Cairns, "Have We an Evangelistic Policy?" *CG*, 13 October 1909, 24.

124 "The Evangelistic Policy," *CG*, 8 December 1909, 24.

125 Allen, *The Social Passion*, 16 describes Shearer as "pre-eminent among a roster of Presbyterian social gospellers," and considered by some as "the mouthpiece of the social conscience of Canadian Christianity".

126 W. Lashley Hall, "A Great Revival in Fernie," *CG*, 12 May 1909, 7. For an account of similar activities in the Maritimes, see "Dr. Chown in Halifax," *CG*, 17 April 1907, 16.

127 "A Deep Gulf Laid Bare," *CG*, 23 January 1889, 56.

128 "Higher Criticism in America," *CG*, 5 July 1899, 424 and "Dr. Munhall and Higher Critics," *CG*, 2 August 1899, 488. Courtice countered Munhall by referring to the exemplary teaching of Burwash. Munhall, one of the few Methodists involved with the prophetic conferences, later left the denomination; see Sandeen, *The Roots of Fundamentalism*, 163.

129 "Modern Evangelism vs. Modern Scholarship," *CG*, 16 August 1899, 516 was the first of a series of articles and published correspondence between Eby and Munhall that continued until November (cf. 530, 546, 562, 581, 597, 610, 650, 754, 761). Eby had earlier written articles for a holiness movement publication and praised the work of the Salvation Army; ten years after this series of *CG* articles he founded a Socialist church in Toronto.

130 "Revival of Religion and Higher Criticism," *CG*, 3 January 1906, 6.

131 "Mr. Campbell's New Book," *CG*, 10 April 1907, 3–4.

132 Ernest Thomas [Edward Trelawney], "Rev. R.J. Campbell's New Theology," *CG*, 27 February 1907, 8.

133 "Theological Controversy," *CG*, 27 February 1907, 5.

134 "The New Theology," *CG*, 10 April 1907, 5.

135 "Note and Comment," *CG*, 3 July 1907, 2.

136 *CG*, 1 November 1911, 7.

137 *CG*, 20 December 1911, 7.

138 "Rev. George Jackson, b.a., of Edinburgh," *CG*, 21 May 1902, 328. For this emphasis in his speeches, see the transcript of Jackson's address before the British and Foreign Bible Society, "The Best Apologetic," *CG*, 14 May and 28 May 1902. (The best apologetic, according to Jackson, came not from the scholar, but from the preacher, missionary, and evangelist.)

139 "London Conference," *CG*, 18 June 1902, 393. When Jackson delivered a similar address at the Toronto Conference, the motion of thanks was moved by E.H. Dewart; see *CG*, 18 June 1902, 386.

140 "'Chadwick of Leeds' and Rev. George Jackson of Edinburgh," *CG*, 22 July 1903, 21.

141 "Essential Methodism," *CG*, 8 July 1903, 5.

142 In Annie Jackson, ed., *George Jackson*, 7 she describes Hughes as "the most powerful magnet for him."

143 Ibid., 29.

144 Ibid., 28–9 details the circumstances of his decision, his health being one consideration after what his wife described as a bad nervous breakdown in 1905.

145 Sinclair-Faulkner, "Theory Divided from Practice," especially 333–43.

146 "The Call to Aggressive Evangelism," *CG*, 10 October 1906, 7.

147 Jackson, *The Old Methodism and the New*, 57–8.

148 Ibid., 60.

149 Ibid., 32.

150 J. Findlater to Albert Carman, 30 March 1909, George Jackson Papers. This is only one of numerous letters about the incident in the collections of personal papers at the Archives. For other examples, see the Burwash and Carman Papers.

151 "A Leader in Sherbourne St. Criticizes Rev. Geo. Jackson," *Toronto Star*, 17 February 1909; clipping in George Jackson Papers.

152 Annie Jackson, ed., *George Jackson*, 33.

153 For example Allen, *The Social Passion*, 5–6 restricts his discussion of the connection to the mid-century revivals, an interpretation which he bases on Timothy Smith's research. His discussion of "new evangelism" comes after his account of the major developments of the social gospel movement and does not connect it with late-nineteenth-century revivalism. For an interesting discussion of the relation of the "new evangelism" to the American social gospel movement, see Hudson, "Walter Rauschenbusch and the New Evangelism," 412–30, in which he maintains that in his own mind, Rauschenbusch considered himself an evangelist in the tradition of the great revivalists.

154 Ernest Thomas [Edward Trelawney], "The Test of Social Reform," *CG*, 6 May 1908, 11. For other examples of this trend compare "Saving Souls," *CG*, 23 November 1910, 7 with "Each and All," *CG*, 30 November 1910, 7; and "The Ground of Our Faith" with "The Layman's Evangelistic Responsibility," both in *CG*, 25 August 1909.

155 "Saving Men's Souls," *CG*, 13 May 1908, 5. Compare George Jackson, *The Old Methodism and the New*, 57–8.

156 S.D. Chown, "Revival Our Greatest Need – A Plea for the Times," *CG*, 6 April 1910, 8.

157 Ibid.

CHAPTER FOUR

1 J.S. Woodsworth, *My Neighbor*, 24 and Frye, *The Modern Century*, 11.

2 Carman, *The Preparation of Ryerson Embury*. The experience of the fictional hero was probably not uncommon; see Hutchison, "Cultural Strain and Protestant Liberalism," 400, 403, and the account of J.S.

Woodsworth below. The romantic end is different from the outcome of the story of the unconverted man who sought the hand of Barbara Heck's daughter recounted in chapter 1.

3 "Address by James Allen at H.A. Massey Funeral," *CG*, 11 March 1896, 162.

4 Chown, Sermon on "Return we beseech thee" ("The Growth of Methodism"), Chown Papers, box 8/216, 7. This is an undated address, but the references to the recent temperance campaign place it around 1902.

5 Ibid., 7–8.

6 William Hincks, "My Eighty Years on Earth," 2 vols., 1939–40, Hincks Papers, UCA, 1:160–1. He continued to defend Decision Days as an improvement over "explosive" evangelism; see 2:62–3.

7 Ibid., 2:74–5.

8 "Hindrance to Revivals," *CG*, 23 January 1895, 56. A.B. McKillop's work on the ideas presented in the classrooms of the theological colleges is particularly useful here, although it is not clear how or whether these ideas were presented in the pulpits.

9 "Toronto Conference," *CG*, 23 June 1909, 18.

10 "Toronto Conference," *CG*, 22 June 1910, 24.

11 "B.C. Conference," *CG*, 31 May 1911, 18–19.

12 "Glimpses of the Spirit," *CG*, 13 August 1924, 15. Robert Pearson, "Some Impressions of Alberta Methodist Conference," *Morning Albertan*, 30 May 1914 [clipping in Bland Papers] makes special note of the absence of the "vision bordering on the supernatural" that usually accompanied the accounts of calling in past years.

13 For the impact of James on religion, see Browning, *Pluralism and Personality*; Clebsch, *American Religious Thought*; and Levinson, *The Religious Investigations of William James*. On Coe, see Hutchison, *The Modernist Impulse in American Protestantism*, 156–64; H. Shelton Smith, "George Albert Coe: Revaluer of Values," 46–57 and the entire issue of *Religious Education* 47 (March-April 1952).

14 Hutchison, *The Modernist Impulse in American Protestantism*, 157. Coe refers to "the disappointment of my adolescence, when the promised and sought-for mystical 'witness of the Spirit' did not come" in *The Psychology of Religion*, xiii–xiv.

15 Coe, "A Study of Religious Dynamics," in *The Spiritual Life*, 104–50; also "Are Conversions Going out of Date," in *The Religion of a Mature Mind*, 253–90; and "Conversion" in *The Psychology of Religion*, 152–74.

16 Coe dedicated one of his books to the study of "the human naturalness of religion"; see *The Psychology of Religion*, vii.

17 "Preaching to the Wrong People," *CG*, 29 April 1903, 4–5.

18 "The Law of Average in Religious Life," *CG*, 31 August 1904, 5.

19 "The Age of Conversion," *CG*, 1 June 1904, 5.

20 "Professor Coe's Resignation," *CG*, 21 October 1908, 3. In a letter to a student discussing the job opening created at Northwestern, Burwash wrote: "Things became a little too hot for him at Evanston as they are not disposed to go any very great length in the direction of modern speculations on that particular subject [psychology of religion]"; Nathanael Burwash to A.D. Miller, 4 February 1909, Burwash Papers, box 3/44. Burwash's letter to Miller, 10 February 1909, Burwash Papers, box 3/44 concedes that Coe had gone further than Burwash could follow him.

21 R.O. Armstrong, "A Leader in the Armchair: Interview with Prof. George Albert Coe," *CG*, 27 August 1919, 8. The article described Coe's first book as "epoch-making," and *The Religion of a Mature Mind* as "one of the largest sellers."

22 James, *The Varieties of Religious Experience*, xxi.

23 Cook, *The Regenerators*, 86–104.

24 For Alline's conversion, see Rawlyk, *Ravished by the Spirit*, especially 3–35.

25 A.D. Watson, "The Psychology of Revivals," *CMR* 7, no. 5 (1895):377–88 notes some of the dangers, while maintaining that in revivals "Methodism should furnish the norm, after which all revival methods should be modelled." For criticisms of the holiness movement based on psychological interpretation, see series by W. Pyke, "Religious Manifestations," *CG*, 3 August 1892, 483–4; 17 August 1892, 515–16; 31 August 1892, 547; 5 October 1892, 627.

26 S.T. Bartlett to Burwash, March 1907, Burwash Papers, box 2/25.

27 Nathanael Burwash, "A Serious Danger," [letter to the editor of the *Epworth Era*], 15 April 1907, Burwash Papers, box 2/25.

28 Nathanael Burwash, "The Spiritual Life: Its Birth in a Definite Religious Experience," *CG*, 28 September 1910, 10–11.

29 S.D. Chown, "Ordination Sermon," Chown Papers, box 4/104, 9. The sermon is not dated, but a reference to Coe's work having been published nearly twenty-five years previous places it around 1924. For similar concerns about psychology from George Jackson, see *The Old Methodism and the New*, 37 and *The Preacher and the Modern Mind*, 50, 236.

30 S.D. Chown, "The Betrayal of Speech or Accent," Chown Papers, box 4/100, 13–14 and "Pastoral Address," 21 April 1921, Chown Papers, box 12/315, 4–5.

31 For example, "The Betrayal of Speech or Accent," 14.

32 S.D. Chown, "The Present Need," *CG*, 14 August 1912, 17 included James's ideas as developments (along with changes in theology and social science) which had greatly affected the preacher in recent years.

For similar versions of this address, see "Toronto Conference," *CG*, 3 July 1912, 21; "The Present Need of Christian Thinkers," Chown Papers, box 11/296; and *Some Causes of the Decline of the Earlier Typical Evangelism*. For Chown's assessment of the impact of the social sciences on theological education, see "A Search for Reality in Religion," *Biblical Review*, 16, no. 4 (1931):505–18.

33 Chown, "The Present Need," Chown Papers, box 11/296, 17.

34 Chown, "Ordination Sermon," Chown Papers, box 4/104, 3.

35 Ibid., 8.

36 Chown, *Some Causes of the Decline of the Earlier Typical Evangelism*, 15. He linked this to the rise of Christian Science as well, 14–15, a connection that deserves more study for its impact on religious life at the turn of the century. Also deserving more attention is the impact of psychology on the handling of revivalism in the secular press. The results of such scientific studies are specifically referred to in a lukewarm editorial on the subject in the *Manitoba Free Press*, 24 March 1907, 4, with a different assessment of Moody's effectiveness from the same paper's coverage of Moody's visit to Winnipeg less than a decade before.

37 "The Value of Children to the Church," *CG*, 5 June 1918, 5–6.

38 Ibid., 6. See also "Decision Day and After," *CG*, 10 March 1920, 7–8.

39 "The Child and the Church," *CG*, 11 May 1921, 8, 11.

40 The subject provoked a heated discussion in the *Guardian* and at conferences for over a decade. For a sampling of the issues involved, see "General Conference," *CG*, 21 September 1898, 594–5; S.P. Rose, "Canadian Methodism and Popular Amusements," *CG*, 15 January 1902, 34; Salem Bland, "Our Rules," *CG*, 5 February 1902, 82; S. Bond, "Our General Rules and the Note," *CG*, 5 February 1902, 83; Albert Carman, "The Rev. R. Hobbs on 'The Church and Amusements,'" *CG*, 26 March 1902, 194; Salem Bland, "A Meditation on Some Recent Letters in the *Guardian*," *CG*, 15 April 1903, 8; "Footnotes – Old and New," *CG*, 21 September 1910, 5.

41 "Federal Council of Churches in America," *CG*, 23 December 1908, 8 noted that the meeting which had recently passed resolutions strongly supporting labour had its largest representation from Methodist bodies. Grant, *The Church in the Canadian Era*, 102 states that in Canada "Methodists welcomed the social gospel with a fervour unmatched elsewhere". Also see Allen, *The Social Passion*, 5, 16 and Emery, "The Origins of Canadian Methodist Involvement in the Social Gospel Movement," 105, 113.

42 Luker, "Liberal Theology and Social Conservatism," 193–204.

43 Niebuhr, *The Kingdom of God in America*.

44 Graves, "Converting Individuals, Converting the World," 7ff.

45 Hutchison, *The Modernist Impulse in American Protestantism*, 165, note 36. Theological differences are related to Allen's classification of the degrees of commitment to the social gospel as conservative, progressive, or radical. However, there are still problems; for example, Carman is explicitly excluded, despite his ardent support for the temperance movement; see *The Social Passion*, 19.

46 "Some Dangerous Tendencies," *CG*, 10 November 1880, 356. Dewart often made this criticism in the context of arguing against those who believed that nothing one could *do* affected one's salvation – his interpretation of what the Plymouth Brethren taught.

47 "Ministers and Social Questions," *CG*, 23 March 1892, 184; also see "The Pulpit and Social Science," *CG*, 6 January 1892, 8.

48 "Questionable Teaching about Christian Socialism," *CG*, 2 May 1894, 280.

49 "Not Ethics but Dynamics," *CG*, 7 January 1903, 6; also "Do Men Just Need Patching Up?" *CG*, 26 September 1900, 616 and "The Church and Its Social Mission," *CG*, 16 July 1902, 456.

50 "What We Would Like to See in 1907," *CG*, 2 January 1907, 5. "The Rights of Labor," *CG*, 17 July 1902, 5 predicted that religion confined to the pulpit and prayer-meeting would die.

51 "Individualistic Religion," *CG*, 1 May 1907, 5; "The Church and Politics," *CG*, 24 October 1906, 5; "Everyday Religion," *CG*, 23 January 1907, 5; "Religion and Politics," *CG*, 5 August 1914, 5.

52 "Spirituality in Religion," *CG*, 4 December 1907, 7; "The Home-land" *CG*, 24 July 1907, 5.

53 "The Church and the Social Order," *CG*, 1 April 1908, 5.

54 "Was Jesus a Socialist?" *CG*, 14 February 1912, 5; also see "Saving Souls," *CG*, 23 November 1910, 7 and "Each and All," *CG*, 30 November 1910, 7.

55 Emery, "The Origins of Canadian Methodist Involvement in the Social Gospel Movement," 105. The article is flawed by a confusing use of terminology. Emery misrepresents Methodists as premillennialists and uses the terms "evangelical" and "pietist" in unconventional ways without explaining what he means by them. Richard Allen in *The Social Passion* wisely focuses his attention on post-war developments.

56 "The Report of the Committee on Sociological Questions," *CG*, 3 October 1906, 12.

57 Allen, *The Social Passion*, 71.

58 Ibid., 74.

59 Ibid., 73.

60 "The General Conference," *CG*, 23 October 1918, 6.

61 "Pious Twaddle," *CG*, 28 May 1919, 5–6.

62 Allen, *The Social Passion*, 123.

63 Ibid., 75, quoting from the Methodist *Journal of Proceedings*.
64 For example, "Holiness Cranks," *CG*, 16 May 1906, 5. On the holiness movement, see chapter 2 above; also Timothy L. Smith, "Righteousness and Hope: Christian Holiness and the Millennial Vision in America, 1800–1900," 114–47.
65 Grant, *The Church in the Canadian Era*, 103 sees this emphasis as part of Methodism's attraction to the social gospel, which he describes as having "authentic roots in Wesley's doctrine of Christian perfection."
66 Dieter, *The Holiness Revival of the Nineteenth Century*, 147.
67 C.S. Eby, "To the Angel of the Church of Canadian Methodism," *CG*, 20 August 1902, 533.
68 Allen, *The Social Passion*, 127.
69 Ernest Thomas [Edward Trelawney], "Evangelism and Moral Reform," *CG*, 22 June 1910, 9–10. See his UCA biography file and correspondence between E. Lloyd Morrow and Ernest Thomas, T. Albert Moore Papers, box 8/173. Thomas was asked to write the article on the union movement for the University of Chicago's *Journal of Religion* and was a regular correspondent to the *Christian Century* which had some ties to the University of Chicago through several professors who were frequent contributors.
70 Ernest Thomas, "The Deposit and Decline of Methodism," *CG*, 22 February 1905, 8.
71 Ernest Thomas [Edward Trelawney], "Conference Moods and Men," *CG*, 23 October 1918, 11.
72 McKillop, *A Disciplined Intelligence*, 225–7; "John Watson and the Idealist Legacy," 84 This assessment is based largely on the lectures which Chown gave as part of his work for the Department of Temperance and Moral Reform; see Chown Papers, box 13/379–83.
73 S.D. Chown, "Revival Our Greatest Need – A Plea for the Times," *CG*, 6 April 1910, 8.
74 S.D. Chown, "Revival Now," *CG*, 17 December 1913, 8.
75 S.D. Chown, Sermon on Holiness, Part v, Chown Papers, box 3/82, 3.
76 S.D. Chown, Sermon on "And the very God of peace sanctify you wholly" ("Work of Department of Temperance and Moral Reform"), Chown Papers, box 5/134, 6. In this address Chown relates his own experience of seeking sanctification as a blessing; see 7.
77 S.D. Chown, "The Evolution of Evangelism," Sermon on Holiness, series III, Chown Papers, box 3/80, 5, 7, 11.
78 S.D. Chown, "A Word to the Wise," *CG*, 5 March 1913, 8–9. See also his address at a reception given in his honour, 24 November 1914, Chown Papers, box 11/301, 8.
79 Chown, "The Betrayal of Speech or Accent," Chown Papers, box 4/100, 14. This is in the context of commenting on the damaging influence of the psychology of religion.

80 S.D. Chown, "Intensive Spiritual Cultivation," *CG*, 20 April 1921, 10; "Winning 100,000 Souls for Christ," *CG*, 28 April 1920, 15.

81 "Preaching the Gospel," *CG*, 30 April 1919, 5; also "The Problem of Methodism," *CG*, 22 May 1907, 5.

82 Chiles, *Theological Transition in American Methodism*, 71–2.

83 "Missions and the New Theology," *CG*, 20 October 1886, 664.

84 S.D. Chown, "The Present Need," *CG*, 14 August 1912, 17.

85 S.D. Chown, "The Vitality of Religion," *CG*, 7 October 1914, 13, 21.

86 "Relation of Negative Criticism to Evangelical Faith," *CG*, 5 August 1891, 488.

87 "What Is the Authority for Religious Belief," *CG*, 20 July 1892, 456. "Wesley's quadrilateral" also included the Bible, reason, and the tradition of the church as sources of authority, but the impact of revivalism had tended to erode the latter three by the end of the nineteenth century.

88 Mead, *The Lively Experiment*, 172.

89 J.S. Woodsworth to Nathanael Burwash, 14 January 1902, Burwash Papers, box 1/14.

90 J.S. Woodsworth, *Following the Gleam*, 8.

91 Ibid.

92 Ibid. For more on Woodsworth and the social gospel, see Allen, *The Social Passion*, especially 45–50, 81–103; McKillop, *A Disciplined Intelligence*, 223–4; McNaught, *A Prophet in Politics*, especially 3–131; Cook, *The Regenerators*, 213–27.

93 McNaught, *A Prophet in Politics*, 7.

94 For the impact of those educated elsewhere on biblical studies in Canada, see Moir, *A History of Biblical Studies in Canada*, passim. For the impact of Canadians elsewhere, see Handy, "The Influence of Canadians on Baptist Theological Education in the United States," 42–56.

95 George Workman had connections to the organization, and was listed as an associate with William Rainey Harper and the Institute in a pamphlet distributed from Chicago criticizing their work; see *CG*, 27 January 1892, 51. For praise of the work of AISL see "A Helpful Service," *CG*, 21 February 1923, 8.

96 Morley Pettit to Nathanael Burwash, 11 February 1908, Burwash Papers, box 3/34. The letter to Albert Carman from William Metford, 26 February 1909, George Jackson Papers, mentions a student who left Victoria to go to Moody Bible Institute.

97 Information from the account of his life in *This One Thing*.

98 Manson, "Liberal Theology and United College: Ideas, Faith and Feelings in a United Church Seminary, 1938–1960."

99 Lorne Pierce, "Searching Can We Find God?" [review of *Theology as an Empirical Science*], *CG*, 3 November 1920, 9. On Chicago's modernism,

see Hutchison, *The Modernist Impulse in American Protestantism*, 114–15, 225.

100 There are points of contact between Mathews and George Workman, whose understanding of "Atonement in Service" was described by Creighton as the basis for a strong appeal for social service as a practical method of "getting individuals right with God." See "At Onement: On Reconciliation with God" [review of Workman's book], *CG*, 25 October 1911, 6.

101 Methodism's first important idealist philosopher, George Blewett, began teaching in 1901; he died eleven years later in a drowning accident. The publication of Blewett's first book, Chown's sociological lectures, and increased attention to the subject in the *Guardian* all came at mid-decade. On theology in the universities see Fraser, "'The Christianization of Our Civilization,'" 35–44; McKillop, *A Disciplined Intelligence*; and Van Die, *An Evangelical Mind*. The impact of this educational experience is difficult to assess because there are few indications of how it affected the work of young ministers in their first pastoral charges. Marshall, "The Clerical Response to Secularization: Canadian Methodists and Presbyterians, 1860–1940," 226, note 62 assesses the impact of idealism as marginal. For examples of Methodism's use of idealism, see articles by Ernest Thomas [Edward Trelawney], "Society Life – A Means of Grace," *CG*, 6 February 1907, 8; "Professor McBride on Religion and Science," *CG*, 20 February 1907, 10; and "Evangelism and Moral Reform," *CG*, 22 June 1910, 9–10; J.H. Philp, "Another Point of View," *CG*, 3 April 1907, 27; and W.F. Osborn, "The Study of Nature and the Vision of God" [review of Blewett's book], *CG*, 17 April 1907, 9.

102 Bland, *James Henderson*, 25–6. Bland's biographical account of Henderson's journey parallels much of his own. The book includes many of Henderson's sermons and long excerpts from correspondence.

103 Ibid., 27.

104 Ibid., 28.

105 Ibid., 8–9.

106 Ibid., 14.

107 Ibid., 20–1.

108 Ibid., 48.

109 Ibid., 53.

110 Ibid., Letter to W.R. Wornell, 59.

111 Ibid., 65.

112 Ibid., 106.

113 Ibid., 193; see newspaper synopsis of Henderson's sermon on Christian socialism, 142–3, and the text of a sermon for that title, 324–32.

114 Ibid., 108.

115 Ibid., 147.
116 Ibid., 147–9.
117 Ibid., 311–12.
118 Ibid., xv.
119 Ibid., xvii–xviii. Henderson's impact is difficult to assess but seems to have been widespread; he was, for example, travelling across Canada as Associate Secretary of Missions in the critical years between 1896 and 1907.
120 Ibid., 218–19.
121 Ibid., xv.
122 Ibid., 321. For a sermon explicating his approach to doctrine, see "Old Creeds in the Modern Crucible," 298–305.
123 "Orthodoxy of the Heart," CG, 19 September 1923, 6.
124 "Lay Agencies and the Church," CG, 6 March 1907, 7.
125 Burwash, "Life and Labors of Nathanael Burwash," Burwash Papers, box 28/622–37 [continuation of section on "Inductive Theology"], 2.
126 "Class-meeting Superseded," CG, 16 October 1918, 29.
127 Apparently the growth of Methodism at the end of the century was due in large part to adding these converted children as members. Some had already expressed concern over the lack of adult conversions; eventually there were worries that children were no longer being converted. See "Confessing Our Faults," CG, 3 January 1912, 5.
128 James Speakman, "The Children and Church Membership," CG, 8 January 1908, 8–9.
129 Ernest Thomas [Edward Trelawney], "The Glory of Religious Education," CG, 23 May 1923, 13.
130 Brown, "The Sunday School Movement in the Methodist Church in Canada, 1875–1925," 136.
131 "A Boy's Religion," CG, 23 April 1919, 5. For Creighton's response to criticism, see CG, 11 June 1919, 2. For what "a girl's religion" would have been like in this period, see Prang, "'The Girl God Would Have Me Be,'" 154–84.
132 Frank Langford, "The Work of Educational Evangelism," CG, 11 May 1921, 11. This was printed as a response to Chown, who was perceived as being critical of this approach. For Chown's affirmation of the strengths he saw in the "preaching of the fathers," see "The Springs of Evangelistic Power," Biblical Review 13, no. 2 (1928):232–43.
133 R.E. Fairbairn, "Educational Evangelism," CG, 1 January 1920, 9. He rejected the traditional idea of regeneration: "Nothing like this happens in the spiritual order. The regenerate man has not a new nature though it may be renewed."
134 "The Church in Testing Times," CG, 26 June 1912, 5.

CHAPTER FIVE

1 John Hay's eulogy to President McKinley cited in Sklar, *The Corporate Reconstruction of American Capitalism, 1890–1916,* 440 and Walter Lippman, cited in Chambers, *The Tyranny of Change,* 231.

2 Carman and Chown, *The Address of the General Superintendents to the General Conference of 1914,* 25. The drafts and correspondence between Chown and Carman indicate that Chown wrote this section; see Carman Papers, box 26/150.

3 Sklar, *The Corporate Reconstruction of American Capitalism, 1890–1916,* 432.

4 For an interesting discussion of the "culture of abundance," see Susman, *Culture as History;* also see Lears, "From Salvation to Self-Realization," 3–38. For a suggestive essay on the implications of consumerism for revivalism in Canada, see Rawlyk, *Wrapped Up in God,* 136–40.

5 Rybczynski, *Home,* 219–20.

6 King, "The Role of Auxiliary Ministries in Late Nineteenth-Century Methodism," 167 and Meyer, "American Intellectuals and the Victorian Crisis of Faith," 595. Gilbert, *Religion and Society in Industrial England,* 186 links growing prosperity with the "crisis of plausibility" of evangelicalism's religious world view, which had been shaped in the context of early industrialism with its economic insecurity.

7 The studies of women and domesticity are numerous. See as examples the influential studies of Barbara Welter on the cult of true womanhood and the feminization of religion in *Dimity Convictions.* Epstein, *The Politics of Domesticity* has examined the relationship of temperance and domesticity. For Canadian developments see Prentice et al., *Canadian Women,* 113–211 and Warne, "Literature as Pulpit." The influence of progressivist assumptions on the concept of "family" raises interesting questions, some of which are explored in Fishburn, *The Fatherhood of God and the Victorian Family;* Huff, "Social Christian Clergymen and Feminism during the Progressive Era, 1890–1920"; and Airhart, "Sobriety, Sentimentality and Science."

8 Rutherford, *Saving the Canadian City,* ix.

9 Rutherford, "Tomorrow's Metropolis," 447–8. On the rise of technical expertise and the resulting regulation of society see Weaver, "'Tomorrow's Metropolis' Revisited," 465–70. In view of these developments, Fraser has aptly titled his study of Presbyterian reformers *The Social Uplifters.* For an interesting study of the impact of sociology on religion (including a chapter on the social survey) see Vidich and Lyman, *American Sociology.*

10 As an illustration of the importance of statistics in presenting the so-
    cial gospel agenda, see J.S. Woodsworth, *My Neighbor*. Between 1913
    and 1915 the Board of Temperance and Moral Reform of the Method-
    ist Church and the Board of Social Service and Evangelism of the
    Presbyterian Church published social survey reports on both rural
    areas (Swan River Valley and Turtle Mountain District in Manitoba,
    Huron County in Ontario, and Pictou District in Nova Scotia) and
    urban centres (Hamilton, London, Fort William, Port Arthur,
    St Catharines, Regina, and Sydney). An interdenominational survey
    of Toronto was made in 1915 in conjunction with the Social Survey
    Commission. W.A. Riddell was a key participant and reported on the
    method at the Social Service Congress held in Ottawa in 1914; see his
    essay on "The Value of the Social Survey," *Social Service Congress: Re-
    port of Addresses and Proceedings*, 54–9.
11 Friesen, *The Canadian Prairies*, 312–16.
12 Boyer, "*In His Steps*: A Reappraisal," 73. Marty has suggested that it
    might be helpful to describe what is referred to as "secularization" as
    a migration of religiosity away from organized institutions to individu-
    als themselves; see "Social Service: Godly and Godless," 463–81.
13 See Stokes, *Ministry after Freud*, 3–36; Holifield, *A History of Pastoral
    Care in America*, 159–258; and Lears, "From Salvation to Self-Realiza-
    tion," 3–38.
14 Park, "Biological Thought, Athletics and the Formation of a 'Man of
    Character': 1830–1900," 7–34 and Rotundo, "Learning about Man-
    hood," 35–51 provide interesting perspectives on the concept of "mus-
    cular Christianity" found in such social gospel writings as the novels
    of Ralph Connor. On temperance and health, see Airhart, "Sobriety,
    Sentimentality and Science."
15 The press's challenge to the clergy in championing social salvation
    and church union is discussed by Rutherford, *A Victorian Authority*,
    200–2. He notes the inadequacy of older institutions such as the
    church to meet the new social needs of the early-twentieth-century
    bourgeois democracy; the press filled the vacuum for knowledge
    about how to vote, what to buy, where to invest, where to get a job –
    and even what to believe.
16 King, "The Role of Auxiliary Ministries in Late Nineteenth-Century
    Methodism," 171–2.
17 Sklar, *The Corporate Reconstruction of American Capitalism, 1890–1916*,
    437–9 notes the emphasis on an associative outlook and its affinity
    with corporate liberalism: "Corporate-liberal thought did acknowledge
    and affirm the displacement of the individual by the group (or associ-
    ation) as the basic fundamental unit of a modern capitalist economy,

but it was a group that the individual might freely join or quit." Yet rights and obligations, Sklar maintains, continued to be perceived in terms of the individual.

18 Foster, "The Imperialism of Righteousness," 23–7. On missionary work in China, see Austin, *Saving China*. For a discussion of the missionary movement in the context of American progressivism, see Hutchison, *Errand to the World*.

19 Foster, "The Imperialism of Righteousness," 31–3 for Stephenson's work; on the SCM, see Kirkey, "'Building the City of God.'"

20 For a more detailed discussion of the Layman's Missionary Movement (from which the information for this section is drawn) see Foster, "The Imperialism of Righteousness," 36–50. Assessing the movement's decline, he notes that the businessmen's attention turned from evangelization of the world to reconstruction of it. Organizational energies were directed to the "United National Campaign: An Inter-Church Forward Movement." Support for Methodism's Laymen's Missionary Movement came from very generous contributions of executives, lawyers, and brokers concentrated in the three wealthiest Toronto churches; it did not catch on as well in other congregations. Theological liberalism and the concern of church members for solving social problems at home combined with the hostility of journalists, novelists, and academics towards the missionary enterprise; see 43–7. For a discussion of the Presbyterian wing of the movement see Moir, "Canadian Presbyterians and the Laymen's Missionary Movement."

21 "Publication of Census Figures," *CG*, 23 May 1923, 3. Methodists, Baptists, and Roman Catholics lost ground in terms of percentage of the total population.

22 "The Unrecorded Growth," *CG*, 2 October 1918, 5.

23 Fundamentalists organized associations that worked on parallel lines; see Sawatsky, "'Looking for That Blessed Hope'" and Carpenter, "Fundamentalist Institutions and the Rise of Evangelical Protestantism, 1929–1942," 62–75.

24 Nathanael Burwash to Margaret Burwash, 18 August 1910, Burwash Papers, box 10/144.

25 "Methodism and Evangelism," *CG*, 21 September 1910, 6.

26 "The Revival – Is It Coming? Or Is It Here?" *CG*, 12 October 1910, 5. See also C.E. Bland, "The Revival at Hand," *CG*, 2 November 1910, 8. A brother to Salem, his address at the General Conference was reported as having been very influential; see "Methodism and Evangelism," *CG*, 21 September 1910, 6. In his article, he distinguished between "evangelism" and "revival meetings," describing evangelism as not so much a method as a way of life. He was appointed to the Committee on Evangelism.

27 "Close of Chapman-Alexander Campaign," *CG*, 8 February 1911, 6.

28 "What Was There in the Chapman-Alexander Campaign?" *CG*, 8 February 1911, 6. In the recommendations sent to Creighton, support for "personal work," not "social evangelism," was proposed as the alternative to mass meetings. A report in the same issue continued to urge a return to "the methods of the fathers" which had "made Methodism a soul-saving power," 26. For Creighton's reservations about the memories of past revivals, see *CG*, 21 June 1911, 5.

29 "Where We Get Our Members," *CG*, 11 October 1911, 5.

30 "A Summing Up of Evangelism," *CG*, 18 October 1911, 5.

31 "Editorial in Brief," *CG*, 10 April 1912, 7.

32 "Serving the Community," *CG*, 8 January 1913, 5.

33 C.E. Bland, "Evangelism and Social Reconstruction," *CG*, 19 February 1913, 27 (note Creighton's reply); also see "Evangelism and the Evangelistic Committee," *CG*, 15 February 1911, 8.

34 "The Evangelism for To-day," *CG*, 21 January 1920, 7. For suggestions to broaden the concept of evangelism, see S.P. Rose, "The Religion of a Great City," *CG*, 3 April 1907, 6; 10 April, 8; and 17 April, 8; C.H. Huestis, "The Mission of the Christian Church," *CG*, 11 September 1907, 8–9; C.H. Cross, "Aggressive Evangelism," *CG*, 16 October 1907, 9–10; H.G. Cairns, "What Is the Business of the Church?" *CG*, 9 April 1913, 11 and "Present-day Evangelism – The Need and the Method," *CG*, 23 April 1913, 10–11; Fred W. Langford, "Religious Education and Training for the Ministry," *CG*, 2 October 1918, 7; R.E. Fairbairn, "The Church and the New Civilization," *CG*, 9 April 1919, 7 and "What Is Christianity Coming To?" *CG*, 4 May 1921, 18; Fred C. Middleton, "'My Creed': An Experiment in Educational Evangelism," *CG*, 11 February 1925, 5. On the disillusionment with the idea of "sacrificial service" see Bliss, "The Methodist Church and World War I," 213–33 and Marshall, "Methodism Embattled," 48–64. As examples of Creighton's impatience with those who held different views, see the editor's reply to E.W.S. Coates, *CG*, 9 April 1919, 22 and his reply to S.G. Mulhall, "Some Advice to the Editor," *CG*, 5 October 1921, 13 where his response to Mulhall's explanation that many were driven to the *Sunday School Times* because their own paper did not find their views worthy of consideration was simply, "When, oh when, did we do and be all these naughty, terrible things."

35 R.E. Fairbairn, "The Problem of Church Membership," *CG*, 7 February 1923, 4.

36 H.F. Ball, "Conversion, or Consecration, Which?" *CG*, 27 March 1918, 8.

37 J.S. Williamson, "Conversion or Consecration," *CG*, 24 April 1918, 20.

38 Ibid., 20–1.

39 "What Is a Christian," *CG*, 22 May 1918, 6.
40 "H.A. Seed," "The Winning of Men," *CG*, 19 November 1913, 25. Dissatisfaction with the urban environment in which theological education of the clergy took place continued, contributing, for example, to the growth of sectarian movements; see Mann, *Sect, Cult and Church in Alberta*, 82–112.
41 For examples in the 1880s and 1890s see "Is the World Getting Worse?" *CG*, 11 February 1880, 44; "Pre-millennial Views," *CG*, 28 October 1885, 680; "Pre-millennialism," *CG*, 28 March 1888, 194; "Mr. Moody and His Work," *CG*, 21 November 1894, 744; John Laing, "The Premillenarian Theory," *CMM* 23, no. 3 (March 1886):274–7; G.A. Cleveland, "The Millennium," *CMM* 26, no. 4 (October 1887):368–73. The last is an abridgment of an article by William Rainey Harper.
42 "A Complex Theological Question," *CG*, 29 March 1893, 200. On its significance for fundamentalism, see Sandeen, *The Roots of Fundamentalism*, 103–31 and Marsden, *Fundamentalism and American Culture*, 56–7, 113–15.
43 *CG*, 18 March 1914, 7. For a discussion of the conference, see Sandeen, *The Roots of Fundamentalism*, 224–6, who says that "at no previous conference was the emphasis upon the details of the Darbyite dispensationalist doctrines so explicit and dogmatic as at this gathering."
44 A. McKibbin, "That Pre-millennial Conference," *CG*, 22 April 1914, 27 claimed that it was a Methodist doctrine, and in "That Premillennial Matter," 3 June 1914, 2 stated that the presentation of it in a book recommended by Torrey was "a sufficient guarantee that it is safe." T.L. Wilkenson, "The Pre-millennial Question," *CG*, 20 May 1914, 27 denied that it had ever been a doctrine of Methodism, and stated that though he was an old man, he had met only one or two Methodist ministers who believed it.
45 "The Collapse of Civilization," *CG*, 26 August 1914, 6.
46 "What Next," *CG*, 17 April 1918, 6.
47 "An Unreliable Spiritual Guide," *CG*, 14 April 1920, 7.
48 Byron J. Stauffer, "Worse World or Better World?" *CG*, 19 May 1920, 7.
49 "Dr. Torrey and Dr. Mathews," *CG*, 4 June 1919, 4.
50 "Editorial in Brief," *CG*, 16 February 1921, 9.
51 J.H. Philp, "Religious Education: A Survey," *CG*, 26 January 1921, 5.
52 Bassett, "The Fundamentalist Leavening of the Holiness Movement: 1914–1940," 65–85. If one looks for a "schism" in Methodism related to the fundamentalist-modernist debate, the holiness movement and Pentecostalism may be the place to find it. Again, it is manifested in a

different way, focusing more on the the experiences of conversion, sanctification, and, later, speaking in tongues than on issues like higher criticism and evolution.

53 The six-part series was titled *The Christian Hope*. The most interesting in this context is "Redemption by Revolution," from which the quotations used here are taken. Criticism of premillennialism came from a number of prominent Methodists. George Workman wrote two pamphlets dealing with questions about it; see *Armageddon; or, The World Movement* and *Is Jesus Coming Again?*. There is also a manuscript of a book on the Second Coming in his papers, which he apparently had difficulty publishing in book form. In "A Note from Dr. Workman," *CG*, 26 October 1921, 16 he expressed regret that Macmillan had turned down the manuscript which many had asked him to prepare, but that he was willing to preach on the subject. S.D. Chown, "The Methodist Attitude toward Christian Doctrine," *CG*, 29 March 1922, 13, argued that premillennialism had no place in Methodism's theology of experience. S.G. Bland gave a series of talks on "A Christianity for To-day" at the London Annual Conference where he reportedly discussed the fallacy of premillennialism for three or four mornings; see *CG*, 23 June 1920, 21.

54 "News from Manitoba," *CG*, 17 September 1924, 12. Price's visit to Manitoba followed his evangelistic work in British Columbia, during which questions were raised on his healing ministry; for a discussion of Price's work and its relationship to the holiness movement and Pentecostalism, see Burkinshaw, "Strangers and Pilgrims in Lotus Land," 146–63.

55 "Protestant Federation," *CMM* 22, no. 6 (December 1885):561. I have not been able to find out when the practice of union revivals began in Canada; however, they seem to have become more commonplace during the 1880s and 1890s. Though Hunter left the team in 1910 because of poor health, Crossley continued his union revivals until after 1925; see "A Letter from Dr. Crossley," *CG*, 31 December 1924, 16.

56 Nathanael Burwash, "To the Members of the Methodist Ecumenical Conference," [1911], Burwash Papers, box 8/107, 3.

57 Ibid., 3.

58 Ibid., 5.

59 Ibid., 5–6. Ironically, this was the same conference where revivalism was severely criticized.

60 Nathanael Burwash, "Our Federated Divinity Schools," *CG*, 17 October 1894, 661.

61 [Anon.], "The Confessions of a University Graduate," *CG*, 1 February 1899, 74.

62 Kilpatrick, *New Testament Evangelism*, 137–8. For Moody's role in shap-

ing the liberal evangelicalism of Scotland, see Fraser, "'The Christianization of Our Civilization,'" 35–44.

63 Ernest Thomas [Edward Trelawney], "Church Union and Personal Religion," *CG*, 9 December 1908, 7. Thomas had earlier moved the resolution for union in the Montreal Conference on the same basis: "And
whereas the propagation and culture of scriptural holiness is now accepted by all evangelical churches as the goal of their activities, and
the test of their methods, thus ensuring the permanent success of the
mission of Methodism; ... we affirm that the fulfilment of the mission
of Methodism is no longer bound up with a separate organization";
see *CG*, 17 June 1903, 15.

64 Even Creighton, who had developed reservations by this time, was
concerned, criticizing Kilpatrick's tendency to link revivalism with vice
and his seeming fear of revivalism; see "'New Testament Evangelism,'" *CG*, 14 June 1911, 5.

65 Robert Milliken, "The Message of Methodism: What Will Be Her Contribution to the United Church," *CG*, 18 February 1925, 5. On Methodism's contribution from its top official's point of view see S.D.
Chown, "The Vitality of Religion," Sermon to the 1914 General Conference, Chown Papers, box 3/90, 7–8. There was less said in these
discussions about the Congregational contribution, partly because the
denomination was small.

66 "Methodism Still Fights Evil Forces: The Story of the Board of Evangelism and Social Service," *CG*, 3 December 1924, 17. The article notes
that it was a response to the anti-union Presbyterians.

67 Lucas, "Wesley Heritage in the United Church of Canada," 140–76.
See also Clifford, "The Impact of the Presbyterian Controversy over
Church Union on the Methodist Church in Canada," 1–7, where he
notes that Methodists relied on Presbyterians to defend them when
they were verbally attacked by the non-concurring Presbyterians.

68 Evangelism had already become professionalized and social work was
to become more so; see Marty, "Social Service: Godly and Godless."

69 S.D. Chown, "Fundamentalists and Modernists," Chown Papers,
box 5/129, 9–10; also see "Modernism and Fundamentalism," Chown
Papers, box 14/401.

70 "Methodist Emphasis," *CG*, 21 January 1925, 2.

EPILOGUE

1 Whitehead, *Adventures of Ideas*, 238.

2 Stockton, "An Exploration of Some of the Factors Causing the Decline
of the United Church in the Rural Areas," 7–16. Stockton is the
daughter born in 1937; the decision not to baptize her came after ob-

jections from a cousin who had joined the Brethren; see 18–19. The Zion United Church, closed by the presbytery in 1969, is an interesting study of the connection of spiritual alienation to institutional alienation. It would be interesting to see if the discontents of such congregations have more recently found expression through groups like the United Church Renewal Fellowship.

3 Mead, "The Rise of the Evangelical Conception of Ministry," 224.
4 Shils, *Tradition*, 280.

Bibliography

PRIMARY SOURCES

Books and Pamphlets

Bland, Salem. *The New Christianity; or, The Religion of the New Age.* Toronto: McClelland and Stewart, 1920. 2nd ed., edited by Richard Allen. Toronto: University of Toronto Press 1977.
– *James Henderson.* Toronto: McClelland and Stewart 1926.
Burwash, E.M. *The New Theology.* Toronto: William Briggs 1910.
Burwash, Nathanael. *The Relation of Children to the Fall, the Atonement, and the Church.* Toronto: William Briggs 1882.
– *Inductive Studies in Theology.* Toronto: William Briggs 1896.
– *Manual of Christian Theology on the Inductive Method.* 2 vols. London: Horace Marshall and Son 1900.
– *The History of Victoria College.* Toronto: Victoria College Press 1927.
Burwash, Nathanael, ed. *Wesley's Doctrinal Standards: The Sermons, with Introduction, Analysis and Notes.* Toronto: William Briggs 1881.
Carman, Albert. *The Guiding Eye; or, the Holy Spirit's Guidance of the Believer.* Toronto: William Briggs 1889.
Carman, Albert, and S.D. Chown. *The Address of the General Superintendents to the General Conference of 1914.* Toronto: William Briggs 1914.
Carman, Albert A. *The Preparation of Ryerson Embury: A Purpose.* Toronto: Publishers' Syndicate 1900.
Carlile, John. *An Exposé of and a Red Hot Protest against a Damnable Heresy, Smuggled into Methodism and Taught by Rev. Professor Workman of Victoria University, and Approved of by Rev. Professor Burwash.* Peterborough: Examiner Print [1891].
Carroll, John. *Case and His Cotemporaries; or, The Canadian Itinerants' Memorial.* 5 vols. Toronto: S. Rose 1867–77.

Chown, Samuel Dwight. *Some Causes of the Decline of the Earlier Typical Evangelism.* Toronto: Ryerson Press 1930.

– *The Story of Church Union in Canada.* Toronto: Ryerson Press 1930.

Coe, George. *The Spiritual Life: Studies in the Science of Religion.* New York: Eaton and Mains 1900.

– *The Religion of a Mature Mind.* Chicago: Fleming H. Revell 1903.

– *The Psychology of Religion.* Chicago: University of Chicago Press 1916.

Dewart, E.H. *Broken Reeds; or, The Heresies of the Plymouth Brethren Shown to be Contrary to Scripture and Reason.* Toronto: Wesleyan Conference Office 1869.

– "The Development of Doctrine." Address to the Theological Union of Victoria College. Toronto: Methodist Conference Printing Office 1879.

– *Jesus the Messiah in Prophecy and Fulfilment: A Review and Refutation of the Negative Theory of Messianic Prophecy.* Toronto: William Briggs 1891.

– *The Bible under Higher Criticism: A View of the Current Evolution Theories about the Old Testament.* Toronto: William Briggs 1900.

– *Misleading Lights: A Review of Current Antinomian Theories of the Atonement and Justification.* Toronto: Christian Guardian Office n.d.

General Conference. *Centennial of Canadian Methodism.* Toronto: William Briggs 1891.

Grant, John Webster, ed. *Salvation! O the Joyful Sound: The Selected Writings of John Carroll.* Toronto: Oxford University Press 1967.

Horner, Ralph C. *Ralph C. Horner, Evangelist: Reminiscences from His Own Pen.* Edited by A.E. Horner. Brockville: Standard Church Book Room n.d.

Jackson, George. *The Old Methodism and the New.* London: Hodder and Stoughton 1903.

– *The Fact of Conversion.* New York: Revell 1908.

– *The Preacher and the Modern Mind.* London: Kelly 1912.

Jones, Sam, and Sam Small. *Sam Jones and Sam Small in Toronto.* Toronto: Rose Publishing Co. 1886.

Kilpatrick, T.B. *New Testament Evangelism.* New York: George H. Doran 1911.

Kilpatrick, T.B., and J.G. Shearer. *The Kootenay Campaign.* Toronto: General Assembly Committee on Evangelism [1910].

McClung, Nellie L. *Clearing in the West: My Own Story.* Toronto: Thomas Allen 1935, 1964.

MacDougall, John. *Rural Life in Canada: Its Trends and Tasks.* 1913; 2nd ed. Toronto: University of Toronto Press 1973.

Methodist Church of Canada. *The Christian Hope.* Toronto: Board of Evangelism and Social Service [1922–3].

Nevin, John W. *The Anxious Bench.* Chambersburg, Pennsylvania: Publication Office of the German Reformed Church 1844.

Richey, Matthew. *A Memoir of the Late Rev. William Black, Wesleyan Minister.* Halifax: William Cunnabell 1839.

Ryerson, Egerton. *Scriptural Rights of the Members of Christ's Visible Church.* Toronto: Brewer 1854.

Smith, Hannah Whitall. *The Unselfishness of God and How I Discovered It.* New York: Fleming H. Revell 1903.

Social Service Congress. *Report of Addresses and Proceedings.* Toronto: Social Service Council of Canada [1914].

Steele, Daniel. *Antinomianism Revived; or, The Theology of the So-Called Plymouth Brethren Examined and Refuted.* Boston: McDonald, Gill and Company 1887.

Stevens, Abel. *Life and Times of Nathan Bangs.* New York: Carlton and Porter 1863.

Strachan, R. *Wandering Lights: A Stricture on the Doctrines and Methods of Brethrenism.* Toronto: William Briggs n.d.

Truax, A., ed. *Autobiography of the Late Rev. Nelson Burns.* Toronto: Christian Association n.d.

Withrow, W.H. *Barbara Heck: A Tale of Early Methodism.* Toronto: William Briggs [1895].

Woodsworth, James. *Thirty Years in the Canadian North-West.* Toronto: McClelland, Goodchild and Stewart 1917.

Woodsworth, J.S. *Strangers within Our Gates or Coming Canadians.* Toronto: Missionary Society of the Methodist Church, Canada 1909.

– *My Neighbor: A Study of Social Conditions, A Plea for Social Service.* Toronto: Missionary Society of the Methodist Church, Canada 1911.

– *Following the Gleam: A Modern Pilgrim's Progress to Date.* Ottawa: n.p. 1926.

Workman, George Coulson. *Messianic Prophecy Vindicated.* Toronto: William Briggs 1899.

– *At Onement; or Reconciliation with God.* New York: Revell 1911.

– *Armageddon; or, The World Movement.* Toronto: William Briggs 1917.

– *Is Jesus Coming Again?* Toronto: Ryerson Press 1922.

Young, George. *Manitoba Memories: Leaves from My Life in the Prairie Province, 1868–1884.* Toronto: William Briggs 1897.

Periodical Literature

Canadian Methodist Magazine, 1875–95
Canadian Methodist Magazine and Review, 1896–1906
Canadian Methodist Quarterly, 1889–95
Christian Guardian, 1880–1925
Expositor of Holiness (Canada Holiness Association), 1882–94

Manuscript Collections

ARCHIVES OF THE UNITED CHURCH OF CANADA, TORONTO, ONTARIO
Biographical Files

Bland, Salem Goldsworth. Personal Papers
Burwash, Nathanael. Personal Papers
Carman, Albert. Personal Papers
Chown, Samuel Dwight. Personal Papers
Church Union Collection
Department of Temperance, Prohibition and Moral Reform; Department of
    Social Service and Evangelism; and Department of Evangelism and Social
    Service Papers
Hincks, William. Personal Papers
Jackson, George. Personal Papers
Moore, T. Albert. Personal Papers
Workman, George Coulson. Personal Papers

SECONDARY WORKS

Acquaviva, S.S. *The Decline of the Sacred in Industrial Society.* Oxford: Basil
    Blackwell 1979.
Ahlstrom, Sydney E. *A Religious History of the American People.* New Haven:
    Yale University Press 1972.
Aikens, Alden Warren. "Christian Perfection in Central Canadian Meth-
    odism 1828–1884." Ph.D. dissertation, McGill University 1987.
– "Christian Perfection in Four Representative Canadian Methodists." Vic-
    toria, BC: Papers of the Canadian Methodist Historical Society, volume
    6, 1987.
Airhart, Phyllis D. "Sobriety, Sentimentality and Science: The W.C.T.U. and
    the Reconstruction of Christian 'Womanhood.'" Papers of the Canadian
    Methodist Historical Society, volume 8, 1991.
Allen, Richard. *The Social Passion: Religion and Reform in Canada, 1914–28.*
    Toronto: University of Toronto Press 1971.
– "Children of Prophecy: Wesley College Students in an Age of Reform."
    Red River Valley Historian (Summer, 1974): 15–20.
– "Salem Bland: The Young Preacher." *Bulletin* (Committee on Archives of
    The United Church of Canada) 26 (1977): 75–93.
Altick, Richard D. *The English Common Reader: A Social History of the
    Mass Reading Public, 1800–1900.* Chicago: University of Chicago Press
    1957.
– *Victorian People and Ideas.* New York: W.W. Norton 1973.
Arndt, Ruth Spence. *Prohibition in Canada.* Toronto: Ontario Branch of the
    Dominion Alliance 1919.
Austin, Alvyn J. *Saving China: Canadian Missionaries in the Middle Kingdom,
    1888–1959.* Toronto: University of Toronto Press 1986.
Ballard, Paul. "Evangelical Experience: Notes on the History of a Tradition."
    Journal of Ecumenical Studies 13 (1976): 51–68.

Ban, Joseph D., and Paul R. Dekar, eds. *In the Great Tradition*. Valley Forge, Pennsylvania: Judson Press 1982.

Bannister, Robert. *Social Darwinism: Science and Myth in Anglo-American Social Thought*. Philadelphia: Temple University Press 1970.

Barron, F.L. "The American Origins of the Temperance Movement in Ontario, 1828–1850." *Canadian Review of American Studies* 11, no. 2 (Fall 1980): 131–50.

Bassett, Paul. "The Fundamentalist Leavening of the Holiness Movement: 1914–1940." *Wesleyan Theological Journal* 13 (Spring 1978): 65–91.

Baumer, Franklin L. "Intellectual History and Its Problems." *Journal of Modern History* 21 (1949): 191–203.

Bebbington, D.W. *Evangelicalism in Modern Britain: A History from the 1730s to the 1980s*. London: Unwin Hyman 1989.

Bell, David, ed. *New Light Baptist Journals of James Manning and James Innes*. Hantsport, Nova Scotia: Lancelot Press 1984.

Berger, Peter L. *The Sacred Canopy: Elements of a Sociological Theory of Religion*. New York: Doubleday 1967; Anchor Books 1969.

Berger, Peter L., and Thomas Luckmann. *The Social Construction of Reality: A Treatise in the Sociology of Knowledge*. New York: Doubleday 1966; Anchor Books 1967.

Berkhofer, Robert F. *A Behavioral Approach to Historical Analysis*. New York: Macmillan 1969.

Bliss, Michael. "The Methodist Church and World War I." *Canadian Historical Review* 44 (1968): 213–33.

– *A Canadian Millionaire: The Life and Business Times of Sir Joseph Flavelle, Bart., 1858–1939*. Toronto: University of Toronto Press 1978.

– *Northern Enterprise: Five Centuries of Canada Business*. Toronto: McClelland and Stewart 1987.

Boyer, Paul *"In His Steps*: A Reappraisal." *American Quarterly* 23 (1971): 60–78.

Boylan, Anne M. "Evangelical Womanhood in the Nineteenth Century: The Role of Women in Sunday Schools." *Feminist Studies* 4 (1978): 62–80.

– *Sunday School: The Formation of an American Institution*. New Haven: Yale University Press 1988.

Boyle, George Alfred. "Higher Criticism and the Struggle for Academic Freedom in Canadian Methodism." Th.D. dissertation, Victoria University 1965.

Bradley, Ian C. *The Call to Seriousness: The Evangelical Impact on the Victorians*. New York: Macmillan 1976.

Brantley, Richard E. *Locke, Wesley, and the Method of English Romanticism*. Gainesville: University of Florida Press 1984.

Brauer, Jerald C. "Conversion: From Puritanism to Revivalism." *Journal of Religion* 58 (1978): 227–43.

- "Revivalism and Millenarianism in America." In *In the Great Tradition*, 147–59. Edited by Joseph D. Ban and Paul R. Dekar. Valley Forge, Pennsylvania: Judson Press 1982.
Brooks, William H. "The Uniqueness of Western Canadian Methodism, 1840–1925." *Bulletin* (Committee on Archives of The United Church of Canada) 26 (1977): 57–74.
Brown, W.L. "The Sunday School Movement in the Methodist Church in Canada, 1875–1925." Th.M. thesis, University of Toronto 1959.
Browning, Don S. *Pluralism and Personality: William James and Some Contemporary Cultures of Psychology.* Lewisbury: Bucknell University Press 1980.
Bruce, Dickson. *And They All Sang Hallelujah: Plain-Folk Camp-meeting Religion, 1800–1845.* Knoxville: University of Tennessee Press 1974.
Burkinshaw, Robert Kenneth. "Strangers and Pilgrims in Lotus Land: Conservative Protestantism in British Columbia, 1917–1981." Ph.D. dissertation, University of British Columbia 1988.
Burrell, Sidney A., ed. *The Role of Religion in Modern European History.* New York: Macmillan 1964.
Bush, Peter. "James Caughey, Phoebe and Walter Palmer and the Methodist Revival Experience in Canada West, 1850–1858." MA thesis, Queen's University 1985.
- "The Reverend James Caughey and Wesleyan Methodist Revivalism in Canada West, 1851–1856." *Ontario History* 79 (1987): 231–50.
Calderwood, Robert Charles. "The Fundamentalist Movement in the Methodist Episcopal Church." AM thesis, University of Chicago 1927.
Carpenter, Joel A. "Fundamentalist Institutions and the Rise of Evangelical Protestantism, 1929–1942." *Church History* 49, no. 1 (1980): 62–75.
Carter, Paul. A. *The Spiritual Crisis of the Gilded Age.* DeKalb: Northern Illinois University Press 1971.
Carwardine, Richard. "The Second Great Awakening in Urban Centers: An Examination of Methodism and the 'New Measures.'" *Journal of American History* 59 (1972): 327–40.
- *Transatlantic Revivalism: Popular Evangelicalism in Britain and America, 1790–1865.* Westport, Connecticut: Greenwood Press 1978.
Chadwick, Owen. *The Victorian Church.* 2 vols. London: Adam and Charles Black 1966.
- *The Secularization of the European Mind in the Nineteenth Century.* London: Cambridge University Press 1977.
Chambers, John Whiteclay. *The Tyranny of Change: America in the Progressive Age, 1900–1917.* New York: St Martin's Press 1980.
Chiles, Robert Eugene. *Theological Transition in American Methodism, 1790–1935.* Nashville: Abingdon Press 1965.
Clark. S.D. *Church and Sect in Canada.* Toronto: University of Toronto Press 1948.

Clebsch, William. *American Religious Thought: A History*. Chicago: University of Chicago Press 1973.

Clemens, James M. "Taste Not; Touch Not; Handle Not: A Study of the Social Assumptions of the Temperance Literature and Temperance Supporters in Canada West between 1839 and 1859." *Ontario History* 64, no. 3 (1972): 142–60.

Clifford, N.K. "Religion and the Development of Canadian Society: An Historiographical Analysis." *Church History* 38 (1969): 506–23.

– "His Dominion: A Vision in Crisis." *Studies in Religion* 2 (1973): 315–26.

– "The Origins of the Church Union Controversy." *Journal of the Canadian Church Historical Society* 18 (June–September 1976): 34–52.

– "The Interpreters of the United Church of Canada." *Church History* 46 (1977): 203–14.

– "The Impact of the Presbyterian Controversy over Church Union on the Methodist Church in Canada." Papers of the Canadian Methodist Historical Society, volume 2, 1977–80.

Cohen, Marjorie Griffin. *Women's Work, Markets, and Economic Development in Nineteenth-Century Canada*. Toronto: University of Toronto Press 1988.

Cook, Ramsay. *The Regenerators: Social Criticism in Late Victorian English Canada*. Toronto: University of Toronto Press 1985.

Creighton, Donald. "My Father and the United Church." In *The Passionate Observer: Selected Writings*, 94–9. Toronto: McClelland and Stewart 1980.

Cross, Whitney R. *The Burned-over District: The Social and Intellectual History of Enthusiastic Religion in Western New York, 1800–1850*. Ithaca: Cornell University Press 1950.

Crysdale, Stewart. *The Changing Church in Canada: Beliefs and Social Attitudes of United Church People*. Toronto: United Church House 1965.

Currie, Robert. *Methodism Divided: A Study in the Sociology of Ecumenicalism*. London: Faber and Faber 1968.

Currie, Robert, A. D. Gilbert, and H. Horsley. *Churches and Churchgoers: Patterns of Church Growth in the British Isles since 1700*. Oxford: Clarendon Press 1977.

Dayton, Donald W. *Discovering an Evangelical Heritage*. New York: Harper and Row 1976.

– "The Social and Political Conservatism of American Evangelicalism." *Union Seminary Quarterly Review* 23 (1977): 71–80.

– "Whither Evangelicalism?" In *Sanctification and Liberation*, 42–63. Edited by Theodore Runyon. Nashville: Abingdon Press 1981.

Dieter, Melvin Easterday. *The Holiness Revival of the Nineteenth Century*. Metuchen, New Jersey: Scarecrow Press 1980.

Dimond, Sydney G. *The Psychology of the Methodist Revival: An Empirical and Descriptive Study*. London: Oxford University Press 1926.

Douglas, Mary, and Steven M. Tipton. *Religion and America: Spirituality in a Secular Age*. Boston: Beacon Press 1983.

Dreyer, Frederick. "Faith and Experience in the Thought of John Wesley." *American Historical Review* 88 (1983): 12–30.

Emery, George N. "The Methodist Church and the 'European Foreigners' of Winnipeg: The All People's Mission 1889–1914." *Historical and Scientific Society of Manitoba*, series III, no. 28 (1971–2): 85–100.

– "Ontario Denied: The Methodist Church on the Prairies 1896–1914." In *Aspects of Nineteenth-Century Ontario*, 312–26. Edited by F.H. Armstrong, H.A. Stevenson, and J.D. Wilson. Toronto: University of Toronto Press [in association with University of Western Ontario] 1974.

– "The Origins of Canadian Methodist Involvement in the Social Gospel Movement, 1890–1914." *Bulletin* (Committee on Archives of The United Church of Canada) 26 (1977): 104–19.

Epstein, Barbara. *The Politics of Domesticity: Women, Evangelism, and Temperance in Nineteenth-Century America*. Middletown: Wesleyan University Press 1981.

File, Edgar Francis. "A Sociological Analysis of Church Union in Canada." Ph.D. dissertation, Boston University 1961.

Finlay, J.F. *Dwight L. Moody: American Evangelist*. Chicago: University of Chicago Press 1969.

Finlay, John L. *Canada in the North Atlantic Triangle: Two Centuries of Social Change*. Toronto: Oxford University Press 1975.

Fishburn, Janet Forsythe. *The Fatherhood of God and the Victorian Family: The Social Gospel in America*. Philadelphia: Fortress Press 1981.

Foster, John William. "The Imperialism of Righteousness: Canadian Protestant Missions and the Chinese Revolution, 1925–1928." Ph.D. dissertation, University of Toronto 1977.

Fraser, Brian J. "Theology and the Social Gospel among Canadian Presbyterians: A Case Study." *Studies in Religion* 8 (1979): 35–46.

– "'The Christianization of Our Civilization': Presbyterian Reformers and Their Defence of a Protestant Canada, 1875–1914." Ph.D. dissertation, York University 1982.

– *The Social Uplifters: Presbyterian Progressives and the Social Gospel*. Waterloo: Wilfrid Laurier University Press 1988.

French, Goldwin. *Parsons and Politics: The Role of the Wesleyan Methodists in Upper Canada and the Maritimes from 1850 to 1855*. Toronto: Ryerson Press 1962.

– "The People Called Methodists in Canada." In *The Churches and the Canadian Experience*, 69–80. Edited by John Webster Grant. Toronto: Ryerson Press 1963.

– "The Evangelical Creed in Canada." In *The Shield of Achilles: Aspects of Canada in the Victorian Age*, 15–35. Edited by W.L. Morton. Toronto: McClelland and Stewart 1968.

Friesen, Gerald. *The Canadian Prairies: A History*. Toronto: University of Toronto Press 1984.

Frye, Northrop. *The Modern Century*. Toronto: Oxford University Press 1967.

Gabriel, Ralph H. "Evangelical Religion and Popular Romanticism in Early Nineteenth-Century America." *Church History* 19 (1950): 34–47.

Garland, M.A., and J.J. Talman. "Pioneer Drinking Habits and the Rise of Temperance Agitation in Upper Canada Prior to 1840." In *Aspects of Nineteenth-Century Ontario*, 171–93. Edited by F.H. Armstrong, H.A. Stevenson, and J.D. Wilson. Toronto: University of Toronto Press [in association with University of Western Ontario] 1974.

Gauvreau, Michael. "The Taming of History: Reflections on the Canadian Methodist Encounter with Biblical Criticism, 1830–1900." *Canadian Historical Review* 65: (1984): 315–46.

Geertz, Clifford. *Interpretation of Cultures: Selected Essays*. New York: Basic Books 1973.

Gellner, Ernest. *Thought and Change*. Chicago: University of Chicago Press 1964; Midway reprint 1978.

Gerrish, B.A. *Tradition and the Modern World: Reformed Theology in the Nineteenth Century*. Chicago: University of Chicago Press 1978.

Gilbert, A.D. *Religion and Society in Industrial England: Church, Chapel, and Social Change*. New York: Longman 1976.

– *The Making of Post-Christian Britain: A History of the Secularization of Modern Society*. New York: Longman 1980.

Goen, C.C. "The 'Methodist Age' in American Church History." *Religion in Life* 34 (1965): 562–72.

Goetzmann, William H. *The American Hegelians: An Intellectual Episode in the History of Western America*. New York: Knopf 1973.

Gordon-McCutcheon, R.C. "Great Awakenings?" *Sociological Analysis* 44 (1983): 83–96.

Gorrell, Donald K. *The Age of Social Responsibility: The Social Gospel in the Progressive Era*. Macon, Georgia: Mercer University Press 1988.

Graham, W.H. *Greenbank: Country Matters in Nineteenth-Century Ontario*. Peterborough: Broadview Press 1988.

Grant, John Webster. "Asking Questions of the Canadian Past." *Canadian Journal of Theology* 1 (1955): 98–104.

– "Blending Traditions: The United Church of Canada." In *The Churches and the Canadian Experience*, 133–44. Toronto: Ryerson Press 1963.

– *The Canadian Experience of Church Union*. Richmond, Virginia: John Knox Press 1967.

– *The Church in the Canadian Era: The First Century of Confederation*. Toronto: McGraw-Hill Ryerson 1972.

– "The United Church and Its Heritage in Evangelism." *Touchstone* 1 (October 1983): 6–13.

– *A Profusion of Spires: Religion in Nineteenth-Century Ontario*. Toronto: University of Toronto Press 1988.

Grant, John Webster, ed. *The Churches and the Canadian Experience*. Toronto: Ryerson Press 1963.

Graves, Louise. "Converting Individuals, Converting the World: A Look at the Life and Work of the Crossley and Hunter Evangelistic Team." Seminar paper, Emmanuel College 1986.

Hammond, John L. "The Reality of Revivals." *Sociological Analysis* 44 (1983): 111–16.

Handy, Robert T. *A Christian America: Protestant Hopes and Historical Realities*. New York: Oxford University Press 1971.

– *A History of the Churches in the United States and Canada*. New York: Oxford University Press 1976.

– "The Influence of Canadians on Baptist Theological Education in the United States." *Foundations* 23 (1980): 42–56.

Handy, Robert T., ed. *The Social Gospel in America, 1870–1920*. New York: Oxford University Press 1966.

Hassey, Janette. *No Time for Silence: Evangelical Women in Public Ministry around the Turn of the Century*. Grand Rapids: Zondervan Publishing House 1986.

Hatch, Nathan. *The Democratization of American Christianity*. Yale University Press 1989.

Heyck. T.W. *The Transformation of Intellectual Life in Victorian England*. New York: St Martin's Press 1982.

Hiller, Harry. "Continentalism and the Third Force in Religion." *Canadian Journal of Sociology* 3 (1978): 183–207.

Hirschman, Albert O. "Reactionary Rhetoric." *Atlantic Monthly*, May 1989, 63–70.

Hofstadter, Richard. *Social Darwinism in American Thought, 1860–1915*. Philadelphia: University of Pennsylvania Press 1944.

-- *The Age of Reform: From Bryan to F.D.R.* New York: Random House 1955.

Holifield, Brooks. *A History of Pastoral Care in America: From Salvation to Self-Realization*. Nashville: Abingdon Press 1983.

Hopkins, C.H. *The Rise of the Social Gospel in American Protestantism, 1865–1915*. New Haven: Yale University Press 1940.

Houghton, Walter E. "Victorian Anti-Intellectualism." *Journal of the History of Ideas* 13 (1952): 291–313.

– *The Victorian Frame of Mind, 1830–1870*. New Haven: Yale University Press 1957.

Hudson, Winthrop S. "Walter Rauschenbusch and the New Evangelism." *Religion in Life* 30 (1961): 412–30.

– "The Methodist Age in America." *Methodist History* 3 (1974): 3–15.

– *Religion in America*. 3rd. ed. New York: Charles Scribner's Sons 1981.

Huff, Ronald Paul. "Social Christian Clergymen and Feminism during the Progressive Era, 1890–1920." Ph.D. dissertation, Union Theological Seminary 1978.

Hughes, H. Stuart. *History as Art and as Science: Twin Vistas on the Past.* Chicago: University of Chicago Press 1964; Midway reprint 1975.

Hughes, Norah L. "A History of the Development of Ministerial Education in Canada from Its Inception until 1925 in Those Churches Which Were Tributary to the United Church of Canada in Ontario, Quebec, and the Maritime Provinces of Canada." Ph.D. dissertation, University of Chicago 1945.

Hunter, James Davison. *American Evangelicals: Conservative Religion and the Quandary of Modernity.* New Brunswick, New Jersey: Rutgers University Press 1983.

Hutchison, William R. "Cultural Strain and Protestant Liberalism." *American Historical Review* 76 (1971): 386–411.

– *The Modernist Impulse in American Protestantism.* 2nd. ed. New York: Oxford University Press 1982.

– *Errand to the World: American Protestant Thought and Foreign Missions.* Chicago: University of Chicago Press 1987.

Jackson, Annie. *George Jackson: A Commemorative Volume.* London: Epworth Press 1949.

James, William. *The Varieties of Religious Experience.* Introduced and edited by Martin E. Marty. New York: Penguin Books 1982.

Johnson, Dale A. "The Methodist Quest for an Educated Ministry." *Church History* 51 (1982): 304–20.

Kaye, Howard L. *The Social Meaning of Modern Biology: From Social Darwinism to Sociobiology.* New Haven: Yale University Press 1986.

Kent, John. *Holding the Fort: Studies in Victorian Revivalism.* London: Epworth Press 1978.

Kett, Joseph F. *Rites of Passage: Adolescence in America, 1790 to the Present.* New York: Basic Books 1977.

Kewley, Arthur. "Mass Evangelism in Upper Canada before 1830." Th.D. dissertation, Victoria University 1960.

– "Camp Meetings in Early Canadian Methodism." Papers of the Canadian Methodism Historical Society, volume 2, 1977–80.

Kiesekamp, Burkhard. "Presbyterians and Methodist Divines: Their Case for a National Church in Canada, 1875–1900." *Studies in Religion* 2 (1973): 289–302.

King, William McGuire. "The Role of Auxiliary Ministries in Late Nineteenth-Century Methodism." In *Rethinking Methodist History*, 167–72. Edited by Russell E. Richey and Kenneth E. Rowe. Nashville: Kingswood Books 1985.

Kirkey, Donald Layton. "'Building the City of God': The Founding of the

Student Christian Movement of Canada." MA thesis, McMaster University 1983.

Lawrie, Bruce. "An Historical Overview of the Canadian Methodist Mission in West China, 1891–1925." Papers of the Canadian Methodist Historical Society, volume 2, 1977–80.

Lears, T.J. Jackson. "From Salvation to Self-Realization: Advertising and the Therapeutic Roots of the Consumer Culture." In *The Culture of Consumption: Critical Essays in American History, 1880–1980*, 3–38. Edited by Richard Wightman Fox and T.J. Jackson Lears. New York: Pantheon Books 1983.

Lenhart, Thomas Emerson. "Methodist Piety in an Industrializing Society, 1865–1914." Ph.D. dissertation, Northwestern University 1981.

Levinson, Henry S. *The Religious Investigations of William James*. Chapel Hill: University of North Carolina Press 1981.

Lindbeck, George A. *The Nature of Doctrine: Religion and Theology in a Postliberal Age*. Philadelphia: Westminster Press 1984.

Lucas, Glenn. "Wesley Heritage in the United Church of Canada." In *Dig or Die*, 140–76. Edited by James S. Udy and Eric G. Clancy. Sydney: World Methodist Historical Society 1981.

Luckmann, Thomas. *The Invisible Religion*. New York: Macmillan 1967.

Luker, Ralph E. "Liberal Theology and Social Conservatism: A Southern Tradition, 1840–1920." *Church History* 50 (1981): 193–204.

Lynn, Robert W., and Elliott Wright. *The Big Little School: Two Hundred Years of the Sunday School*. Nashville: Abingdon Press 1971; rev. ed. 1980.

McCalla, Douglas. "An Introduction to the Nineteenth-Century Business World." In *Essays in Canadian Business History*, 13–23. Edited by Tom Traves. Toronto: McClelland and Stewart 1984.

McCulloh, Gerald O. *Ministerial Education in the American Methodist Movement*. Nashville: United Methodist Board of Higher Education and Ministry 1980.

MacIntyre, Alasdair. *Secularization and Moral Change*. London: Oxford University Press 1967.

McKillop, A.B. *A Disciplined Intelligence: Critical Inquiry and Canadian Thought in the Victorian Era*. Montreal: McGill-Queen's University Press 1979.

– "John Watson and the Idealist Legacy." *Journal of Canadian Literature* 83 (1979): 72–88.

– "Canadian Methodism in 1884." Papers of the Canadian Methodist Historical Society, volume 4, 1984.

McLeod, Hugh. *Religion and the People of Western Europe, 1789–1970*. London: Oxford University Press 1981.

McLoughlin, William G. *Modern Revivalism: Charles G. Finney to Billy Graham*. New York: Ronald Press 1959.

– *Revivals, Awakenings, and Reform*. Chicago: University of Chicago Press 1978.

- "Timepieces and Butterflies: A Note on the Great-Awakening-Construct and Its Critics." *Sociological Analysis* 44 (1983): 103–10.
McNaught, Kenneth W. *A Prophet in Politics: A Biography of J.S. Woodsworth.* Toronto: University of Toronto Press 1959.
Magney, William H. "The Methodist Church and the National Gospel." *Bulletin* (Committee on Archives of The United Church of Canada) 20 (1968): 3–95.
Magnuson, Norris. *Salvation in the Slums.* Metuchen, New Jersey: Scarecrow Press 1977.
Mann, William E. *Sect, Cult and Church in Alberta.* Toronto: University of Toronto Press 1955.
Manning, Harry. "Changes in Evangelism within the Methodist Church of Canada during the Time of Carman and Chown, 1884–1925: A Study of the Causes for and Shifts in Evangelism." MA thesis, University of Toronto 1975.
Manning, William E. *Sect, Cult and Church in Alberta.* Toronto: University of Toronto Press 1955.
Manson, Ian M. "Liberal Theology and United College: Ideas, Faith and Feelings in a United Church Seminary, 1938–1960." Seminar paper, Emmanuel College 1986.
- "Serving God and Country: Evangelical Piety and the Presbyterian Church in Manitoba." MA thesis, University of Manitoba 1986.
- "The Religious Thought of Hugh Price Hughes." Seminar Paper, Trinity College 1990.
Margolis, Maxine L. *Mothers and Such: Views of American Women and Why They Changed.* Berkeley: University of California Press 1984.
Markell, H. Keith. "Canadian Protestantism against the Background of Urbanization and Industrialization in the Period from 1885 to 1914." Ph.D. dissertation, University of Chicago 1971.
Marsden, George M. *Fundamentalism and American Culture: The Shaping of Twentieth-Century Evangelicalism, 1870–1925.* New York: Oxford University Press 1980.
Marshall, David. "Methodism Embattled: A Reconsideration of the Methodist Church and World War I." *Canadian Historical Review* 66 (1985): 48–64.
- "The Clerical Response to Secularization: Canadian Methodists and Presbyterians, 1860–1940." Ph.D. dissertation, University of Toronto 1986.
Marty, Martin E. *The Modern Schism: Three Paths to the Secular.* New York: Harper and Row 1969.
- *Righteous Empire: The Protestant Experience in America.* New York: Dial Press 1970.
- *A Nation of Behavers.* Chicago: University of Chicago Press 1976
- "Social Service: Godly and Godless." *Social Service Review* 54 (1980): 463–81.

– "From Personal to Private, from Political to Public Religion." Inaugural Lecture on Religion and Public Life, University of Notre Dame 9 February 1984.

– *Modern American Religion: The Irony of It All.* Chicago: University of Chicago Press 1986

Mathews, Donald G. "The Second Great Awakening as an Organizing Process, 1780–1830." *American Quarterly* 21 (1969): 23–43.

Matthews, William. *Canadian Diaries and Autobiographies.* Berkeley: University of California Press 1950.

Mead, Sidney E. "The Rise of the Evangelical Conception of the Ministry in America: 1607–1850." In *The Ministry in Historical Perspectives*, 207–49. Edited by H. Richard Niebuhr and Daniel Day Williams. New York: Harper and Row 1956.

– *The Lively Experiment: The Shaping of Christianity in America.* New York: Harper and Row 1963.

Meyer, D.H. "American Intellectuals and the Victorian Crisis of Faith." *American Quarterly* 27 (1975): 585–603.

Miller, Doris I. "Unfermented Wine on the Lord's Table: Origins and Implementation in Nineteenth-Century Methodism." *Methodist History* 29:1 (1990): 3–13.

Miller, Jean Padberg. "Souls or the Social Order: Polemic in American Protestantism." Ph.D. dissertation, University of Chicago 1969.

Moberg, David. *The Great Reversal: Evangelism vs. Social Concern* Philadelphia: Lippincott 1972.

Moir, John S. *A History of Biblical Studies in Canada: A Sense of Proportion.* Chico, California: Scholars Press 1982.

– "Canadian Presbyterians and the Laymen's Missionary Movement." Papers of the Canadian Society of Presbyterian History 1983.

Moore, James R. *The Post-Darwinian Controversies: A Study of the Protestant Struggle to Come to Terms with Darwin in Great Britain and America, 1870–1900.* Cambridge: Cambridge University Press 1979.

Moore, R. Laurence Moore. *Religious Outsiders and the Making of Americans.* New York: Oxford University Press 1986.

Moyles, R.G. *The Blood and the Fire in Canada: A History of the Salvation Army in the Dominion, 1882–1976.* Toronto: Peter Martin Associates 1977.

Muelder, Walter George. *Methodism and Society in the Twentieth Century.* Nashville: Abingdon Press 1961.

Murphy, Howard R. "The Ethical Revolt against Christian Orthodoxy in Early Victorian England." *American Historical Review* 60 (1955): 800–17.

Nicholl, Grier. "The Christian Social Novel and Social Gospel Evangelism." *Religion in Life* 34 (1965): 548–61.

Niebuhr, H. Richard. *The Kingdom of God in America.* New York: Harper and Bros. 1937.

Norwood, Frederick A. "The Shaping of Methodist Ministry." *Religion in Life* 22 (1953): 337–51.

Pannenberg, Wolfhart. *Christian Spirituality*. Philadelphia: Westminster Press 1983.

Park, Roberta J. "Biological Thought, Athletics and the Formation of a 'Man of Character': 1830–1900." In *Manliness and Morality: Middle-class Masculinity in Britain and America*, 7–34. Edited by J.A. Mangan and James Walvin. Manchester: Manchester University Press 1987.

Paterson, Morton. "The Mind of a Methodist: The Personalist Theology of George John Blewett in Its Historical Context." *Bulletin* (Committee on Archives of The United Church of Canada) 27 (1978): 5–42.

Playter, George F. *The History of Methodism in Canada*. Toronto: A. Green 1862.

Porter, John. *The Vertical Mosaic: An Analysis of Social Class and Power in Canada*. Toronto: University of Toronto Press 1965.

Prang, Margaret. *N.W. Rowell: Ontario Nationalist*. Toronto: University of Toronto Press 1975.

– "'The Girl God Would Have Me Be': The Canadian Girls in Training, 1915–39." *Canadian Historical Review* 66 (1985): 154–84.

Prentice, Alison, et al. *Canadian Women: A History* Toronto: Harcourt Brace Jovanovich 1988.

Rack, Henry. "The Decline of the Class-meeting and the Problems of Church Membership in Nineteenth-Century Methodism." *Wesleyan Historical Society Proceedings* 39 (1973–4): 12–21.

Randall, John Herman. "The Changing Impact of Darwin on Philosophy." In *The Role of Religion in Modern European History*, 122–9. Edited by Sidney A. Burrell. New York: Macmillan 1964.

Rawlyk, George. *Ravished by the Spirit: Religious Revivals, Baptists and Henry Alline*. Montreal and Kingston: McGill-Queen's University Press 1984.

– *Wrapped Up in God: A Study of Several Canadian Revivals and Revivalists* Burlington: G.R. Welch 1988.

Reid, John G. *Mount Allison University: A History, to 1963*. Toronto: University of Toronto Press 1984.

Reynolds, Lindsay. "The Great 'Plymouth Brethren' Controversy in South Western Ontario, 1872–73." Unpublished manuscript. Toronto: United Church Archives 1979.

Rhodes, Aaron Anthony. "The Tradition of Enthusiasm." Ph.D. dissertation, University of Chicago 1980.

Richey, Russell E. "Evolving Patterns of Methodist Ministry." *Methodist History* 22 (1983–4): 20–37.

Riddell, J.H. *Methodism in the Middle West*. Toronto: Ryerson Press 1946.

Rosenberg, Carroll Smith. *Religion and the Rise of the American City*. Ithaca: Cornell University Press 1971. *See also* Smith-Rosenberg.

Ross, Brian R. "Ralph Cecil Horner: A Methodist Sectarian Deposed, 1887–1895." *Bulletin* (Committee on Archives of The United Church of Canada) 26 (1977): 94–103.

Rotundo, Anthony. "Learning about Manhood: Gender Ideals and the Middle-class Family in Nineteenth-Century America." In *Manliness and Morality: Middle-class Masculinity in Britain and America*, 35–51. Edited by J.A. Mangan and James Walvin. Manchester: Manchester University Press 1987.

Runyon, Theodore. "Wesley and 'Right Experience.'" Papers of the World Methodist Historical Society, volume 7, 1989.

Ruse, Michael. *The Darwinian Revolution: Science Red in Tooth and Claw.* Chicago: University of Chicago Press 1979.

Rutherford, Paul. *Saving the Canadian City: The First Phase, 1880–1920.* Toronto: University of Toronto Press 1974.

– *The Making of the Canadian Media.* Toronto: McGraw-Hill Ryerson 1978.

– *A Victorian Authority: The Daily Press in Late-Nineteenth-Century Canada.* Toronto: University of Toronto Press 1982.

– "Tomorrow's Metropolis: The Urban Reform Movement in Canada." In *The Canadian City: Essays in Urban and Social History*, 435–55. Edited by Gilbert A. Stelter and Alan F.J. Artibise. Ottawa: Carleton University Press 1984.

Rybczynski, Witold. *Home: A Short History of an Idea.* New York: Viking Penguin 1986.

Ryerson, Egerton. *Canadian Methodism: Its Epochs and Characteristics.* Toronto: William Briggs 1882.

Sandeen, Ernest R. "Towards a Historical Interpretation of the Origins of Fundamentalism." *Church History* 36 (1967): 66–83.

– *The Roots of Fundamentalism: British and American Millenarianism, 1800–1930.* Chicago: University of Chicago Press 1970; reprint ed., Grant Rapids, Michigan: Baker Book House 1970.

Sawatsky, Ronald George. "'Unholy Contentions about Holiness': The Canada Holiness Association and the Methodist Church, 1875–1894." Papers of the Canadian Society of Church History 1982.

– "'Looking for That Blessed Hope': The Roots of Fundamentalism in Canada, 1878–1914." Ph.D. dissertation, University of Toronto 1985.

Schroeder, Gordon. "The Role of Theology in Church Union: Discussion and Controversy." Course paper, University of Toronto 1978.

Schwartz, Edward R. "Samuel Dwight Chown: Architect of Church Union." Ph.D. dissertation, Boston University 1961.

Scott, Donald M. *From Office to Profession: The New England Ministry, 1750–1850.* Philadelphia: University of Pennsylvania Press 1978.

Semple, Neil. "The Decline of Revival in Nineteenth Century Central-

Canadian Methodism: The Extraordinary Means of Grace." Papers of the Canadian Methodist Historical Society, volume 2, 1977–80.

- "The Impact of Urbanization on the Methodist Church in Central Canada, 1854–1884." Ph.D. dissertation, Victoria University 1979.
- "'The Nurture and Admonition of the Lord': Nineteenth-Century Canadian Methodism's Response to 'Childhood.'" *Histoire Sociale/Social History* 14 (1981): 157–75.

Shils, Edward. *The Intellectuals and the Powers*. Chicago: University of Chicago Press 1972.

- *Center and Periphery*. Chicago: University of Chicago Press 1975.
- *Tradition*. Chicago: University of Chicago Press 1981.

Sinclair-Faulkner, Tom. "Theory Divided from Practice: The Introduction of the Higher Criticism into Canadian Protestant Seminaries." *Studies in Religion* 10 (1981): 321–43.

Sizer, Sandra S. *Gospel Hymns and Social Religion: The Rhetoric of Nineteenth-Century Revivalism*. Philadelphia: Temple University Press 1978.

Sklar, Martin J. *The Corporate Reconstruction of American Capitalism, 1890–1916*. New York: Cambridge University Press 1988.

Smith, H. Shelton. "George Albert Coe: Revaluer of Values," *Religion in Life* 22 (1952): 46–57.

Smith, Timothy L. *Called unto Holiness: The Story of the Nazarenes*. Kansas City, Missouri: Beacon Hill Press 1962.

- "John Wesley and the Wholeness of Scripture." *Interpretation* 39 (1985): 246–62.
- "My Rejection of a Cyclical View of 'Great Awakenings.'" *Sociological Analysis* 44 (1983): 97–102.
- *Revivalism and Social Reform: American Protestantism on the Eve of the Civil War*. Nashville: Abingdon Press 1957; reprint ed., Gloucester, Massachusetts: Peter Smith 1976.
- "Righteousness and Hope: Christian Holiness and the Millennial Vision in America, 1800–1900." *American Quarterly* 31 (1979): 21–45.

Smith-Rosenberg, Carroll. "Women and Religious Revivals: Anti-Ritualism, Liminality, and the Emergence of the American Bourgeoisie." In *The Evangelical Tradition in America*, 199–231. Edited by Leonard Sweet. Macon, Georgia: Mercer University Press 1984.

- *Disorderly Conduct: Visions of Gender in Victorian America*. New York: Oxford University Press 1985. *See also* Rosenberg.

Stockton, Jessica. "An Exploration of Some of the Factors Causing the Decline of the United Church in the Rural Areas as Evidenced in the History of Zion United Church, Monteagle Township." Seminar paper, Emmanuel College 1990.

Stokes, Allison. *Ministry after Freud*. New York: Pilgrim Press 1985.

Susman, Warren I. *Culture as History: The Transformation of American Society in the Twentieth Century.* New York: Pantheon Books 1973, 1984.

Sweet, Leonard I., ed. *The Evangelical Tradition in America.* Macon, Georgia: Mercer University Press 1984.

Sweet, William Warren. *Revivalism in America: Its Origin, Growth and Decline.* New York: Charles Scribner's 1945.

Symondson, Anthony. *The Victorian Crisis of Faith.* London: SPCK 1970.

Szasz, French Morton. *The Divided Mind of Protestant America, 1880–1930.* University: University of Alabama Press 1982.

Taylor, Robert John. "The Darwinian Revolution: The Responses of Four Canadian Scholars." Ph.D. dissertation, McMaster University 1976.

Thomas, John D. "Servants of the Church: Canadian Methodist Deaconess Work, 1890–1926." *Canadian Historical Review* 65 (1984): 371–95.

Tipson, Baird. "How Can the Religious Experience of the Past Be Recovered?: The Examples of Puritanism and Pietism." *Journal of the American Academy of Religion* 43 (1975): 695–708.

Trivett, Timothy Roy. "The Doctrine of Perfection in Nineteenth-Century America and the Holiness Schism in American Methodism." MA thesis, University of Manitoba 1987.

Turner, James. *Without God, Without Creed: The Origins of Unbelief in America.* Baltimore: Johns Hopkins University Press 1985.

Unger, Walter. "'Earnestly Contending for the Faith': The Role of the Niagara Bible Conference in the Emergence of American Fundamentalism, 1875–1900." Ph.D. dissertation, Simon Fraser University 1981.

Van Die, Marguerite. "Nathanael Burwash and 'The Conscientious Search for Truth.'" Papers of the Canadian Methodist Historical Society, volume 3, 1982–83.

– "Nathanael Burwash: A Study in Revivalism and Canadian Culture, 1839–1918." Ph.D. dissertation, University of Western Ontario 1987.

– *An Evangelical Mind: Nathanael Burwash and the Methodist Tradition in Canada, 1939–1918.* Kingston, Montreal, London: McGill-Queen's University Press 1989.

Vidich, Arthur J., and Stanford M. Lyman. *American Sociology: Worldly Rejections of Religion and Their Directions.* New Haven: Yale University Press 1985.

Wach, Joachim. *Types of Religious Experience: Christian and Non-Christian.* Chicago: University of Chicago Press 1951.

Wacker, Grant. "The Holy Spirit and the Spirit of the Age in American Protestantism, 1880–1910." *Journal of American History* 72, no. 1 (1985): 45–62.

Wakefield, Gordon S. *Methodist Devotion: The Spiritual Life in the Methodist Tradition, 1791–1945.* London: Epworth Press 1966.

Wallace, W. Stewart. *The Ryerson Imprint.* Toronto: Ryerson Press 1954.

Walsh, H.H. *The Christian Church in Canada*. Toronto: Ryerson Press 1956.

Warne, R.R. "Literature as Pulpit: Narrative as a Vehicle for the Transmission and Transformation of Values in the Christian Social Activism of Nellie L. McClung." Ph.D. dissertation, University of Toronto 1988.

Watson, David. "Methodist Spirituality." In *Protestant Spiritual Traditions*, 217–73. Edited by Frank C. Senn. New York: Paulist Press 1986.

– *The Early Methodist Class Meeting*. Nashville: Discipleship Resources 1987.

Weaver, John C. "'Tomorrow's Metropolis' Revisited: A Critical Assessment of Urban Reform in Canada." In *The Canadian City: Essays in Urban and Social History*, 456–77. Edited by Gilbert A. Stelter and Alan F.J. Artibise. Ottawa: Carleton University Press 1984.

Weber, Timothy. *Living in the Shadow of the Second Coming: American Premillennialism, 1875–1925*. New York: Oxford University Press 1979.

Weisberger, Bernard A. *They Gathered at the River: The Story of the Great Revivalists and Their Impact upon Religion in America*. Boston: Little, Brown and Co. 1958.

Welter, Barbara. *Dimity Convictions: American Women in the Nineteenth Century*. Columbus: Ohio State University Press 1976.

Westfall, William, "The Sacred and the Secular: Studies in the Cultural History of Protestant Ontario in the Victorian Period." Ph.D. dissertation, University of Toronto 1976.

– "Order and Experience: Patterns of Religious Metaphor in Early Nineteenth-Century Upper Canada." *Journal of Canadian Studies* 20 (1985): 5–23.

– *Two Worlds: The Protestant Culture of Nineteenth-Century Ontario*. Kingston, Montreal, London: McGill-Queen's University Press 1989.

White, Charles Edward. *The Beauty of Holiness: Phoebe Palmer as Theologian, Revivalist, Feminist and Humanitarian*. Grand Rapids: Francis Asbury Press 1986.

Whiteley, Marilyn Färdig. "Modest, Unaffected and Fully Consecrated: Lady Evangelists in Canadian Methodism." Papers of the Canadian Methodist Historical Society, volume 6, 1987.

– "Called to a More Suitable Mission: Conversion in the Life of Annie Leake Tuttle." Papers of the Canadian Methodist Historical Society, volume 8, 1991.

Whitehead, Alfred North. *Adventures of Ideas*. New York: Free Press 1933.

Wiebe, Robert, *The Search for Order, 1877–1920*. New York: Hill and Wang 1967.

Williams, Peter. *Popular Religion in America: Symbolic Change and the Modernization Process*. Englewood Cliffs, New Jersey: Prentice-Hall 1980.

Wilson, Christopher P. "The Rhetoric of Consumption: Mass-Market Magazines and the Demise of the Gentle Reader, 1880–1920." In *The Culture of Consumption: Critical Essays in American History, 1880–1980,* 36–64. Edited by Richard Wightman Fox and T.J. Jackson Lears. New York: Pantheon Books 1983.

Wilson, John F. "Perspectives on the Historiography of Religious Awakenings." *Sociological Analysis* 44 (1983): 117–20.

Wilson, Major L. "Paradox Lost: Order and Progress in Evangelical Thought of Mid-Nineteenth-Century America." *Church History* 44 (1975): 352–66.

Wise, S.F. "Sermon Literature and Canadian Intellectual History." *Bulletin* (Committee on Archives of The United Church of Canada) 18 (1965): 3–18.

Index